CHASING DOWN A DREAM

Tales from the Middle of the Pack

JAMES H. RIEHL, JR.

Charleston, SC

www.PalmettoPublishing.com

Chasing Down a Dream

First Edition

Certain of the individuals' names in this autobiographical memoir have been changed to protect their privacy

ISBN: 978-1-63837-776-4

Advance Praise for...
Chasing Down a Dream:
Tales from the Middle of the Pack

"I loved *Chasing Down a Dream*, and Jim's look at life and how distance running became such a key part of his journey. His funny commentary spices up the story, as in the end, he found the athletic success he was looking for...and so much more!"

Bill Rodgers
Four Time Boston Marathon & Four Time New York City
Marathon Champion

"Jim has packed a lot of energy and activity into his twin passions of marathoning and marketing. In this breezy book he weaves together both stories in an entertaining and informative manner."

Amby Burfoot
1968 Boston Marathon Champion & Former Executive Editor,
Runner's World

"A great read over a beer or two for any runner, especially those who lived the running boom of the '70s and the early '80s. I put my stamp of approval on this book and agree with Jim that, 'All my running adventures are experiences I wouldn't trade for anything.'"

Bill Squires
Former Coach, Greater Boston Track Club

"*Chasing Down a Dream* is a coming-of-age memoir that chronicles Jim's various and sundry adventures as a childhood athlete, a prep school and college student, a junior high school teacher, an MBA candidate, a summer intern and a marketeer, with long-distance running as its unifying theme. Entertaining, humorous, self-deprecating and inspirational, it has Walt Disney's words as its motto, 'If you can dream it, you can do it.'"

Libby Connolly Alexander
Former CEO and Vice Chairman of Cotiviti, Inc.

"A laurel wreath for this 'middle of the pack' runner and ardent all-around athlete! Jim's writings bring back rich, vibrant memories of the 1970's running 'boom' and remind us that there was also life beyond it in this humorous and entertaining read for both runners and non-runners alike."

Scott Graham
Educator, PhD Educational Research

"Do understand, Jim was not born to run. Imagine a fire hydrant with short legs and the shortest stride on earth...Sure, hard to visualize. But, run he did, training like no other. While most slept in those early morning hours, Jim was always out running to greet the sun as it came to work. Yes, he was the pure definition of tenacity and now he has the audacity to tell his story. Enjoy this auspicious journey through his words...."

C. David Gelly
Author of the Best-Selling *Gap* Series of Novels
Fancy Gap, Orchard Gap, Piper's Gap* and *Volunteer Gap

DEDICATION

To Denise...

For her love and support as I chased down my dream—
in fact, several of them—
at the expense of several of her own.

Run Free
Words and Music by
Willie Nile and Frankie Lee

Ain't nothin' wrong with a house on a hill,
But I've been too long standin' still

I'm gonna chase that sky for the mystery
'Cause there ain't no chain got a hold on me
It's why I breathe, I gotta run free

Gonna take a ride, on a river of steel,
I wanna go where the dreams are real

I'm gonna chase that sky for the mystery
'Cause there ain't no chain got a hold on me
It's why I breathe, I gotta run free

I gotta run free, I gotta run free

I'm gonna chase that sky for the mystery
'Cause there ain't no chain got a hold on me
It's why I breathe, I gotta run free.

I gotta run free, I gotta run free
I gotta run free, I gotta run free

I'm gonna chase that sky for the mystery
'Cause there ain't no chain got a hold on me
It's why I breathe, I gotta run free

I'm gonna raise my hand, gonna climb that wall,
Gonna hear those bells of freedom call
It's why I breathe, I gotta run free

I gotta run free, I gotta run free
I gotta run free, I gotta run free

Contents

FOREWORD

THREE DIVERSE INFLUENCES CAME TOGETHER TO CREATE THIS AUTOBIOGRAPH-ical coming-of-age memoir.

One factor was the COVID-19 pandemic in the spring and summer of 2020, which forced me to slow down long enough to first, do some reading, and second, do some writing.

The second factor was the reading I did, of three books that characterized that magical era in the 1970s and early 1980s that was distance running:

- *Kings of the Roads: How Frank Shorter, Bill Rodgers and Alberto Salazar Made Running Go Boom* by Cameron Stracher
- *Marathon Man: My 26.2 Mile Journey From Grad Student to the Top of the Running World* by Bill Rodgers and Matthew Shepatin
- *14 Minutes: A Running Legend's Life and Death and Life* by Alberto Salazar and John Brant.

The third factor was the inspiration I got from working with Libby Connolly Alexander, former CEO and Vice Chairman of Cotiviti Inc., on her book *Figuring It Out: A Memoir About Connolly, Inc's Journey To The Top.* With a front row seat as Libby made it happen, I learned that the book that I had always felt was somewhere inside of me might finally make its way into the light of day.

PROLOGUE

The running boom of the 1970s and early 1980s.

Practically overnight, an entire subculture was born.

The names of the swiftest were on everyone's lips...

Frank Shorter, Bill Rodgers, Alberto Salazar and Dick Beardsley.

Champions all.

But what about the runner a few steps behind them,

sharing the vision but not necessarily the talent?

What became of him when his aspirations collided with reality?

When his limitations clouded his dreams?

Or when injuries and life's demands curbed his ability to achieve?

That's what this story is all about...

IN THE BEGINNING...

**"A story should have a beginning, a middle and
an end, but not necessarily in that order."**

—Jean-Luc Godard, French-Swiss Film Director

EVEN AS A KID, AS YOUNG AS SEVEN OR EIGHT, I ALWAYS LOVED SPORTS.

I was constantly playing sandlot baseball with three or four chums in western New York, where I grew up. And then when we moved to northeastern Ohio, it was touch football with my buddies there. I was short but fast with good hand-eye coordination. As it turned out, I had apparently started playing before a lot of my peers, so I had, as they say in business, first mover advantage.

Early on, I was the star. My first experience in organized baseball was in something called the farm league. The only thing I remember is I hit a home run. Of course, it was really a single, with the other three bases reached on errors because the other team could neither field nor throw, but in my eyes that did not tarnish my achievement.

And in pickup football games, I was always the one with the ball in my hands. I even won the local Ford dealer's Punt, Pass and Kick competition when I was eleven or twelve, bringing home a Cleveland Browns team jacket for my efforts.

There were experiments in other sports. I learned how to swim but didn't race well because I couldn't stay straight in the lanes. I sort of learned how to dive, but a poorly executed springboard flip ruptured my eardrum and ended that promising career. Then there was basketball...well, suffice it to say—as I did in the paragraph above—I was short. And tennis? Anyone but me.

I'm not really sure why I was drawn toward sports, specifically baseball and football. Maybe it was the fielder's glove my uncle gave me for my eighth birthday or the youth-sized football I got when I was ten. Heck, my parents gave me a baseball bat one time that I even took to sleep with me that night. Pretty weird, huh?

With two older sisters, Nicky and Susie, and two younger sisters, Laurie and Liz, I was the proverbial crème in the Oreo cookie, starved for a brother in some form or fashion.

Fortunately for me, when I was in sixth or seventh grade, my oldest sister, Nicky, started dating Dave Kispert, the starting quarterback on the high school football team. How cool was that? Dave used to throw me bullets across the front yard until the inside of my forearms were a stinging bright red from the impact of the pigskin. Dave was my idol, my brother from another mother, and yes, I was going to collect multiple high school varsity letters, just like he did.

AN IDLE MIND: EPISODE 1

"...children are virtuosos of imagination."

—Benjamin Spock

IT'S NOT LIKE KIDS IN THE MID-1960S HAD A LOT OF CONSTRUCTIVE ALTERNA-tives for spending their spare time. No organized play dates. No video games. Aside from sandlot sports, some of the stuff we used to do tended to get us into trouble. "An idle mind," as the saying goes.

For instance...

When I was around eight or nine, there was a group of four of us kids who hung out together, Warren, Stevie, Larry, and me. Every couple of weeks, each of us would get into a knock-down, drag-out fight with one of the others, only to retreat home with cuts and bruises, to face a withering parental interrogation.

Why did we do this? To this day, I have no idea. I guess we were on our way to becoming alpha males.

Another disturbing pastime involved the assembly of plastic scale model airplanes or ships. Certainly, that activity in and of itself was constructive. But what happened next really wasn't.

I would destroy said plastic model in one of three ways...by riddling it with BBs, igniting it with airplane glue, or exploding it with a firecracker.

When a demolition charge being loaded into a model F-104 Starfighter for later ignition went off prematurely in the basement, I was grounded for weeks. And my ears didn't stop ringing for almost that long, either.

Of course, there were other adventures with fireworks too harrowing to relate here, but suffice it to say, sports became my safest and most legitimate passion at an early age, taking me in some interesting directions, directions that will be the subject of most of my subsequent musings in this space.

GETTING ORGANIZED

**"When did I know I had talent? I think it started when
I first started playing sports, organized sports."**

—LeBron James, Los Angeles Lakers

B EING A BACKYARD SANDLOT STAR IS ALL WELL AND GOOD. BUT AS THEY SAY IN the investment business, past performance does not guarantee future returns.

My earlier farm league experience notwithstanding, when, as a worldly nine-year-old, I graduated into organized sports in the form of Little League baseball tryouts, it was intimidating. In my hometown of Fredonia, New York, there were six teams—VFW (black uniforms), Youth Council (red), Carl Vincent (yellow), Policemen (blue), Firemen (green), and one other I don't remember.

It certainly wasn't the Red Sox or the Yankees.

I tried out for the Firemen and didn't make it. I was crushed. Not only that. I was deeply insulted when, Larry, one of my so-called friends, one of the kids with whom I regularly tussled in our alpha male fights, made it as an outfielder on the Youth Council team. However, as I guiltily reflected all these years later, vindication was mine as I watched at a Little League game when an easy grounder trickled between Larry's legs to the outfield wall.

It took me two more years and a move to the small town of Hudson, in northeast Ohio, before I could resurrect my juvenile baseball career as a second baseman and pitcher on the maroon-clad Village team. In my time on that squad, I was a two-time All-Star, batted .538, and pitching in one two-inning span, I struck out four batters. In each league All-Star game, I made a clutch play, including throwing out a slothful runner at first base from right field.

I swear, there were Cleveland Indians scouts in the stands.

It was also in Hudson that I was introduced to organized football. Unlike baseball, that didn't go so well. Kids were starting to catch up—well, actually, surpass me—in size and speed. Throw in the fact that on my first team, the Western Reserve Spartans, I was playing with kids two years older than me, and the future didn't look especially rosy.

In a harbinger of things to come, the coach parked me on the offensive line. The kid, me, who once always had the ball in his hands, now touched it only occasionally as the long-snapping center in punt formation. From that position, with head down, looking through my legs to make sure my snap went where it was supposed to, I was defenseless, sure to be obliterated by the onrushing enemy once I served up the pigskin. It was not pretty.

But I always had baseball, right? My career rejuvenated, right?

Fast forward to the end of eighth grade. Babe Ruth League. More try-outs. More anxiety. The good news…I made the team. The bad news…I was exiled from second base to the wilderness of center field. I could hear the crickets out there.

The worse news…I was now playing against high school kids with high school fastballs. My legs would tremble when I would step into the batter's box against one speed baller in particular by the name of Bill Conway. Nevertheless, for a rookie I was more or less holding my own until I interrupted the season to take an ill-advised Nantucket vacation as the babysitting enforcer for my unruly seven- and nine-year-old cousins.

While in the Bay State, I learned that the island's name originated from the Native American Algonquin term meaning "far away land." Returning home later that summer, deprived of the batting reps I needed during the season, I discovered that my skills at the plate were likewise far away, very far away.

I never hit as well again.

BEING SCHOOLED

"This fall I think you're riding for—it's a special kind of fall. A horrible kind. The man falling isn't permitted to feel or hear himself hit bottom. He just keeps falling and falling."

—Mr. Antolini to Holden Caulfield, *The Catcher in the Rye*

THEN ALL OF A SUDDEN, AFTER THAT BABE RUTH SUMMER, I WAS STARTING high school in the fall of 1966, still in Ohio. Of course, I went out for the freshmen football team, not fully realizing that my diminutive size was putting me at more and more of a disadvantage with each passing day. Since I had been playing the game for longer than many of my new teammates, I gravitated back to the skill positions of halfback, safety, and kick returner.

It was during the two-a-day summer practices for that season that I recall my first positive running experience. We were about two weeks into two-a-day practices, which got very tiresome very quickly. So, I audaciously skipped a morning session without a legitimate excuse, returning to practice that afternoon.

As a reward for my transgression, the coach demanded that I run ten laps of the high school's athletic complex, probably three miles distance in all. And as I did my penance, I actually enjoyed it. There was a cadence to it, a rhythm; somehow it felt natural. And it certainly involved a lot less exertion and discomfort than the practice I had cut.

Despite this egregious violation of our athletic brotherhood, I was somehow named co-captain for our inaugural game against Field High School, which we tied 6-6. Coincidentally, the other co-captain was a guy by the name of Jim Conway, whose older brother, Bill, possessed the aforementioned frightening fastball. Jim later joined me as a member of the Class of 1974 at Dartmouth College.

The season was all downhill from that first contest, as we lost the remainder of our games, including one to Kent Davey by the humiliating score of 54-6. During halftime of that game, one of our coaches screamed at us, tabbing our squad "a bunch of cake-eaters!" If his intent was to stem the avalanche of opposing touchdowns, it didn't happen. And it wasn't especially helpful to our self-esteem, nor did it facilitate our enjoyment of the experience.

After fall term of freshman year, my family moved from Hudson to Illinois, and I enrolled in Lake Forest Academy, a private boys prep school. Academically, it was a lot more challenging, and my grades definitely suffered. Somewhat obtusely, I tried out for the basketball team, and the coaches demonstrated their excellent talent assessment skills by promptly cutting me.

Good thing. More time for the books.

Baseball in the spring of 1967 confirmed my Babe Ruth experience of the year before. Now I was nothing more than a mediocre denizen of the diamond at best, even though I loved playing the game.

Then, to use a sports analogy, I encountered another curve ball at the end of my freshman year, as we moved again, this time to Valparaiso, Indiana. In an impressive show of astute organizational planning, my father's company, Interstate-United, had transferred him to Chicago and then, six months later, transferred him to Northwest Indiana. To give me some educational stability for the remainder of my high school years, I was enrolled in the fall of 1967 at The Hill School, another all-boys private school, in Pottstown, Pennsylvania.

Three different schools and four different states within ten months. No wonder I developed an affinity for road maps!

The Hill actually required every student to participate in a sport every afternoon after class. This was something new and different (and perhaps frightening) for a lot of the kids, but not for me. What was frightening for me was going 700 miles away from home to school as a fifteen-year-old, but with time I got over it.

Predictably, I had fall and spring covered, respectively, with football and baseball. The winter, however, was a dilemma. My incompetence in basketball had already been abundantly demonstrated. Ice hockey was out of the question. I had absolutely no experience, and it was not a sport one picks up at age fifteen without the risk of certain death. Squash? Never really a consideration because of earlier negative experiences with its racqueted relative, tennis.

That left wrestling. I really don't remember how I settled on that. It might well have been because the head football coach, Dick O'Shaughnessy, was the assistant wrestling coach, and I still had dreams of cracking the varsity football squad and garnering multiple football varsity letters at my new school.

Talk about a character builder. Wrestling was macho with a capital "M," which fit my aspirational image of myself. It required strength, balance, finesse, conditioning, discipline, and endurance. I was never more exhausted—even after running my fastest marathon—than I was after grappling a six-minute match. Wrestling taught me new things about myself, especially about self-discipline and adhering to a program. But I was kidding myself if I was ever going to be more than an occasional junior varsity grappler. The other kids had too big a head start.

Plus, at the end of the day, wrestling really wasn't any fun.

For fun, I could always look forward to spring and baseball. And although I continued to love playing the game, my malaise, which began in Babe Ruth League and continued at Lake Forest Academy—mostly followed me to The Hill. Part of one season, I suffered a cracked right thumb, courtesy of a misjudged fly ball. Working my way back into the infield at shortstop, I did break up one game with a clutch double, as reported in an article I still have from *The Hill News*.

However, on balance I was condemned to an endless succession of junior varsity games, never displaying the superlative talent relative to my peers that I had earlier in my youth.

So, the last shot at that elusive varsity "H" for this five-foot, seven, 135-pound kid was via the Hill football program. Yeah, that'll work. By this time, I had been relegated to the role of offensive guard and defensive linebacker, and a couple of developments during the summer before my senior year assured that I would never don a letter sweater.

One, Coach O'Shaughnessy announced that, for the first time since I had matriculated, he was bringing in a handful of post-graduate students. "PGs," as we called them, were accomplished football players from public high schools who would attend The Hill for one year in order improve their odds of gaining admission to a better college. They would inevitably steal playing time from the most marginal of players on the team, which of course happened to include me.

Two, in order to qualify for even the meager amount of playing time that would remain, I would have to physically survive the double practice sessions during the two weeks preceding classes. As the fates would have it, that just wasn't going to happen.

On a stifling, late-August Pottstown morning, the linemen all assembled for the infamous one-on-one "nutcracker" drill, in which an offensive blocker (in this case, me) tries to prevent a defensive player from getting around him to tackle the ball carrier.

My opponent happened to be one of the PGs, Maury Benton. Maury weighed 270, which, for those readers lacking in math skills, meant he was *twice* my size. (By the way, he made the most of his PG year by subsequently gaining admission to Harvard, where he was a standout defensive lineman.)

Well, the drill was bound to end badly, and it did, as I dislocated my left shoulder. Coach O'Shaughnessy promptly popped it back into place, but despite my macho pleas to rejoin practice, I ended up missing several games.

Not that I would have played anyway. When I returned, dressing for varsity games in my jersey number 60 and wearing a bulky shoulder brace, there was one final indignity that was reserved especially for me.

Despite bringing in the PGs, the Hill football squad was mired in the midst of a 3-win 5-loss campaign and was desperate and willing to try anything for a win. So, in midseason, the staff recruited anyone they thought might help, including George Berleson, a very athletic, strong swimmer, and gave him jersey number 79, as a defensive tackle.

In George's first game, a home tilt against Penn Charter, the defensive coordinator decided George would be more effective playing directly across from the opposing team's center, as nose tackle instead of as defensive tackle. However, the rules stated that, in order to play that position, George was required to wear a jersey number between 60 and 69. Consequently, I was summoned over to the sideline and ordered to give my jersey to George so he could go back into the game at his new position. Shirtless and head hanging low, I shuffled back over to the bench and took a seat.

Aside from some garbage time in The Hill's season-ending 26-2 loss to archrival Lawrenceville, that was pretty much the end of my football career. I never realized the irony of that final score until some fifty-one years later, when I was compiling these notes.*

---

*   A marathon is 26.2 miles in length.

ANOTHER SUCCESSFUL TRYOUT

"A journey of a thousand miles begins with a single step."

—Chinese Proverb

WITHOUT NECESSARILY REALIZING IT, I HAD TAKEN MY FIRST HALTING STEPS toward becoming a runner a few months earlier, before my ill-fated final season of football.

The previous spring, as a junior, I had participated in a school event called "The Hill Marathon," which wasn't really a regulation 26.2-mile marathon but rather an eight-mile road run from the campus to some subsequently forgotten point off campus. The competition couldn't have been particularly distinguished, because I finished fourth. Impressed that I could run that far without any special training and excited by my high finish, I enjoyed the experience and its aftermath tremendously.

That set the gears in my mind turning. I reached out to my classmate and roommate-to-be in senior year, John Ford. John was on the Hill cross-country team, which would go an undefeated 11-0 in the fall.

Perhaps anticipating the disastrous results of the approaching football season, I queried John, "What do you think about me going out for cross country?"

Without a moment's hesitation, John replied, "Let's talk to Coach Lawson."

Clifford Lawson was head coach of the cross-country team, and when we approached him with my proposition, he agreed to a tryout of sorts. Yes, another tryout.

"Jim, let me watch you run," he said, "and then I'll tell you what I think."

So, a day or two later, I met Coach Lawson at the Hill track. Now, I must admit to having a very unorthodox running style. Folks much later labeled it a "shuffle." My stride was very short and choppy. My feet did not rise very far off the ground. It was anything but graceful and fluid. And unlike my younger self, I was not especially speedy. But I was determined to give it my best shot.

Once I strutted my stuff on the cinders, Coach Lawson gave me his blunt assessment.

"Jim, stick to football."

And so I did.

We've already seen what a rousing success that turned out to be.

AN IDLE MIND: EPISODE 2

**"In view of the kind of matter we work with, it will never
be possible to avoid little laboratory explosions."**

—Sigmund Freud

SO THAT WAS IT. I WAS A CUM LAUDE GRADUATE OF THE HILL SCHOOL, RANKED seventh in my class, and headed for Dartmouth College in the fall of 1970.* Sounds pretty impressive, right?

However, a part of me, at least, saw the glass as half empty. I had failed to letter in any varsity sport in high school. Not only that; I lacked the athletic street cred (not to mention the size or talent!) to play intercollegiate football or baseball at an ultracompetitive school like Dartmouth. And this after sports had been a focal point, a passion to me for so much of my life.

All of a sudden, I was a man without a sport.

---

*   Coincidentally, one of the other colleges I applied to, Wesleyan University in Middletown, Connecticut, counted among its alumni Amby Burfoot, who won the Boston Marathon in 1968, and Bill Rodgers, who would win it in 1975, 1978, 1979, and 1980. Unfortunately, admission was denied me because The Hill's college admissions advisor forgot to submit my academic credentials to Wesleyan. No big deal. Amby and Bill would have been gone by the time I got there anyway.

I mean, we had dorm intramurals...touch football and softball. But those were just games. About having fun but not about continuing to improve yourself athletically, which I guess subconsciously I still wanted to do.

I struggled with that during freshman year. I knew how to study, and I respected the sacrifice my parents were making to put me through school, so grades weren't going to be an issue. But without a full-time sport, I had a lot of time on my hands for mischief, such as beer drinking, contact explosives and fireworks.

In regard to the last two items, let me relate an incident in order to provide some perspective.

One evening, I had taken a study break to go down to the tube room to watch the Browns-Jets game during the premiere season telecast of Monday Night Football on ABC. During my absence, a cerebral sophomore chemistry major named Bob Aronson mixed up a batch of contact explosives and poured it on the seat of my desk chair. By the time I returned and plunked down to complete my term paper, it had dried, and I experienced a most unpleasant crackling sensation on my underside.

Of course, Bob had notified the entire hall of his prank, and I ended up being—what else?—the butt of his joke that evening.

However, Bob's treachery did not go unavenged.

A couple of days later, fetching an M-80 super firecracker from my arsenal, I cadged a Camel straight from Bob's roommate, Jim Winter, and repaired to my dorm room. Safely behind closed doors, I chewed three sticks of Juicy Fruit, lit the cigarette, slipped it over the M-80's fuse, and slapped the gum onto the body of the firecracker. Thus, my explosive device was armed. I then strolled back into Bob's sleeping quarters, humming "Smoke on the Water," stuck the bomb on the back of his dresser and beat a hasty retreat.

In a few minutes, a staccato blast was heard, and smoke could be seen issuing from the room. Appropriately chastened, Bob apologized for instigating the war and let me inspect the damage, which included a sizable hole in the back of his dresser and several pairs of singed undershorts.

And while perhaps this adventure is amusing in the retelling, at the end of the day, it was not a constructive use of time or resources. Instead, it was bordering on the dangerous. I think I got that and realized I needed to find something better to do.

But what? It was winter, and I was in New Hampshire. What better place to ski? Well, perhaps Austria, but you get my drift. My roommate, Chris Wiley, and another close friend, John Larson, were skiers, going up to the Dartmouth Skiway almost every afternoon after classes. But I was very sensitive to the expense involved and so chose not to go that route.

Instead, for the first time, I began running regularly. Avoiding the snowy roads, I did a lot of my runs in the college's Leverone Field House, which had a one-eighth-mile track. And although it was nice to be able to run inside, the place had a dirt floor that churned up clouds of choking dust whenever there was any activity. Come spring, it was a delight to go out on the roads and feel the warm sun on my back and the fresh air on my face.

Perhaps I was onto something here.

TROT, TROT TO BOSTON

"They are here because they want to be here. Nobody
makes them come to Boston. Nobody forces them. They
are here because at the heart of it all is the fact that they
wouldn't be any place else on the third Monday of April,
which is Patriots' Day, the day of the Boston Marathon."

—Joe Falls, Author, *The Boston Marathon*

SOMETIME SOON AFTER BEGINNING THOSE REGULAR DAILY RUNS IN THE MID-
dle of freshman year, early 1971, I became obsessed with running the
Boston Marathon.

I'm not sure exactly why. There might have been any number of reasons.

One of the teachers at The Hill while I was there, Bruce Bergstrom, ran
Boston in 1969. As I began running, I subscribed to *Runner's World* magazine, which covered competitive track and road races, including Boston.
Particularly vivid in my memory are also a *Runner's World* pamphlet on the
marathon and a *National Geographic* article about it.

I would devour everything I could find about the event, always held on
Patriots' Day, the third Monday in April to commemorate the battles of
Lexington and Concord, and dream about the day I would run in it.

THE UNKINDEST CUT OF ALL: EPISODE 1

"How implausible that a trip to the Windy City would improve my odds of being drafted."

—Jim Riehl

O F COURSE, DREAMING OF RUNNING IN THE BOSTON MARATHON AND ACTU-ally running in it were two entirely different things, especially for a kid just starting to run on a regular basis. But before I could worry about that, I had to navigate a different sort of detour.

I came back home to Indiana from Dartmouth after my freshman year. By that time, my left shoulder had become a chronic problem because of that old football injury, courtesy of my friend Maury Benton, who by now was at Harvard terrorizing enemy running backs. My shoulder dislocated all the time—heck, once even when I was minding my own business, lying face down asleep in bed.

So, my parents booked me for something called Putti-Platt shoulder surgery, which would basically shorten my upper arm muscle such that, ostensibly, my shoulder would never dislocate ever again. The operation would be done by Dr. Frank Harold, who had actually invented the procedure. The venue was Presbyterian St. Luke's Hospital in Chicago, about forty miles away.

The only disconcerting aspect of this entire affair was that, in the summer of 1971, the Vietnam War was going full tilt. Two years earlier, in 1969, the US government had instituted a military draft lottery in which the birthdates of all men born in a given year would be selected at random. Those with birthdates selected earlier in the lottery were eligible to be drafted sooner than those selected later.

As I reported for surgery in Chicago in June, I was not eligible for the draft. I had something called a 2-S, a student deferment, which meant I couldn't be drafted because I was in college. However, later that summer the lottery was conducted for those in my birth year, 1952, and my birth date, May 12, was drawn at fifty-two. That meant that, as long as I stayed in college, I was fine. But as soon as I was out, I could be inducted into the military because my birthdate was drawn so early in the lottery.

With the chronic dislocating shoulder condition, I would have been protected from the draft whether in school or not, via a 4-F classification, a physical deferment. But with my shoulder repair completed, the 4-F went away. It wasn't that I refused to serve our country; it was that I did not want to serve our country in Vietnam because I agreed with neither the US rationale for involvement nor the conduct of the war.

Consequently, the shoulder surgery became a source of anxiety for me because, potentially, it qualified me for military service in a conflict I did not support. What's more, my unwillingness to serve in Vietnam, should I need to act upon it, was bound to become a source of conflict with my father, who flew an Army Air Force attack bomber in World War II.

However, I had just completed my freshman year of college and would be protected by my student deferment for the next three years. So I chose not to raise the subject, and the surgery went on.

ISN'T IT IRONIC... DON'T YOU THINK?

**"I've worried about many things that ended
up never happening to me."**

—Anonymous

OR ME, GETTING DRAFTED INTO THE MILITARY WAS ONE OF THOSE THINGS, something about which I needlessly worried.

Even though the shoulder surgery was successful and I remained in college with my 2-S deferment, eleven months later, in May of 1972, I decided to voluntarily report to the US military induction center in Manchester, New Hampshire for my pre-draft physical.

The Manchester center reportedly had a higher rejection rate of draftees for physical disabilities than in the Midwest, and I thought I might be rejected, either because my shoulder had been surgically repaired or because of a medical condition called nephritis—or inflammation of the kidneys—that I had suffered in my senior year at The Hill.

I'll never forget the morning of the physical. The local draft board supplied a bus to ferry those taking the physical from Lebanon, a few miles southeast of Dartmouth, to Manchester. There were Vietnam War protesters there, people chanting, "Don't ride the death bus" and lying down in the street to prevent our departure.

Some of the guys on the bus were frantic, Dartmouth seniors facing induction upon graduation, including at least one member of the varsity football team, willing to do just about anything to be disqualified from the draft. Some had stayed up all night, consuming copious amounts of NoDoz and coffee in the hope that a racing pulse and an elevated blood pressure might save them from the clutches of the US Army.

My decision to go to Manchester turned out to be a good one. After a medical exam, I was rejected. I was now officially 4-F and could never be drafted into the military.

Ironically, I ended up not needing the 4-F anyway, because the Selective Service suspended the draft in January of 1973, a full eighteen months before my 2-S student deferment expired when I graduated from Dartmouth.

On the same day of my draft physical, May 15, 1972, Alabama Governor and Democratic Presidential candidate George Wallace was shot five times by Arthur Bremer, effectively ending Wallace's Chief Executive bid. One of the bullets lodged in his spinal column, leaving him paralyzed for the remainder of his life.

And there was additional irony associated with my shoulder surgery. Although I would have gladly taken a pass on the Putti-Platt procedure to preserve my 4-F draft status, that was not an option because my parents insisted the surgery needed to be done. As I recovered in the hospital, I had an extremely uncomfortable and vocal roommate, suffering from excruciating burns, whose outbursts sent me into the corridors seeking some peace and relative quiet.

In my travels, I encountered a sunny, smart, very pretty, blonde seventeen-year-old, Denise Dahle, a patient herself, who was in for abdominal surgery. Just weeks past her high school graduation and having just broken up with her boyfriend, she lived north of Chicago in Lake Bluff, about five miles from where my family had lived during my brief and questionably scholarly existence at Lake Forest Academy.

We seemed to hit it off during our time at Presbyterian St. Luke's, though our stays only overlapped for a few days. Given my monastic background at all-boys institutions, I was incredibly uncomfortable around girls who didn't happen to be my sisters, but somehow this was different. We had some things in common, and she actually laughed at my lame attempts at humor, although after her surgery, those chuckles caused her a great amount of discomfort.

I was instantly smitten, and the rest, as they say, is history.

Had I not submitted to an operation that I did not want performed, I would never have met the woman I ended up marrying.

Yes, ironic, I really do think.

BACK ON THE ROAD AGAIN

"Running is the thing I love more than anything in the world. Tell me it's worthless and idiotic. Point out that there's no money in it. Tell me I'd be better off looking for a job. Do all this. I'm still going to run ten miles before work. Better yet, I'm going to run another six miles when I get home."

—Bill Rodgers

POST-SURGERY, I WAS TIED UP IN A SLING FOR A FEW WEEKS, BUT I WAS MO-bile enough by mid-July to attend a Creedence Clearwater Revival concert in Chicago with my good buddy Rob Harkel. CCR shared the bill with Tower of Power. I had invited Denise to join us, but she was still in recovery mode. Before the show, we visited Old Town on Chicago's North Side, and I remember seeing a bumper sticker in a head shop that read "Pull Out Like Nixon's Father Should Have," in reference to the Vietnam war.

I also was able to resume my running regimen again and, toward the end of the summer, was running twice a day in the Indiana heat, seven-plus miles a pop, to record my first-ever 100-mile week. I think this was in part a ploy to impress Denise, whom I was now avidly pursuing from the longest of distances, whether it was eighty miles away when I was in Valparaiso or half a country away once I returned to school in New Hampshire.

But it wasn't only to impress Denise. Running had become my sport. It was something I could do whenever I wanted at whatever intensity I wanted. Nobody could tell me I had to play this position or that I didn't make the varsity or that I had to sit on the bench.

And I believed I could be as good a runner as I wanted to be. It was all up to me and how hard I was willing to work. And I knew what it was to be disciplined and work hard in sports. Credit Coach O'Shaughnessy and The Hill School wrestling program. At least I got something out of that experience.

And this was 1971, well before the running boom. The first New York City Marathon had occurred the preceding year. The course was not the current five-borough extravaganza but rather four loops around Central Park. There were 127 participants, 100 spectators, and the winning time was 2:31. And the granddaddy of them all—Boston? In 1971, a mere 1,067 runners toed the starting line in Hopkinton.

So, when I was out there on the road, I was an oddity. Fortunately, I never encountered anything of a violent or verbally abusive nature. Mostly just folks who couldn't quite understand why I was doing what I was doing and who would yell things like, "Get a horse!" Nobody ever tried to run me off the road with their car, throw a full can of beer at me, or swear at me, fortunately. And when I think about all the miles I ran in all the different places I ran, I look back and find it pretty amazing. But then again, those were different times.

And don't get me started on the running shoes of the time. They weren't much. Early on, I ran in a pair of white Onitsuka Tiger shoes with red and blue striping, I think, because I had some Tiger wrestling shoes at The Hill. Pretty sterling endorsement there...from the mat to the macadam. Then some white and blue Puma flats—probably because that's what my roommate, John Ford, and The Hill School cross-country team were wearing. They had virtually no shock absorbing cushioning compared to the shoes of today, and what's more, they only came in one width.

For me, that "one-width-fits-all" thing became a problem over time, as my D-width dogs would inevitably pop through the upper as the miles accumulated, bringing my sockless, bare outer foot in contact with the road surface.

History tells us that in 1960, at the Olympic Games in Rome, a barefoot Ethiopian runner named Abebe Bikila won the marathon. As I ran, I kept telling myself that at least Abebe and I had one thing in common.

THE SOPHOMORIC SOPHOMORE

"Go fast enough to get there, but slow enough to see."

—Jimmy Buffett, American Singer and Songwriter

A S I HEADED BACK TO COLLEGE IN THE FALL OF 1971, THE RUNNING CONTINUED.

And there is no more spectacular place to run in the autumn than in the hills of New Hampshire and Vermont surrounding Dartmouth College. After class, in midafternoon, I would pull on some shorts and a polo shirt, lace up my shoes, and take off, bounding down across the Hanover green, onto Wheelock Street, and then down the hill to the Connecticut River. From there, it was up a hill into Norwich, Vermont and then a series of lefts and rights, up along rustic New England farm roads, then turning back down the valley to see the Baker Library clock tower while starting the return trek to the college amid the blazing fall colors.

At the time, I was rooming in Fayerweather Hall with lifelong friends John Larson and Chris Wiley. Both guys, as I mentioned earlier, were skiers. John was good. Chris, however, was otherworldly. He grew up in Laconia, New Hampshire and was pretty much born on skis. He was even a ski jumper on his high school ski team. That was until one of his binders broke just after he cleared the jump, kind of like that guy at the beginning of ABC's *Wide World of Sports*. Despite landing on his head, Chris insisted afterward he was OK.

Anyhow, Chris did not ski on the Dartmouth ski team, but he did know some of the team members. Occasionally he would participate with them in something interestingly called "dry land" exercises. These were various calisthenics and twelve- to eighteen-mile runs, which they did in the fall to improve their conditioning prior to ski season.

Well, one day, Chris said, "Hey, Riehl-Man, why don't you come along?"

So here we went. I think it was a twelve-mile run that day. I won't burden the reader with the specifics, because I don't really remember them, other than the fact that there were eight or ten of us. It was more of a cross-country than a road run. The captain of the team's name was George Perkins, and I stayed with—and some might say, crushed—them all. These were elite skiers, well-conditioned college athletes, and I came away from my engagement with them feeling very confident about my running progress.

Though I knew my ultimate goal was to run and complete the Boston Marathon, I hadn't really gamed it out yet. I hadn't plotted out what the things were that I needed to do or when I needed to do them in order to get to the starting line on Patriots' Day. I don't even think I knew which Patriots' Day in which year I was gunning for. I was just running for the joy of running. Running to build a base and running every day to get just a little bit stronger and a little bit better.

If I did that, I believed, the Boston Marathon would come to me.

THE SHORTER HEARD ROUND THE WORLD

"The Olympic Games are the quadrennial celebration of the springtime of humanity."

**—Pierre de Coubertin,
Founder and Second President of the
International Olympic Committee**

A ND RUNNING WASN'T THE ONLY THING IN MY LIFE.

Academics were certainly key, and I was falling in love. Denise and I had a few weekend dates before I returned to school. Then she came up to Dartmouth in November, when the football Indians—as they were called at the time—stuffed Cornell's NCAA leading rusher Ed Marinaro, winning 24-14 en route to a share of the Ivy League championship.

We had a fabulous time together, including a concert by Mary Travers—of *Peter, Paul and Mary* fame. When Mary sang the tune "Jet Plane" as her last number, it really resonated. I just felt special in Denise's presence.

Then came the summer of 1972 and the Munich Summer Olympic Games.

This was the Olympiad of American swimmer Mark Spitz's seven gold medals (a world record at the time), Soviet gymnast Olga Korbut's gold in the team competition, and Finn runner Lasse Viren's double victory in the 5,000- and 10,000-meter runs. In the final of men's basketball, the United States appeared to have defeated the Soviet Union 50-49, with time almost expired. However, the final three seconds of the game were replayed thrice until the USSR emerged victorious, 51-50. Seems like somebody put in the fix.

Just before dawn on September 5, eight members of the Palestinian Black September terrorist group scaled a cyclone fence and entered an Olympic Village dormitory, taking eleven Israeli athletes, coaches and officials hostage. During the break-in, two resisting hostages were killed, and the resulting standoff between police and the terrorists lasted over seventeen hours.

Late that evening, the hostages and their captors were helicoptered to a military airport outside of Munich, where they expected to board a jet to an unnamed Arab state. Instead, German authorities ambushed them, and the terrorists retaliated, detonating a grenade inside the chopper and then shooting all the Israelis to death. All but three of the Palestinians also died.

As ABC anchorman Jim McKay memorably recounted on US television, "Our worst fears have been realized tonight. They have now said there were eleven hostages. Two were killed in their rooms yesterday morning. Nine were killed at the airport tonight. They're all gone."

The Olympics were halted briefly after the initial attack, and there was some question as to whether the rest of the games, including the marathon some five days later, would be canceled. However, Avery Brundage, president of the International Olympic Committee, declared that the twentieth Olympiad would continue.

Favorites in the marathon included Ron Hill of Great Britain, Mamo Wolde of Ethiopia, Karel Lismont of Belgium, and Jack Bacheler and Frank Shorter of the United States. Shorter, coincidentally born in Munich, had begun running in seventh grade to alleviate anxiety from the extensive child abuse he suffered at the hands of his father.

At age fifteen, Frank, a high school sophomore, entered the Mount Hermon School, a Massachusetts all-boys boarding school, where he was playing JV baseball and football. In the spring of that year, on a lark, pretty much untrained, he signed up for the obscurely named Bemis-Forslund Pie Race. This was a 4.3-mile run through the campus and adjacent town, with every Mount Hermon boy who cracked the 33-minute barrier scoring his own apple pie. Exuberantly rolling through his run, Frank was the seventh finisher behind the school's five championship cross-country runners and the captain of the Nordic ski team.

After he was recruited for the Mount Hermon harriers by the cross-country coach, Frank's running took off. Upon graduation, he headed to Yale, where he won the NCAA six-mile run as a senior. In 1970 and 1971, he captured US national titles at 3 miles, 6 miles and 10,000 meters/6 miles. He made the 1972 US Olympic marathon team with fellow Americans Bacheler and Kenny Moore, ultimately winning the event with a time of 2:12:19.

Late in that marathon, Frank was cruising along the course that had been laid out in the shape of the Olympic mascot dog, Waldi the dachshund, having built over a two-minute lead over Belgium's Karel Lismont by virtue of a 4-minute 30-second per mile surge he threw in at mile 9.

As the triumphant American was approaching the finish, an imposter named Norbert Sudhaus, wearing a West German track uniform, jumped on the course and ran into the stadium ahead of him. ABC TV announcer and *Love Story* author Erich Segal, who had been one of Shorter's professors at Yale, exclaimed, "That's not Frank. It's an imposter. Get that guy off the track! It's a fraud, Frank!"

Certainly not Erich's most erudite commentary—but accurate, nonetheless.

Initially thinking Sudhaus was the winner, the Munich crowd lustily cheered their homie, but officials soon recognized the hoax and pulled him off the track. Subsequently whisked away by security, Norbert's ultimate fate remains undetermined to this day. Perhaps he was executed and reincarnated at the 1980 Boston Marathon as Rosie Ruiz. But more about that later.

Although nobody knew it at the time, Shorter's win was the match that lit the fuse of the US running boom.

And I was still at it, putting in my miles, though I'm not sure how many because the log I was using then has vanished in the sands of time. My mantra at the time was LSD. Not as in the mind-altering drug, but as in "Long Slow Distance."

I was completely self-coached, which means I wasn't coached at all. Even though I subscribed to *Runner's World* magazine, I read the stories about races and runners, not about coaching and training techniques. In addition, I had yet to tap into the local road race scene, so I had absolutely no clue as to the value of racing in building one's fitness, speed, and endurance.

Clearly, I was just getting started.

THE UNKINDEST CUT OF ALL: EPISODE 2

"Growth is an erratic forward movement.
Two steps forward. One back."

—Julia Cameron, American Teacher, Author and Artist

AFTER SPENDING MOST OF MY HIGH SCHOOL YEARS IN THE PRESENCE OF MEN and only men, it was a bit of an alien—but certainly not unwelcome—concept to me when all-male Dartmouth decided to admit women students beginning in the fall of 1972, my junior year.

Simultaneously, the school introduced the creatively named "Dartmouth Plan" of year-round operation. Under the plan, to encourage year-round attendance, the number of terms required for graduation was reduced from twelve to eleven as long as one of the terms of attendance was a summer term.

Why am I telling you this? Because it changed my life.

Seeking to save my parents one term of tuition, I immediately and unflinchingly signed up for the Dartmouth Plan. That meant, in exchange for attending college that upcoming summer, the summer of 1973, I suddenly had no classes in the winter of 1973.

So, there I was at Chicago's O'Hare Airport in early January, climbing aboard a United Airlines 747 for the eight-hour flight to Honolulu. My old Hill roommate, John Ford, was attending the University of Hawaii, and the plan was for me to crash with him at his Waikiki Beach apartment, find some menial job to cover living expenses, and spend two and a half months learning how to surf.

But, as they say, the best laid plans...

I only lasted two weeks before my money ran out. There were no jobs, menial or otherwise, to be had, not even filling the French frier with vegetable oil at the McDonald's on Waikiki Beach.

And I gave that one my best shot. When told the required wardrobe was black slacks and black shoes, I ponied up for a pair of charcoal Levis at the neighborhood JC Penney's, but budgetarily stressed as I was, I could not afford the requisite ebony footwear. So, I bought a can of black spray paint and tinted my beige desert boots accordingly.

I still didn't get the gig.

Although I felt very cool running through Honolulu, up around Diamond Head and along the Ala Wai Canal, accommodations were a bit tight because Ford also had a girlfriend sharing his place that he hadn't mentioned before I boarded the plane in Chicago.

So, I bade aloha to the fiftieth state, returning to the subarctic Midwest to work for a couple of months to restore my depleted savings before repairing to college in the spring. As an added bonus, I got to see Denise again, so coming back from Hawaii certainly had its upside.

In late January, I went to work at Midwest Steel in Portage, Indiana, where my father knew the mill superintendent. I was working in the shipping department, preparing steel sheets for transit by lowering them onto

4"x 4" wooden beams and wrapping them with metal bands to be loaded on flatbed trucks.

One Saturday night in February, toward the end of a twelve-hour shift, while operating a radial arm saw, I lacerated my left forearm very badly, cutting through the ulnar bone and almost through the radius bone. The ulnar nerve was also severed. It was not pretty, and I nearly lost my hand. I was transported by ambulance to Porter Memorial Hospital in Valparaiso, about thirteen miles away.

Normally, the trip should take about twenty minutes. Not that night.

First, the ambulance had been washed earlier that day, when the mercury was below freezing. Predictably, when the EMTs tried to load me in for the trip to the hospital, the doors were frozen shut. Then, once en route, we were further delayed by a slow freight train crossing Route 130. Although the EMT had placed a tourniquet on my arm, I had lost a great deal of blood by the time we arrived at the emergency room. As I was wheeled in, my heart was beating irregularly. Later, the doctors told me that, if it hadn't been for my excellent cardiovascular condition because I was a runner, the situation could have turned out much worse.

Once I got stabilized, they put me in a double room with a really nice high school kid named Tony Groenings. Coincidentally, Tony was a senior at Portage High School, the same town where Midwest Steel was located, and a starter on their basketball team, the captain, as I recall. As anyone who has seen the movie *Hoosiers* can tell you, high school basketball is an incredibly big deal in Indiana. Tony had hurt himself on that same Saturday, riding a snowmobile. He had hit a tree and really screwed up his leg.

It was a sad time for Tony. After we both got out of the hospital, I went to one of the Portage games. They were in the Indiana state high school tournament. Before the game, they wheeled him out on a gurney and gave him a round of applause. I'm not sure he ever played again or had the op-portunity to go to college.

As a result of my injury, I underwent so many follow up surgeries and therapy sessions in Indiana, New Hampshire, and Massachusetts that I lost count. Finally, I just had to say, "That's it! Time to get on with life." To this day I live with some permanent lack of mobility and numbness in my left hand, but at the time, all that mattered was, unlike Tony and his basketball, I could still run. And I was about to prove it. Sort of.

THE BEANTOWN BANDITS

"There's something very unique about Boston. It is Mecca-like."

—Bill Rodgers

MARCH OF 1973 WAS SPENT RECOVERING FROM MY ARM INJURY, DOING minimal—if any—running; my left forearm wrapped in a huge bundle of bandages that was disturbed only during my all-too-frequent doctor visits.

Miraculously, by April, I was able to talk my parents into letting me out of the house for a road trip. So, one afternoon, after my mother dropped me off at the Valparaiso Trailways bus station, I walked over to Route 49 and began hitchhiking my way north to the Indiana Toll Road.

Once there, I thumbed it east to the Ohio Turnpike and south on I-75 to Bowling Green State University, where my high school pal and original running inspiration, Alan Knobel, was a student. After a night of beer drinking at the Canterbury Inn, we hopped into Alan's car and drove to his parents' house in Canfield, Ohio, outside of Youngstown. I can still hear *Steely Dan's* "Reelin' in the Years" on the car radio.

I'm not sure where or when we got the idea, but we were men on a mission. We were headed to Boston to run in the marathon, which was being held the following Monday, April 16. Of course, we weren't going to run the entire 26.2 miles, silly goose—neither of us was in shape for that—but by running a few miles of the classic, we wanted just a taste of this hallowed event we had heard and read so much about.

And of course, we wouldn't be official entrants either. Rather, we would be "bandits," as they were called, who snuck in at the back of the pack and ran unofficially without race numbers. To be official runners, Alan and I needed to have already run Boston or some other sanctioned marathon in under three and a half hours. And of course, we hadn't done that.

As bandits, we knew we ran the risk of being pulled off the course by one of the race's organizers, the legendary Jock Semple of the Boston Athletic Association.

And Jock's reputation definitely preceded him.

Six years earlier, in 1967, a "K. Switzer" had officially registered for the marathon and started the race along with all the other runners. When Jock, who was riding in a press bus, saw that "K. Switzer" was really *Katherine* Switzer—with women not allowed to run in the marathon at the time—he jumped off the bus and tried to pull her out of the race.

Fortunately for Katherine, a man she was running with gave Jock a body check and sent him over the boards. She finished the marathon that day, the first official* woman ever to do so.

When Alan and I got to Hopkinton, it was sunny with the temperature in the low 70s...not a great day to run a marathon, a little too warm. And it was a total zoo. Admittedly, not compared to what it is now—but runners all over the place. There were 1,574 official starters and an undetermined number of bandits. We just tried to melt into the crowd way at the back

---

*   As a bandit a year prior, in 1966, Roberta "Bobbi" Gibb was the first woman to have run the entire Boston Marathon, and in 1996 she was officially recognized by the Boston Athletic Association for her accomplishment.

of the pack, not attracting any attention, until the starter's gun went off at noon.

When it finally did, we shuffled forward with everyone else, too packed in like sardines in the narrow street to find any decent running room.

It took us several minutes just to cross the starting line, and it was probably a mile before we hit full stride. As we headed down Route 135 out of Hopkinton into Ashland, it was a gentle downhill on the two-lane state highway. Things then flattened out the rest of the way into Framingham, where crowds began to build for the first time since the start. With the huge ball of bandages wrapped around my left arm, I was getting the sympathy vote and felt a bit guilty, knowing I wasn't in it for the long haul.

As we pulled into Framingham, there was a sign in the middle of the road that read "B.A.A. Marathon: 19 and 1/2 Miles To Go." How curious. Normally mile markers are given in even miles so you can pace yourself. Not at the Boston Athletic Association. That's tradition.

Right by that B.A.A. sign, at the 6.72-mile mark across from the Framingham train station, Alan and I dropped out. We were heckled by some of the spectators, who justifiably saw us as true bandits tarnishing those who had the perseverance and guts to go all the way to the finish line at the Prudential Center.

But we had our taste of the Boston Marathon on that April day, and it tasted damn good.

In the words of the immortal General Douglas MacArthur, "I shall return."

CATCHING A BREAK... UNFORTUNATELY

"Life is what happens to us while we are making other plans."

—Allen Saunders, American Writer, Journalist and Cartoonist

AND I STAYED TRUE TO THE GENERAL'S VOW, THOUGH NOT WITH THE GREATest of ease.

In the intervening year before the next Boston, running suffered somewhat as a priority compared to finishing college, continuing to heal from my arm injury, finding a job, and getting ready for a wedding.

To fulfill my end of the Dartmouth Plan and earn my bachelor's degree, classes beckoned in the summer and fall terms of 1973 and the winter term of 1974.

I had been a Town of Hanover volunteer fireman since sophomore year to earn plane fare for Denise to come and visit. When the fire station moved from Main Street to a couple miles north of town, the department offered student volunteers free rooms so there would be someone to ride the rigs during emergencies in the middle of the night. I moved right in at the beginning of the summer to save some money.

In addition, somewhat to the consternation of my parents--to put it mildly—I proposed to Denise right before returning to school in the fall of senior year. Although that was a very young age to get married, especially by today's standards—I would be twenty-two and Denise twenty—we were worried we would grow apart if we waited. My parents, on the other hand, were less than crazy about Denise's pedigree--a Midwesterner with no college degree--and they were concerned that an early betrothal would prevent me from attending graduate school.

But that didn't stop us. We had the master plan perfectly and simply laid out. I would cruise through my remaining academic requirements—which included a stint of practice teaching—take my law and business school board exams, graduate with a history major and education minor, find a teaching job, teach for a couple years, and then go to grad school before the kids came along.

Didn't sound like much time for running. Or breathing, for that matter. Then reality reared its ugly head.

By the fall, my left arm was continuing to heal, though the ulnar bone still had about a one-quarter-inch gap where the saw blade had cut clear through it. You could see it on the x-ray. Interestingly, the doctors had chosen to let the bone heal the entire gap itself. No metal plate, no bone graft. I was told to limit my activity, lest the jarring from running interfere with the healing process.

Over time, I began to grow very impatient with the enforced inactivity. One day, some might say perhaps unwisely, I joined in an impromptu touch football game. Yes, you can see this coming...While I was defending a pass, the receiver gave my left forearm a very slight elbow tap, and the ulna fractured again.

The party line as reported to my parents... I stumbled while climbing some stairs and bumped my arm on the bannister.

A couple days later, after being surgically prepped by former roommate and pre-med wizard Chris Wiley, there I was in the surgical arena at Mary Hitchcock Hospital, undergoing a bone graft from my right hip to my left forearm. Unfortunately, Chris had prepped the *left* hip, but the surgery was successful anyhow. That meant more recovery time, less running.

Despite this setback, through the fall and winter, the academics, practice teaching, and business and law board exams proceeded apace. The running, not so much. Even though I had been at it going on three years, I was not logging my daily efforts. So, I cannot reconstruct what it was I was doing on the roads—or when it was—despite what was apparently pretty limited training, I decided I was going to run Boston in 1974.

And not just some of it.

"The whole freakin' thing," as catcher Jake Taylor remarked in the movie *Major League*.

My training was guided by something with the daunting title "The Collapse Point Theory," as later explained in *The 1975 Marathon Handbook*. I'm not entirely sure where I picked it up. Maybe from Alan Knobel, maybe from *Runner's World* magazine, maybe from a bathroom wall someplace.

Anyhow, the gist of it was that, to successfully complete a 26.2-mile marathon, a runner had to average one-third of that distance—or nine miles—every day for six to eight weeks before the race. If your average was only eight miles, physical collapse came at twenty-four miles. If only seven miles...well, you get the idea. So, I must have been averaging at least nine miles a day.

I do remember one Saturday run with particular clarity. It was the middle of February, spitting snow and probably about twenty-five degrees out, a north wind, overcast, roads wet and sloppy. I headed south from my abode at the fire station on Lyme Road into Hanover to the Dartmouth Green, took a right on Wheelock Street and down the hill across the frozen Connecticut River on the Ledyard Bridge. Once in Vermont, a right along the river on the aptly named River Road, which I followed straight into the wind for about six miles. Back over the river into New Hampshire and south on Lyme Road another four miles back to my point of origin. Probably twelve miles in all. Not bad for a rookie with two months to go until Patriots' Day. Maybe I could do it after all.

But in the meantime, as I prepared for a teaching job, I also needed to find a teaching job. It had been made clear to me, in no uncertain terms by my parents—and I might add appropriately so, after all they had invested in my education—that once I was out of college, I was also out on my own.

My search took on added urgency in that Denise and I tentatively planned our wedding right after my graduation. However, being Mr. Risk Averse, yours truly, I was hesitant to set a wedding date until I had secured an official paying gig. After all, I was going to have a new, albeit brilliant and beautiful, wife to support.

So, I blanketed over twenty-five Northern Illinois, Southeastern Massachusetts, and Central New Hampshire school districts with letters, soliciting an entry-level Social Studies teaching job. Suffice it to say that after an extended crusade, I landed a one-year contract in Norwell, Massachusetts paying $8,450 a year to teach eighth grade US History. The incumbent teacher was going on a twelve-month sabbatical to get his doctorate degree at the University of Tennessee.

A doctorate degree to return to Norwell the following year and teach eighth graders?

Never mind, Jim. A job's a job.

And guess what? Norwell was twenty-six miles from Boston. No doubt about it, must have been harmonic convergence.

So, all of a sudden, it was April of 1974, and miraculously, all the non-running boxes on my to-do list had been checked.

IT'S GREEK... AND BRITISH... TO ME

"Rejoice, we conquer!"

—Pheidippides, Athenian Soldier, Messenger and Runner

NOW IT WAS TIME TO FOCUS ON CHASING DOWN MY DREAM.

Just before the April 15 marathon, I was camped out at my sister Nicky's town house in Duxbury, Massachusetts, on the South Shore about an hour from the starting line at Hopkinton. It had already been a memorable week. On April 8, Henry Aaron had slugged his 715th home run off Al Downing, breaking Babe Ruth's all-time record.

Meanwhile, I was combing through the local sporting goods store, selecting my marathon gear—a blue tank top and baggy white shorts with blue piping, to go with the red, white, and blue elastic headband that held back my flowing blond locks. For footwear, I had graduated from the old Tigers and Pumas to the Adidas brand, training in the Country shoe, which had a white upper white with forest green tri-striping. On Monday, I would run in a brand-new pair of the SL 72 model with blue uppers and white stripes.

I wasn't trying to make a fashion statement by any means. I was trying to fly under the radar. Remember, I was still a bandit, running unofficially, without a number. I didn't want Jock Semple jumping off the press bus to chase me down.

I'd be lying if I said I had studied the course very much. In fact, I'd be lying if I said I had studied the course at all. Pretty much everything I knew could be summed up in one sentence, allowing for a couple of comma faults. The first sixteen miles were flat to slightly downhill, miles 17 to 21 were a series of hills, miles 22 to 26 were downhill to flat. And the hills were famous for killing runners. Well, not literally.

Speaking of killing runners, perhaps a brief history lesson is in order. Unsubstantiated legend has it that the first marathon supposedly was run by a Greek messenger, Pheidippides, in the year 490 BC after the Greek army defeated the invading Persians at the Battle of Marathon. "Rejoice, we conquer," he uttered as he rushed into the Athens marketplace before dropping dead after his run of twenty-something miles from the battle site.

His finishing time was not recorded.

By 1896, that legend had translated to a distance-running event in the modern Olympics called...wait for it...the marathon. The inaugural Olympic marathon, held in Greece,* traced the original route trod by Pheidippides, from the plains of Marathon into the city of Athens and counted among its twenty-five participants one Arthur Blake of the Boston Athletic Association. Although Blake faltered, dropping out at 23 kilometers (14.26 miles) with blood blisters staining his shoes, a seed had been planted.

That first Olympic marathon had mightily impressed some of the Boston Athletic Association officials who accompanied their marathoner, Blake, across the pond, and upon their return to Beantown in late 1896, they began planning Boston's own marathon. Laying out a course that topographically was very similar to the route from Marathon to Athens, the BAA

---

* To the everlasting delight of his countrymen, that first modern Olympic 24.85-mile marathon was won by a twenty-two-year-old Greek named Spiridon Loues in a time of 2:58:50. Seventy-nine years later, that finishing time would have barely qualified him to officially run in the 1976 Boston Marathon.

came up with a course that was 25 miles long and paralleled the Boston and Albany Railroad line from the starting line on Route 135 in Ashland into downtown Boston.

That course—and that distance of 25 miles—would suffice for the first Boston Marathon, held on Patriots' Day, April 19, 1897, when a mere fifteen hardy souls showed up at the starting line and for twenty-six subsequent Boston Marathons.

At the time, there was no such thing as a standard marathon distance. The 1896 Athens Olympic marathon was 24.85 miles. The 1897 Boston Marathon was 25 miles. The 1900 Paris Olympic Marathon was 24.96 miles.

Then, in 1908, the Olympics came to Great Britain. Since the royal family wanted to witness the beginning of the marathon, which was to finish in White City Stadium in London, the starting line was pulled back to within eyeshot of Windsor Castle, making it 26 miles even.

Not only that. Wanting to view the race's completion up close and personal, the royals also had the White City finish line extended another 385 yards so as to end directly in front of their viewing box. Over subsequent years, the 26-mile, 385-yard distance became the marathon standard.

Many is the suffering runner who has launched expletive-laced epithets at the crown in the final stages of a marathon effort.

It wasn't until 1924 that the Boston start was moved back to the burg of Hopkinton, and the course assumed the standard marathon distance of 26 miles, 385 yards.

THERE'S A FIRST TIME FOR EVERYTHING

*"Hooray for me! I scaled Mount Everest, pitched a
no-hitter in the World Series and killed the meanest
bull in Madrid. That's what it felt like when I won the
Boston Marathon in 4 hours and 16 minutes."*

—Richard J. Israel, American Rabbi,
Beekeeper and Marathon Runner

SO HERE I WAS, FIFTY YEARS LATER, A TWENTY-ONE-YEAR-OLD KID SKULKING IN
the back of the pack of 1,741 official starters, hopefully ready to complete my first Boston Marathon. It was great weather to run, fifty-five
degrees and breezy, no need to worry about heat exhaustion.

When the gun sounded at noon, the first quarter of the marathon was
pretty much a rerun (pun intended) of Alan's and my experience year earlier. The only difference: I didn't have a bulky bandage around my left arm,
and I was charged up and ready to chase down a dream three years in
the making.

With basically the first 16 miles of the course flat to downhill and the
crowds steadily building, steadily partying, and steadily cheering, it was
really difficult not to get sucked into going out too fast, especially for a first
timer. However, I wasn't fooling anyone here. I was running to finish, not
so they could perch the winner's laurel wreath on top of my cranium. So, I
kept things very conservative.

Past the train station in Framingham, it was into Natick, past the 10-mile checkpoint, and then on to all-female Wellesley College, the marathon's halfway point. Still feeling pretty fresh, I was buoyed by the wildly cheering women students, whose well wishes carried me another 3 miles, to Newton Lower Falls, the course's low elevation point.

This brought me, in more ways than one, to the moment of truth. Having covered 16 miles, I was about to begin the 5-mile ascent, culminating at the peak of Heartbreak Hill at the end of mile 21. This was the stretch of the course that had crushed countless marathoners, all of them a hell of a lot more experienced I was. To say I wasn't more than a little anxious as I dug into the first hill in front of the Newton Fire Station would be a boldfaced lie.

Confronting the hills, I was also learning that my decision to lace up a spanking-new pair of Adidas SL 72s on race day had been somewhat flawed, if not downright boneheaded. Running as I always did without socks, I could feel the blisters starting to form on the bottom of my right foot. The sole started gradually to burn, but I pushed on as best I could. It really started to sting.

The B.A.A.'s blistered Arthur Blake, from the 1896 Olympic marathon, had nothing on me.

Ever the historian, in an attempt to take my mind off my deteriorating condition, I recalled the hoary legend of how Heartbreak Hill got its name.

In the 1936 edition of the race, a Rhode Island Native American named Ellison "Tarzan" Brown had set a torrid pace and was more than three minutes ahead of the course record as he entered the Newton hills. Then Johnny "The Elder" Kelley, the 1935 marathon winner, wiped out Tarzan's half-mile lead, finally catching him on the final of the four hills.

As Johnny passed him, he patted Tarzan on the back, as if to say, "Nice job, but I've got it from here." Tarzan, incensed, surged ahead to win the race. As *Boston Globe* sportswriter, Jerry Nason, later described the incident; losing to Tarzan, "broke Johnny's heart."

Long story short, my heart unbroken, I made it up and over the hills. There was a loudspeaker at the top of Heartbreak blasting over and over again, "You made it! You beat Heartbreak Hill!" It was a real rush of pride for me as I crested Heartbreak, because even though there were still 5 miles to go, I knew those 5 miles were downhill to flat, and despite my throbbing right foot, I knew I was going to make it.

The crowds were fantastic, pressing in on the runners, except for one thing. As we came down off the inclines, through Cleveland Circle, then Coolidge Corner, Kenmore Square past Fenway Park (where the 12 noon Red Sox game had just finished), onto Massachusetts Avenue, spectators would give radically incorrect mileage information.

They'd say, "Way to go! Great run! Only two miles to go!" Only problem was, they were standing at mile 23, and there were really 3.2 miles to go. That can create a pretty serious buzz kill, even for the euphoric runner who has just conquered Heartbreak Hill.

From Mass Avenue, I took a right on Hereford Street and, after a block, a quick left to cross the finish line in front of the Prudential Center. I had done it! I was caked in sweat, my quadriceps were killing me from all the downhill running, and my fancy new SL 72s—one of them, at least—was soaked in blood.

I limped away from the finish area without even claiming my bowl of beef stew, which the B.A.A. customarily served all runners who completed the race. But—damn it!—I had done it.

THERE'S A FIRST TIME FOR EVERYTHING

My time? Who knows? Distance running in 1974 was in the days before wrist chronographs or computer chips on running shoes. The stopwatch started for everyone when the starter's pistol went off and stopped when those with official numbers each crossed the finish line.

As best I could guess, I ran my first Boston in around 3 hours and 40 minutes, compared to Irish winner Neil Cusack's 2:13. I was an hour and a half behind the winner. My 8:24 per mile compared with Neil's 5:05.

To say there might be room for improvement would be a serious understatement.

THOSE WHO CAN, TEACH

"Tell me and I forget. Teach me and I
remember. Involve me and I learn."

—Benjamin Franklin

WITH SUMMER JUST AROUND THE CORNER, THERE WAS MY GRADUATION IN June, Denise's and my wedding in July, and our move east in August. We drove this huge U-Haul box truck from Chicago to a one-bedroom apartment in Duxbury, towing our blue VW Super Beetle behind us. I had totally overestimated the truck size we needed. Hell, we could have loaded the car *into* the truck and still had plenty of room to spare.

Also in August, until our first paychecks came in, we slept on our apartment floor and subsisted on Bisquick® waffles and pancakes. In other news, flashing a "V" sign as he ducked into Marine One to depart Washington, DC, Richard Nixon resigned as thirty-seventh president of the United States to avoid being impeached for his various transgressions related to the Watergate break-in and its subsequent investigation.

As I settled into my teaching slot in Norwell and Denise found an administrative role at a brokerage firm in Boston, our new life together fell into a happy routine. To be with each other every day was a definite change for the better after trying to maintain a trans-continental relationship for the past three years.

However, I soon found a couple of daunting teaching challenges at Norwell Junior High School.

For one thing, I didn't have enough US History books for the 115 kids in my five classes. What books I did have predated the War of 1812 and may have been used to deflect cannon balls during that conflict, they were in such disrepair.

For another thing, one of my classes in particular must have been the inspiration for the infamous Sweathogs on the '70s TV show *Welcome Back Kotter* starring Gabe Kaplan. The class was composed of about fifteen kids who had ADD, ADHD, learning disabilities, schizophrenia, or perhaps all of the above. They were impossible to control, immune to threats of discipline, and their ringleader was a kid named Paul who was at least fifty pounds heavier than I was and answered to the nickname "Bullet."

I used my creativity to tackle both challenges.

First, the Sweathogs. No US history books for them. Not only could they barely read, but they wouldn't sit still long enough to read, even if they could. They needed their own custom curriculum. Very basic stuff. So I authored it. Like map exercises. Crossword puzzles. Word puzzles. Things that would keep them occupied and reasonably quiet. Not rioting in the halls. Or throwing Molotov cocktails at the Principal's Office.

Second, everybody else. My other 100 scholars. There still weren't enough books to go around, and my educational philosophy was different anyway. I didn't believe that kids learned passively—through reading and being lectured to. I believed that learning was an active process, that children learned more by doing and by actually experiencing. Maybe that was the result of some simulation gaming work I did as part of my education minor at Dartmouth. But more about that shortly.

Consequently, my modus operandi became this...

At the beginning of a study unit, I would prepare a two-page mimeo-graphed summary of the US historical content—names, events, dates, and so forth—for the chapter in question. After distributing my précis as one night's reading assignment, I would spend at most the next two class sessions reviewing the material and saving my young friends twenty to thirty pages of textbook reading.

Which I, of course, made it a point to mention to them.

Then we would spend the next two or three weeks learning by doing, by actually experiencing. Let me offer a couple of examples.

One unit involved the study of the lifestyle of pioneer Americans in the early nineteenth century. To help my charges experience that lifestyle, I assigned them *The Diary of An Early American Boy* by Eric Sloane. In this book, fifteen-year-old Noah Blake narrates his life and times on the 1805 Connecticut frontier. As they read the tome, each pupil was also asked to physically recreate some artifact from those days, many examples of which were sketched out in the book.

Each student's project required my advance approval, and when two boys told me they wanted to build a log cabin, I gave them the green light. The days flew by as if on gossamer wings, and the pioneer lifestyle section was drawing to a close. Most of the kids had handed in their projects or would do so in the next couple of days.

But nothing yet from the log cabin kids. So, after class, I asked them, "Hey, guys, how's your project coming along?"

"We've been working on it, but it's not done yet," one answered.

"Well, the unit's coming to a close," I countered. "Can I see it?"

"Sure," the other replied. "But we'll need to take a ride off campus."

So, the next day, after getting permission from Principal Henry Grandman, the three of us hopped into my trusty VW and drove a couple of miles from the junior high out into the middle of the woods. The boys led me into the brush away from the road, and there it was, the beginnings of their log cabin.

I mean, I had expected something made out of Lincoln Logs or twigs harvested from the local forest preserve. After all, these were scrawny eighty-pound eighth graders, for God's sake! Instead, we're talking a *real* log cabin, four sides, about eight feet wide by ten feet long, four logs high, tree trunks about a foot in diameter, each with the ends notched out, fit together, the whole enchilada. I was blown away.

"Boys!" I exclaimed. "This is incredible!" Then, pausing to collect myself, I asked, "And which one of your parents owns this property?"

They looked at each other, perplexed, and in unison said, "Our parents don't own this property."

We all ran back to the VW, screaming, and jumped in. I gunned the engine, and we sped away.

The lads were given a "B" for their efforts and instructed never to return to the site again.

As a second example of helping my scholars to learn by doing, by actually experiencing, I was really big time into classroom simulation gaming. Simply put, simulation games are re-creations that imitate a real-life situation, and I had a lot of fun devising a number of them in my two years in front of the classroom.

One of these simulation games was cleverly named "A House Divided" and pitted my eighth graders against one another as they refought the US Civil War. Each class was bifurcated—the Union vs. the Confederacy—with each side assigned troops, ships, and resources with which to attack the opposing side's states and ocean zones during ten spring and fall military campaigns.

As in history, with each passing campaign, the Union's strength became more dominant, and wily leadership and luck increasingly became the Confederacy's only hope. In only one of my four classes was the Confederacy able prevent itself from being overrun thanks to that cocktail of wily leadership and luck. Otherwise, the song remained the same as written in the annals of American history.

I knew the simulation had taught the kids something when, on the last day of the Civil War unit, Nancy, certainly far from my most engaged US History scholar, remarked as she walked out of class, "You know, the South never had a chance."

Boo-yah!

THE SECOND COMING

"Are you sure it's a new record? 2:09:55? Honest? This is absurd. I can't run that fast. This is ridiculous. I must be dreaming this whole thing."

—Bill Rodgers

ONCE I GOT OVER THE "I'LL NEVER RUN ANOTHER MARATHON AGAIN" PHASE that practically every first timer goes through, my nascent marathoning career continued. The junior high schedule, with its 2:30 p.m. dismissal time, lent itself perfectly to long afternoon runs, and the scenery along Duxbury's Powder Point and Cape Cod Bay was magnificent.

Although I was still an acolyte of the collapse point theory, my limited recordkeeping suggests that, in addition to increasing my weekly mileage, I was starting to participate in the local road-racing scene. In November of 1974, results from the 4-mile Duxbury Turkey Run showed me to be fourth overall with a time of 22:50, or 5:42 per mile. As we rolled into 1975, in another local run in April, a 10.4 miler, I placed twelfth with a time of 59:48, which translates to 5:45 per mile.

I was getting better. Now if only I could run that much faster for that much farther.

That brings us around to April 21, 1975, Patriots' Day, the bicentennial of the battles of Lexington and Concord and another Boston Marathon.

Beginning in 1972, as previously mentioned, the B.A.A. had imposed a 3-hour, 30-minute Boston Marathon qualifying standard for men ages twenty to thirty-nine because of the increasing number of people who were applying to run. The B.A.A. hierarchy, Race Director Will Cloney, and our old friend Jock Semple were afraid too many runners on the course might compromise what they termed "the Boston Marathon race experience."

So, they wanted to limit how many could run in their race. Truthfully, they were probably on to something, given the pack of runners I had seen in Hopkinton and Ashland the previous two years. And in all honesty, bandits like me were contributing to the problem.

In order to qualify, a runner had to run some other sanctioned marathon under 3:30 in the year before the upcoming Boston and document that performance in their race application to Messrs. Cloney and Semple. I had a 3:40 marathon at Boston in 1974, but of course it was undocumented because I ran as a bandit, and it wasn't under 3:30 anyway.

In the middle of beginning a new career and a new marriage, I don't think I ever seriously entertained entering another marathon to qualify for the 1975 event. So, for the third year in a row, on Patriot's Day, I would be bringing up the rear as a bandit.

The 1975 Boston Marathon itself was pretty unremarkable.

Not!

On a cool day with a southwest tailwind, Bill Rodgers, a relatively unknown Boston College graduate student wearing a shirt on which his girlfriend had crayoned "GBTC BOSTON," won the race and broke Ron Hill's 1970 course record, clocking a 2:09:55 while absolutely thrashing the competition.

Rodgers, who grew up in Newington, Connecticut, avidly chased butterflies as a kid before winning the state high school cross-country championship as a senior. Subsequently, he was recruited to Wesleyan University by Amby Burfoot, whose brother Rodgers beat in that state championship. Bill and Amby roomed together, and Rodgers had a ringside seat as Amby trained to win the 1968 Boston Marathon.

Upon graduation in 1970, Rodgers stepped away from running entirely, enrolling to receive a master's degree in Special Education at Boston College. He had also applied for—and was granted—conscientious objector status, and thus was exempt from the military draft at the height of the Vietnam War. To fulfill his alternative service requirement, he became a service escort manager at Peter Bent Brigham Hospital in Boston, as he put it, "no longer running on the track, but racing to the morgue."

As he performed menial tasks at the hospital and smoked his Winstons, running was the farthest thing from Bill's mind. He even bought a Triumph 650 motorcycle, cruising the bars with his childhood buddy and Back Bay roommate, Jason Kehoe. But when his bike was stolen, he had to begin running again in order to get to work, and he gradually returned to the road-racing scene.

He ran his first Boston Marathon in 1973, a DNF ("Did Not Finish"), and later that year, he won Massachusetts's Bay State Marathon. The next year, Bill came in fourteenth at Boston and fifth at New York before winning the Philadelphia Marathon in November. Along the way, he had joined the Greater Boston Track Club, coached by Bill Squires.

Clearly, now with the course record at Boston, Rodgers was on his way.

For my part, Denise and I got a late start from Duxbury and almost missed the noon starter's gun. After jumping out of the VW, I fell into place just in time, moving slowly out of Hopkinton with the coursing hoard. Again running conservatively—but with a bit more familiarity and a bit less temerity—I proceeded well until an ill-advised swig of Gatorade while climbing the hills at mile 18 induced sharp abdominal cramps that fortunately soon subsided.

Note to self: in the future, stop hydrating after 15 miles.

I crossed the line at the Pru at 3:08:30, a whopping 31 minutes and 30 seconds better than last year. At a pace of 7:12 a mile, a minute and 12 seconds faster than last year. What's more, the 3:08 would have easily qualified me for next year's Boston, had I been officially registered.

It was, like, light years better than the 3:30 qualifying standard.

Now I just needed to register in another sanctioned marathon sometime before the following April and run it under 3:30, and I, the varsity letterless high schooler, the serial bandit, would actually compete in the 1976 Boston Marathon **officially**.

It truly boggled the mind.

SCHOOL'S OUT FOR SUMMER

"To give anything less than your best is to sacrifice the gift."

—Steve Prefontaine, American Distance Runner

OF COURSE, NOW THAT I WAS THIS SUCCESSFUL MARATHONER, I HAD MY first year of teaching to complete. Suffice it to say, most of my eighth graders, perhaps with the exception of Bullet and his crew, idolized me. In fact, during this first season that the sitcom *Happy Days* was on the air, they called me the "Blond Fonz." Behind my back, of course.

The girls, with their Boston-area accents, called me "Mistah Riehl" and catalogued my complete wardrobe, recording exactly what I wore each and every day. Like all the really cool runners of the time, I had a moustache, although because I was blond and very fine-haired, I have to admit it was pretty wimpy. Didn't matter. My female pupils noticed when I shaved my upper lip even before Denise did.

Regarding the boys, perhaps at age twenty-two I should have been less a friend and more of an authority figure. On an occasional Friday after classes, I would change into my running togs and cover the back roads from the junior high school in Norwell to our apartment in Duxbury, about 13 miles. One such Friday, several of my male students came out of the woods on bicycles with ropes and unsuccessfully tried to lasso me. Employing my superior agility and speed, I was able to elude them—and what most likely would have been an unfortunate incident for all of us.

In a much more unfortunate incident a few Fridays later on the opposite coast of the United States, phenomenally talented and intense long-distance runner Steve Prefontaine met his untimely death at age twenty-four in a car accident in Eugene, Oregon. "Pre," as he was called, originally took up cross-country running after getting benched on his junior high school football and basketball teams due to his diminutive stature. I could definitely identify with that.

Running at the University of Oregon for Bill Bowerman and later for the Oregon Track Club, he never lost an NCAA race at 3 miles, 5,000 meters, 6 miles or 10,000 meters, and he set American records at every distance between 2,000 and 10,000 meters. Without exception, he always went out hard from the start, and his mantra was "Somebody may beat me, but they are going to have to bleed to do it." The guy simply resonated with me.

Seven weeks before his death, Pre sent Bill Rodgers a pair of Nike Boston '73 shoes that Billy wore a week and a half later in his record-setting Boston Marathon win.

A couple of weeks after Pre's tragic passing, as I played the *Beach Boys Endless Summer* LP vinyl album on the last day of class, my Norwell contract was up, and I was on to my next—and final—teaching gig.

PLYMOUTH ROCKS

"April showers bring May flowers. And Mayflowers bring Pilgrims."

—Anonymous

A ND WHAT A FORTUITOUS FINAL TEACHING GIG THAT TURNED OUT TO BE.

I had landed at Plymouth-Carver Intermediate School, about twenty minutes south of Duxbury, teaching ninth-grade Civics. PCIS was a brand new, beautiful facility, built at a cost of $8 million a couple of years earlier. The design was something called "open concept," which was a nice way of saying there were no walls or doors between classrooms, just rows of lockers.

It was pretty clear that whoever the architect was hadn't taught school a day in their life. If Johnny in Math class was sitting across from Sara in English and wanted to nail her with a spitball, it happened. Or if a teacher's back was turned, inscribing wisdom on the chalkboard, it was real easy for Claude, the erstwhile scholar, to sail a paper airplane over the lockers into the classroom next door.

But even though PCIS didn't have walls and doors like Norwell Junior High did, I was finding that some of the educational tactics that worked at the old place were going to work at the new place as well. And that was a good thing, because ninth graders are, well...let's just say, a challenging bunch.

One of the tactics that worked again was simulation gaming.

Another of the fun ones I created was called "It's a Mad, Mad World." Every class was divvied up into seven groups, with each group occupying a continent and controlling a different commodity. One continent controlled food, one controlled oil, one controlled precious metal, and so forth. Each continent needed commodities from the other continents to survive. The idea was that the continents had to coexist, negotiate, and trade. I had invented a basic tutorial in international relations.

However, there was one problem. Perhaps none too wisely, I had given two of the continents nuclear weapons, seeking to instruct them also in international diplomacy. Bad idea. Armed accordingly, they blew up the world in the first round of the game. Since I had planned for that unit to last at least two weeks, that was unacceptable! I was forced to change the rules, and we started anew the next day.

A second tactic that worked was Jeopardy.

At Norwell, I had become prolific at drafting Jeopardy games that I employed to kill empty class time on Fridays, sessions before vacations, or when students were especially unruly because of the full moon. These games consisted of three rounds—Jeopardy, Double Jeopardy, and Final Jeopardy—just like on TV. The kids loved them. I could come up with twelve categories of five questions, each in about an hour and a half, and when I shared them with my fellow faculty members, they adored me for it.

Jeopardy turned out to be particularly helpful at PCIS.

As astronaut Jack Swigert of Apollo 13 once said, "Houston, we have a problem." Well, when I arrived at PCIS, I found a problem there too. The problem was a forty-five-minute reading period that some Board of Ed bureaucrat had imposed from 2:00 p.m. to 2:45 p.m. every afternoon, immediately before dismissal. During that time, students were to sit quietly at their desks, reading.

Huh?

What were the odds that energetic, hormone-laden ninth graders were going to sit quietly at their desks, reading, after six hours of inactivity and boring classes (except mine, of course)? I'll tell you--slim and none.

To occupy our young charges and prevent the reading period from becoming three-quarters of an hour of violence and bloodshed, I leveraged my experience gained up the road at Norwell, becoming a Jeopardy game factory and cranking out an original contest daily.

Once again, my fellow faculty members adored me for it.

GREATER BOSTON, THE HOME
OF THE BEAN AND THE COD

"Things always turn out for the best."

—Anonymous

LTHOUGH DEALING WITH THAT ONGOING NINTH-GRADE CIVIL UNREST AT PCIS turned out to be the cloud, I soon found that the cloud had a silver lining, and the silver lining was named Scott Graham. Scott was a Math teacher at PCIS, and he was a runner, a very good runner.

Originally from Melrose, Massachusetts, Scottie had run competitively at and graduated from the University of Bridgeport in Connecticut. Upon returning to Boston, he wanted to continue running. The problem was, once out of college, it was difficult for him to find coaching and other workout partners.

That was before 1973, when a Boston College senior named Jack MacDonald met in a Boston College locker room with four other guys, a six-pack of beer, and Boston State track coach Bill Squires to discuss forming a running club for post-collegiate runners. After kicking around some rather bogus names, like the Boston Beaners and the Boston Codfishers, the group wisely agreed to christen itself the Greater Boston Track Club.

GBTC instantly became a magnet for many aspiring out-of-college tracksters and distance runners in the area, including Scottie and one Bill

Rodgers. In fact, GBTC was a haven for local distance-running luminaries—"sturdleys," as Scottie came to call them. In addition to Scott and Bill, other members of the club included Alberto Salazar, Bob Hodge, Vinnie Fleming, Randy Thomas, Dickie Mahoney, and ultimately, Jim Riehl.

How did that happen? Well, as I got to know Scottie at PCIS, by a huge coincidence, he was renting a place about a half a mile from our Duxbury apartment. We began going for long afternoon runs together after school at an easy 7- or 8-minute-per-mile pace.

Other afternoons, Scott did "fartlek" workouts by himself. At first, I thought that meant he was having a bad intestinal reaction to the food in the school cafeteria. Then he explained that "fartlek" meant "speed play" in Swedish, and in those workouts, he would cruise along at a 7:30 pace and occasionally throw in surges at a 5:00 pace. He did those by himself because I wouldn't have been able to keep up.

Scottie was a real down-to-earth, "aw, shucks" kind of guy, very inclusive, and despite my relative lack of running street cred, he brought me right into his GBTC circle. That meant a lot to me after my intense struggles and spectacular flameouts in my previous sporting ventures.

All of a sudden, I was going up to the Boston College outdoor track in Chestnut Hill when it was warm and to the Tufts University indoor track in Medford when it was cold, doing workouts with Bill Rodgers and a bunch of other running studs. Scottie and I would carpool into Boston after school, do Coach Squires's proscribed workout with all the other guys, and return to Duxbury by around 7:00 p.m.

Squires himself was a bit of a character. He grew up in South Boston, became an All-American, running cross-country and track at Notre Dame, then spent some time in the army before returning to Massachusetts to coach track at Wakefield High School. He himself had run the Boston Marathon, finishing in a very credible 2 hours and 47 minutes. From there he was hired as a professor of Physical Education and track coach at Boston State College. His tutelage of the GBTC was pro bono.

As Alberto Salazar later described him in his book *14 Minutes: A Running Legend's Life and Death and Life*, "He was tall, around 50, with a classic Beantown accent pitched to be heard in the most clamorous Irish barroom. Squires came from the Casey Stengel school of management and elocution. He wouldn't use one word if ten would do, and there was no such thing as a straight line or a simple answer. But Squires was whip smart. No coach understood the marathon in general, and the Boston Marathon in particular, better than Coach Squires."

And Squires's workouts? The GBTC runners had several quirky nicknames for him, but he sure as hell knew what he was doing. It was from Squires that I first learned the value (as did Scottie, Bill, and Alberto) of repeat track intervals combined with hilly distance workouts and 100-plus weekly mileage. That was Squires's secret sauce. Nobody else was training for marathons like that.

Squires's philosophy? It was a three-legged stool.

First, you had to do the miles, but not too many. Everyone was running lots of miles. Everyone had a good enough base to complete the marathon. But the event was evolving from a test of endurance to a test of endurance *and* speed.

Second, how do you build up your speed? You run track intervals and shorter road races in the weeks leading up to the marathon at a per-mile pace *faster* than you are going be running in the actual marathon. That way, when you are running the marathon at a faster pace than your usual road workouts, it feels comfortable.

Third, throw in lots and lots of repeat hills, and just as Manager Jimmy Dugan (aka Tom Hanks) once famously remarked, "There's no crying in baseball," there would be no crashing on Heartbreak Hill.

We would go on the track and run 1/4-mile, 1/2-mile, 3/4-mile, 1-mile, 3/4-mile, 1/2-mile and 1/4-mile "ladders" at race pace on the track with little rest in between. Speed work, Squires called it—as in, as fast as you could run. For some of the guys, that was a sub-60-second quarter mile. For me, my top end might have been 70 or 75 seconds.

Exhausting.

As we got closer to the marathon, the ladder lengths would increase: 1/2-mile, 1-mile, 1 and 1/2-mile, 2-miles, 1 and 1/2 mile, 1-mile, and 1/2 mile.

Brutal.

And then out onto the roads. Boston College was located on the marathon course, in the heart of the Newton hills, including Heartbreak. So, we ran them. Again. And again. Until we knew them like the backs of our hands.

Of course, it was a little embarrassing in that the other guys were running their intervals faster than me. But nobody made light of that; we were all giving it maximum effort. On the roads, it was a similar experience. I went for a run with Bill and Scottie once and could only stay with them for about a mile and a half. But it was incredibly inspiring to be training with, if slightly behind, the reigning Boston Marathon champion and course record holder.

In his book, Salazar recalled one GBTC track workout at Tufts. Coach Squires separated the runners into two groups—the more talented runners, like Rodgers, Scottie, and himself, and the less talented runners, which included me. He christened them the "Sharks" and the "Guppies."

You can guess which was which. No wonder I don't remember that specific workout. But I guess I'd rather be a Guppy in Coach Squires's program than a cake eater in the Hudson football program.

As I look back, this was total and complete serendipity. How could it be possible that, as a humble 3:08 marathoner, I would find myself immersed in world-class talent and technique?

Yes, things always do turn out for the best.

MEET "THE ROOKIE"

"I'd rather run a gutsy race, pushing all the way and
lose, than run a conservative race for a win."

—Alberto Salazar

WHEN I FIRST LAID EYES ON ALBERTO IN JANUARY OF 1976 AT THE TUFTS
University indoor facility, he was a skinny high school senior and
had already been training with GBTC for a year, working out with guys six
to eight years older, who had christened him "The Rookie."

He had quite a story to tell, but you would never know it. He was too
focused on one thing and one thing only. Going faster.

Alberto was born in Cuba, where his father Jose was one of Fidel
Castro's right-hand men as Castro and Che Guevara engineered the Cuban
Revolution that toppled the corrupt US-supported dictator, Fulgencio
Batista. However, as the Castro regime embraced Communism, allied it-
self with the Soviet Union, and squeezed out the Catholic church, Jose
openly denounced Fidel and emigrated with his family, first to Manchester,
Connecticut and later to Wayland, Massachusetts.

Initially, Jose was determined to return to Cuba and was supposed to be
a part of the second wave of the failed 1961 Bay of Pigs invasion, in which
exiled Cuban nationals sponsored by the United States hoped to over-
throw Castro and his cronies. When the insertion failed, Jose rechanneled

75

his considerable energy into becoming, as Alberto put it, "the primary spokesman for the Cuban exile community in New England."

Jose was an intense man, full of anger, bitter over his betrayal, first at the hands of Castro and then at the hands of the United States at the Bay of Pigs. He pushed Alberto relentlessly, admonishing him repeatedly, "A Salazar never quits."

As a youngster, Alberto described himself as "middling" in sports, failing to make Little League teams and getting cut from the Wayland Middle School basketball squad. But then, as a seventh grader, he toasted all his more athletic classmates in the 600-yard run, and the next year, in eighth grade, he began running in high school JV cross-country meets...and winning them.

From there, he hit the Boston summer road-racing scene, competing in 5- to 10-mile events put on around the area by the North Medford Club. Once at Wayland High, Alberto continued to burnish his street cred, going undefeated in cross country as a junior and finishing second in the Massachusetts state championship meet.

It was just after his stellar fall cross-country season that Alberto encountered Kirk Pfrangle, one of the founding members of the GBTC, following an indoor track meet. Kirk asked him to participate in one of the club's workouts, and Alberto agreed, later commenting, "I didn't realize that Kirk's invitation was the equivalent of a high school shortstop being invited to play with the Boston Red Sox, or a garage band drummer being invited to sit in with the Rolling Stones."

I knew exactly what Alberto meant.

PHILADELPHIA FREEDOM

"A runner must have completed any previous
B.A.A. or other sanctioned marathon within 3
hours, 30 minutes within the past year."

—Boston Athletic Association

NOW IT WAS TIME, AFTER THREE YEARS OF UNOFFICIAL BANDITRY, TO *FINALLY* and *officially* qualify for Boston.

In order to do that, remember I had to run some other officially sanctioned marathon in under three and a half hours. Will Cloney and Jock Semple of the B.A.A. said so.

Considering that I had run under 3:09 at Boston back in April and I had Coach Squires's training tools in my kit, a 3:30 time was a "Piece of cake, Gordon," as young Bud Fox said to Gordon Gekko in the movie *Wall Street*.

I had selected my qualifying marathon, the Philadelphia Marathon, to be held the Saturday after Thanksgiving, November 30, 1975. Why I hadn't chosen New York, which was a month earlier, I don't know. Probably so I could train for four more weeks.

So, I pounded the miles: 312 in September, 272 in October, 288 in November. An average of 67 a week. Or 9.5 per day. That meant I wouldn't collapse until the 28.5-mile point, right? In a 4-mile road race the week before the marathon, my per-mile pace was 5:34. As Denise and I climbed into the VW for the trip south, I had never been more prepared for anything.

Arriving in Philadelphia, we bunked with Dartmouth roommate John Larson, who was at the University of Pennsylvania Law School. Another college classmate, John Heywood, had come down from New York for the festivities. Race morning dawned cool and calm, and after listening to some Aerosmith tunes for motivational purposes, we headed out for the Saturday noon start.

Philadelphia was a flat, three-loop course that started adjacent to the Museum of Art and ran along the Schuylkill River. Perfect for pacing out my target three-hour effort—one hour per loop. Since it was exactly a year before the release of the movie *Rocky*, there was no pugilistic statue of Balboa gracing the museum steps just yet.

Once the race began, it was purely a matter of disciplined pacing. The problem was, other than occasional mile split times read to us by officials at the side of the road, we had no idea how fast we were going. We didn't have mile markers every mile or wrist chronographs. That was why it had been beneficial to run a lot of miles; you learned to hit a certain pace and lock in at that pace.

Unlike Boston, this marathon was different. There were absolutely no crowds, nobody cheering to get your adrenaline going, to bilk you into running too fast. In fact, the reverse was true. We were running along a path through the woods next to a river, in effect communing with nature. I half-way expected to see Henry David Thoreau out there. As a result, I ran the first loop too slowly, in slightly over an hour.

As the timer yelled out my split for the first loop, I was not a happy camper. Heywood put it more succinctly: "Man, I could see you were really pissed."

That was the bad news. The good news was that, as a result, I had plenty of energy left to pick up the pace for the second and third loops, and I cruised home in 2 hours, 54 minutes, and 46 seconds. It was official. I was official. I had qualified for the 1976 Boston Marathon by more than 35 minutes.

The Schmidt's beer, brewed in nearby Norristown and the Philadelphia Marathon's one and only sponsor, flowed at the law school that night.

In a somewhat after-the-fact humorous postscript to this triumphant roadshow, Denise had done some shopping, perhaps while I was listening to Aerosmith. Given our extremely limited financials at the time, it was more window shopping than anything else.

However, she had picked up a couple of inexpensive trinkets, one of which was, of all things, an ice cream scoop. With the Christmas holiday approaching, she had also cajoled the retailers she encountered into giving her a number of empty gift boxes, all of which she stashed in the VW, which was parked overnight on Chestnut Street.

Sure enough, on Sunday morning as we prepared to head home, we came to find that the city had contradicted its Brotherly Love moniker by doing us and our beloved Super Beetle wrong. The passenger side window was smashed and all the packages were gone. Of course, we were in for a chilly ride back to Duxbury and a pricey car window repair, but we couldn't help but snicker when we visualized the perps scurrying back to their lair, only to find they had stolen only a bunch of empty boxes and an ice cream scoop.

THE RUN FOR THE HOSES

"If you had the choice of a day on which to run a 26-mile, 385-yard marathon, it would not be April 19, 1976."

—Jerry Nason, *The Boston Globe*

I WAS ON TOP OF THE WORLD, AND I WAS PREPARED TO MAKE THE COMMITMENT to show it.

A Boston qualifier and a member of the Greater Boston Track Club, I was all in, preparing for the 1976 Boston Marathon. I truly believed, as I stood in the shower in our Duxbury apartment, that if I worked hard enough, I could run a 2:20 marathon. Or maybe even faster.

The numbers for January, February, March, and the first half of April don't lie: 1,366 miles in total, including a one-month high in March of 452. Nine GBTC track interval workouts at the Tufts and BC tracks, with quarter and half-mile intervals at a 5:30-minute mile pace. Road races in garden spots like Lynn, Massachusetts (9.75 miles); Newark, New Jersey (12 miles); Providence, Rhode Island (9.32 miles); Holliston, Massachusetts (15.5 miles); and Schenectady, New York (18.6 miles), all run at a pace of around 6 minutes a mile.

If I could sustain that for the entire marathon, we're talking a 2:38.

One anecdote underscores my fanaticism. To achieve my weekly objective of 100-plus miles, I had to run twice a day, at least three days a week. That meant rising early to put in a few miles before heading off to instill some wisdom into the youth of America. Well, one February morning at about 6:15 a.m., the bedside phone rang. Sleepily, Denise picked it up and mumbled into the receiver, "Hello?"

"Is Jim Riehl there? School's been canceled today because of last night's ten-inch snowstorm," declared the caller, a teacher on the PCIS telephone tree.

Rolling over, Denise handed the phone to an empty pillow.

"No," she replied. "He's out running."

Because it was my first year as an official qualifier, I was paranoid about my marathon application being accepted by the B.A.A. Maybe they could ferret out my clandestine history as a three-time bandit. Or discover some other fundamental character flaw of mine and refuse to let me run. So, one afternoon after school in early March, I decided to check on the status of my entry form.

As I dialed into the bowels of the old Boston Garden, who should pick up the phone but Jock Semple, who, in addition to being co-race director of the marathon, worked as a masseuse for the Bruins and Celtics.

"I want to check on my application for the marathon..." I began.

"Stop wastin' me time, lad!" he yelled back in his Scottish brogue. Click!

Somehow the Plymouth paper *Old Colony Memorial* got wind of the fact that, as local PCIS teachers, Scottie and I were going to run in the marathon and sent a reporter out to interview us and take a few photos of us out burning up the roads. We actually made the front page the week before the race, absorbing volumes of abuse from our fellow faculty members as a result. I had yet to be schooled in media relations, and one of the many insightful comments I made in the interview was "Running is like hitting yourself in the head with a hammer. It feels so good when you stop." The news editor did me a huge favor by not running that quote in the article.

The Thursday before Patriots' Day weekend, I decided to roll the dice and take my ninth graders on a field trip to the Prudential Center in Boston. It was a roll of the dice because with kids of that age, when one ventures off school grounds, there's always the possibility that something can go awfully, horribly wrong.

We were headed into the Pru to see a multimedia show called *Where's Boston?* It was put on in the darkened Hynes Auditorium with about fifty Kodak Carousel slide projectors—old school by today's digital standards—simultaneously flipping about a gazillion slides synched up to a killer soundtrack. The program was all about anything and everything having to do with the Boston, the Home of the Cod and the Bean. It was really, really cool.

At the crescendo of the show, Johnny "the Elder" Kelley, who ran sixty-one Boston Marathons before his death in 2004, came on the screen, saying, "I love the Boston Marathon, and I love Boston." It was the perfect thing to get me ready to run on Monday.

Unfortunately, though, the weather was starting to look a great deal less than perfect.

A high-pressure system had moved into the Boston area from the south during the weekend, bringing the temperature on Easter Sunday to ninety-four degrees. As a harbinger of things to come on Monday, my nephew Chip's chocolate bunny melted in the sizzling sunshine. Not a good omen.

But come hell or high water, I was going to run. I had waited five years for this. I was official. I had my number: E 65. I had my red and white singlet that read "Greater Boston." I had trained my butt off. I just had to be careful; that was all. So I took a bunch of salt pills, ate a bunch of bananas—for the potassium, you know—and tried to get some sleep.

The next morning, it was 100 degrees in the sun at Hopkinton. Some of the runners were taking cold showers in the high school locker room **before** the race. Scottie had decided not to waste the effort in the heat and so did a lot of the other registered runners, because there were actually **fewer** starters than in the previous year. Fortunately, there was a lot of water on the course, as spectators were encouraged to run garden hoses out to the street and create fountains to cascade over the sweltering runners.

So, what we ended up experiencing, in fact, was hell **and** high water.

Running carefully, I had no trouble with the heat. As I crested Heartbreak Hill, a meteorological phenomenon called a back door cold front started to approach Boston from the northeast, and temperatures finally began to cool.

Too late for me, though. I was shot. I finished in 3:08:39, nine seconds **slower** than last year.

GO WEST YOUNG MAN: EPISODE 1

"I love the normalcy of Cleveland. There's regular people there."

—Drew Carey, American Comedian and Native Clevelander

T HE 3:08:39 FINISHING TIME AT BOSTON CREATED A REAL DILEMMA FOR ME.

Right after "The Run For The Hoses," Will and Jock had pulled a little switcheroo on me. Having seen the number of runners in the 1976 marathon crest 2,000 for the second year in a row, they lowered the 1977 qualifying time for men ages nineteen to thirty-nine from 3:30 to three hours.

So, first, if I wanted to run Boston again in 1977, it meant I had to requalify, running another marathon eight and a half minutes faster than I just had.

Second, it meant I had to requalify **quickly**, because I had applied to several graduate business schools, and if admitted, I might not have much time for running after classes began right after Labor Day. But more about that later.

So, I took Horace Greeley's advice to "Go west, young man!"

Within hours after finishing Boston in 634th place, rehydrating with a cold one in hand, I was riffling through the March 1976 issue of *Runner's World* magazine, trying to find that next qualifying marathon. It had to be within driving distance of Duxbury and before the dog days of summer set in, or I'd just have another overheated, sweaty 3:09 run and no ticket back to Boston in 1977.

And then, magically, there it was, tucked into an ad on page 117. The first annual Revco Discount Drug Centers Western Reserve Marathon, being held on Mother's Day, May 9. Since 1976 was the 200th anniversary of the Declaration of Independence, the marathon was an Official Cleveland-Akron Area Bicentennial Project.

Man, it doesn't get any better than that!

The course ran from Hudson, Ohio into Cleveland, which was kind of ironic, because as my more attentive readers will recall, Hudson was the small northeastern Ohio town where I lived when I was tearing it up in youth baseball and football. When I used to be really good at sports other than running.

However, the Western Reserve Marathon wasn't the perfect solution. May 9 was twenty days away. Who in their right mind runs another marathon with less than three weeks of recovery time? That kind of advice didn't appear in Coach Squires's playbook. It would be a real test of my fitness. What's more, it was a 680-mile drive from Duxbury. Not exactly a walk in the park.

As I continued running the week after Boston, though, I felt pretty good, and the following Saturday I completed a 10-mile road race in just under an hour, so I knew the marathon had not taken that much out of me. So, I put in 100 miles on the roads the first week of May, and then, irrepressible youths that we were, Denise and I climbed into our dauntless VW and set off for Hudson.

Our hosts and innkeepers once we arrived were Debbie and Alan Knobel. Alan, who ran the first part of the Boston Marathon with me in 1973, had been my former next-door neighbor when I had lived in Hudson and was a very good runner in his own right in his high school and college days. As my original running muse, he also partnered with me in several extremely marginal adolescent garage bands with sketchy names like The Shingles and The Jimi-Ali Spirit.

Mother's Day dawned sunny and a bit warmer than I would have liked. Ultimately, the temperature would climb to almost seventy. The race began at noon at Western Reserve Academy, a private boys college prep school that I would have attended had my family not moved from Hudson in my freshman year. More irony. But that's a story for another time.

The starter's pistol was fired by none other than Jesse Owens, a black man who won four track and field gold medals in the 1936 Berlin Olympics hosted by Adolf Hitler. At the time it was said that, by virtue of his victories, Owens, a Cleveland resident, "singlehandedly crushed Hitler's myth of Aryan supremacy." Pretty inspiring, but I couldn't dwell on it. I had a race to run.

Early on, the miles passed easily. I was right on pace to go under three hours, exactly as planned. Alan decided he would run the first 5 miles with me up Route 91 to Twinsburg and then drop out. Farther along, on the left, I passed a cemetery. "Crown Hill, America's Finest Burial Park," the sign read. Not for me, not today, I hoped.

Approaching the halfway point, where Route 91 intersected Route 87, I encountered a part of the course that, on the map, had been ominously labeled "The Depression." When I queried prior to the race as to what that meant, an official explained that it was a very steep downhill followed immediately by a very steep uphill. He said it was the most difficult section of the marathon.

But, hey, how hard could it be? I was this grizzled veteran of three Boston Marathons and one Philadelphia Marathon. I had put a stake through Heartbreak Hill not once but thrice.

I was going to crush "The Depression" and punch my ticket to the 1977 Boston Marathon.

PRIDE GOETH BEFORE "THE DEPRESSION"

**"Experience is the hardest kind of teacher. It gives
you the test first and the lesson afterward."**

—Oscar Wilde, Irish Poet and Playwright

IT WAS AS I APPROACHED "THE DEPRESSION" THAT 49-PLUS MILES OF RACING
and 180-plus miles of roadwork in the last twenty-one days finally caught
up with me.

As I descended the steep downhill, the climb ahead loomed at a 45- or
50-degree uphill slope. It was a brutal ascent, fortunately only about a quarter of a mile, but by the time I got to the top, my legs were shaking, and I was
a bit light-headed. Somehow, I kept myself from stopping outright, but my
splits for the next couple of miles were atrocious. Fortunately, only the fact
that the course was pancake-flat the rest of the way allowed me to gradually
regain my regular, if shuffling, stride.

I hit the finish line at Cleveland's Case Western Reserve University
in 2:55:38, good enough for 23rd place out of 209 starters. In a first for
me, I spent some time afterward in the medical tent, where I was treated
for dehydration.

Among the other survivors I encountered in there was one finisher who
remarked, "Now, if I can go home and make love to my wife tonight, then
I'll be a real man." Whether he delivered on his conditional comment, this
record shall not reflect.

Yes, runners are indeed cut from different cloth.

Mission accomplished. I was a Boston qualifier for the second time.

But there was no doubt about it. I had dodged a bullet.

THE PLAN, BOSS, THE PLAN: EPISODE 1

"I give you Chicago. It is not London and Harvard. It is not Paris and buttermilk. It is American in every chitling and spare rib. It is alive from snout to tail."

—H. L. Mencken, American Journalist

OH, YEAH, THE PLAN.

Remember? Teach for a couple of years and then on to business school or law school. No question that I had done everything to prepare myself.

Took the appropriate tests back at Dartmouth...the GMAT and the LSAT... while I still remembered how to read and write *before* going into teaching. I watched *The Paper Chase,* that classic movie starring John Houseman as Harvard Law Professor Charles Kingsfield, who gets his jollies tormenting first-year student James Hart. I devoured *The Gospel According to Harvard Business School*, the tome in which b-schooler Peter Cohen details his two years of trials and tribulations on the banks of the Charles.

Yes, I was ready.

In the end, I opted for business school, because its two-year term of incarceration (and consequential tuition-driven indebtedness) was a third less than that of law school.

So, the preceding fall, as I had prepared for the Philadelphia Marathon, I grappled with these incredibly arcane business school applications, which in turn, reminded me of my less-than-sterling wrestling career.

There were four graduate schools on my hit list—the University of Chicago, Harvard, Stanford, and the Wharton School at the University of Pennsylvania in Philadelphia. The application essay questions were way out there. Occasionally I got lucky, like when the answer to Harvard question number 3 also worked for Chicago number 5 and Stanford number 8, but that didn't happen too often.

One question in particular I have never forgotten. It was on the Wharton application and read, "As an individual, what excites you?" Wow. I immediately knew exactly what I wanted to write, but I also knew that if I wrote that, I most definitely would not be accepted. So, my response to that question became one of my first exercises in creative writing.

And it must have worked, because about the time we marathoners were all preparing to shake and bake in the April 1976 "Run for the Hoses," I heard from Wharton, and the news was good. I was in. Next came Chicago. Green light. Then Harvard, which said, "Don't call us. We'll call you." Wait listed. Finally, the guys from the left coast, Stanford, checked in with a bullet. No more California dreamin'.

It was decision time. Given deadlines, we couldn't wait for Harvard. We had to commit to Chicago or Wharton. The reasoning went something like this. We knew Chicago better than Philadelphia. Hell, we'd been robbed in Philadelphia. We had family outside of Chicago. Denise had contacts in Chicago; it would be easier for her to get a job. And yadda, yadda, yadda. So, we ponied up and cut the University of Chicago a huge, nonrefundable deposit check to hold my place in the fall. All of $150. We were committed.

Sayonara, Boston.

TRIAL AND JUBILATION

"When I'm in Boston, I always feel like I'm home. I almost cry, I feel so good."

—Luis Tiant, Pitcher, Boston Red Sox

DENISE AND I HAD RETURNED TO DUXBURY FROM CLEVELAND AND THE Western Reserve Marathon. It was late May, and the ninth-grade academic year was winding down, marked by a dramatic increase in the number of detentions I was forced to issue for spitball incidents and unauthorized paper airplane flights.

Also in late May, the twenty-second, to be exact, the 1976 US Olympic marathon trials were held at Hayward Field in Eugene, Oregon.

Eugene was fast becoming the epicenter of the nascent US running boom. It was the home of the University of Oregon and legendary track and field coach Bill Bowerman, who ultimately won four NCAA titles in his twenty-four years as head coach. He also mentored thirty-one Olympians, including Steve Prefontaine, fifty-one All-Americans, twelve American record holders, twenty-two NCAA champions, and sixteen sub-4-minute milers.

But Bowerman was not just a mere track coach. In 1964, with one of his former Oregon runners named Phil Knight, Bill created a running footwear distribution company creatively called Blue Ribbon Sports. At first, they imported Japanese Onitsuka Tiger running shoes—my old brand—into the United States.

Bowerman soon began tinkering with new shoe designs, incorporating rubber soles he molded using his wife's waffle iron. Reports that he was simultaneously experimenting with maple-syrup-flavored sports drinks were never confirmed. Nonetheless, a few years later, Blue Ribbon Sports became Nike, Bowerman's rubber soles became the Nike Waffle Trainer, and as they say, the rest is history.

At any rate, eighty-seven American runners had qualified for the US marathon trial that May Saturday in Eugene, including a number of the usual suspects—Frank Shorter, Bill Rodgers, Tom Fleming (a perennial runner-up at Boston), Amby Burfoot (the 1968 Boston Marathon winner and Rodgers' Wesleyan roommate), and Jeff Galloway (a Wesleyan classmate of Burfoot and Rodgers).

In the race, Shorter and Rodgers dominated, finishing in a virtual tie at 2:11, with Washington State's Don Kardong finishing third in 2:13. The trio won an all-expenses-paid trip to the Montreal Olympic marathon, to be held in late July.

Meanwhile, back at the ranch, our Duxbury apartment lease was up at the end of July. At that point we would load up our U-Haul and go back to Chicago, from whence we had come two years earlier, towing the indomitable VW Super Beetle behind us.

But I know I wasn't especially happy about leaving Boston. I was incredibly proud of the strides (pun intended) I had made, the contacts I had established, the amazing things I had learned about running and about life. However, sometimes, one just has to move on. We had a future to build. It was what it was.

Then one afternoon in early June, after school, I came back from a 12-mile run and stopped in the tiny vestibule of our apartment at 41 King's Town Way to check the mail. Buried among the varied and sundry bills and solicitations was a business-sized envelope with the return address "Dean of Admissions, Harvard Graduate School of Business, Soldiers Field, Boston, MA, 02163."

"Oh," I thought to myself, "they've finally sent me a bullet to terminate my waiting list status." I climbed the stairs to the apartment, fatalistically concluding, "It'll be nice to get that box checked." Still perspiring from my run, I parked myself cross-legged on the olive-green shag carpet and opened the envelope.

"Dear Mr. Riehl," the letter began, "The Dean of Admissions of the Graduate School of Business at Harvard University is pleased to offer you admission to the MBA Class of 1978."

You could have knocked me over with a feather.

PAAK THE CAAH IN HAAVAAD YAAD

**"You don't run 26 miles at five minutes a mile
on good looks and a secret recipe."**

—Frank Shorter

W HEN DENISE GOT HOME FROM WORK, I SHARED THE NEWS WITH HER. She was as surprised as I was. Maybe even more so, if that was possible. By then I had showered, so we hugged each other, screaming with joy.

With all due respect to the University of Chicago—an outstanding institution where my sister Susie earned her master's in Clinical Social Work—there was never a scintilla of doubt. Not for a second. We were going to Harvard Business School. Chicago could keep our $150. It was like training with GBTC. When you have the opportunity to learn from the very best, you take advantage of it.

We rented a place in Soldiers Field Park, an apartment complex located at the intersection of Soldiers Field Road and Western Avenue, on the Charles River adjacent to the business school campus. It was tiny, one bedroom, up one flight, with a Boston, not a Cambridge, mailing address. Denise liked the fact that it was brand-new construction. That way, she observed, we would graduate before the roaches found their way up to the second floor.

94

My first memory of that apartment was watching the Montreal Olympic marathon on July 31. We had just moved in that day, and even though we didn't have two nickels to rub together, Denise had bought me a $400 Mitsubishi color TV at Lechmere two weeks earlier to watch the opening ceremonies. We expectantly gathered around the tube, adult beverages in hand, with my sister Nicky and her husband Dave, who had helped us move into Boston from Duxbury. Competing for the United States were the top three finishers from the May trial in Eugene, Frank Shorter, Bill Rodgers, and Don Kardong.

In a surprise outcome, unknown East German marathoner Waldemar Cierpinski took the gold medal in 2:09:55, with Shorter copping the silver and Karel Lismont of Belgium scoring bronze. Kardong finished a very credible fourth, and Rodgers, plagued by severe leg cramps just past the halfway point, finished fortieth in 2:35. It just goes to show that even "sturdleys" have their off days.

In a grim postscript, Cierpinski, who also won the 1980 Moscow Olympic marathon, was later implicated in the East German government sponsored performance-enhancing drug program. His name appeared in track and field research files unearthed in the late 1990s, suggesting that in 1976, he was on androgenic steroids. His two gold medals, however, were never taken away. By all appearances, Frank had been robbed of a second consecutive Olympic marathon victory.

Running-wise that summer, I was gradually recovering from my near disaster back in Cleveland, logging between 60- and 80-mile weeks in June and July. I had pretty much regained my leg speed, averaging 6:05 miles in a hot and humid 20-kilometer race in Marshfield, Massachusetts and earning a case of Pepsi® for my thirty-third-place finish.

Once in Beantown, I was also gradually learning the joys of urban running. It reminded me of what I had once heard someone say about runners in traffic-congested Los Angeles: "They resemble their baseball teams. Either they're Dodgers or Angels."

But seriously, running in the city was a whole new experience. No endless stretches of roadway with wide shoulders where you could tool along relatively safely, piling up the miles. No residential streets where the vehicles that were parked outnumbered the vehicles that were moving. Where the only danger was somebody's Fido that you would have to outkick, lest you endure a few fangs in the fanny.

In the city, it was different. Every single block was a challenge. You could never let down your guard. Cars coming out of blind driveways. Signal-less trucks turning directly in front of you. Traffic lights turning ripe just as you reach the intersection. And the air quality. Let's just say that, with all of the exhaust-belching machines in the vicinity, it was somewhat less than pristine. But, as the saying goes, "You get what you get, and you don't get upset."

I was in my beloved Boston. And I was running.

THE GOSPEL ACCORDING TO JIM

"Of all the instruments of fear and terror at the disposal of the
Business School, none can match a WOC's effectiveness in
reducing a healthy first-year body to a mess of gastric disorders,
fluttering eyelids and recurring nightmares that make the poor
bastard jump up in the middle of the night, screaming for Mother."

—Peter Cohen, *The Gospel According to Harvard Business School*

A S THE CALENDAR FLIPPED FROM AUGUST TO SEPTEMBER, THE SIGNIFICANCE
of my commitment to Harvard Business School began to dawn on
me—and not necessarily in a good way.

Here I was, a US History major, a junior high school Social Studies
teacher, for God's sake, about to enter one of the most competitive—if
not **the** most competitive—graduate business programs in the world.
My classmates were bound to be far more seasoned in business than
me; HBS actively discouraged applicants right out of college. Instead,
the ideal candidate had two—or better, three—years of entry-level
business experience at an investment bank, a consulting firm, or some
other Fortune 500 company.

No wonder I initially landed on the waiting list.

And then some of the stuff I read in *The Gospel According to Harvard
Business School* began to eat at me. On the first day of class, one intimidating professor stated, "Look to the left. Look to the right. By Thanksgiving,

one of the three of you isn't going to be here." Washed out. Flunked out. In another of the scribe's recollections, two despondent MBA candidates who couldn't handle the pressure actually committed suicide. Very uplifting.

I was questioning whether I had done the right thing, whether I could really succeed at HBS. One thing I knew for sure. With the tuition loans we had taken out, I was certainly betting the ranch on the fact that I could.

Fortunately, I couldn't stew about those things for too long. Labor Day came and went, and it was the time for me to throw myself off the dock to see if I could swim.

Classes began, three per day, an hour and forty minutes each. Harvard used the case study method, each case presenting a specific real-life business with a specific real-life problem. It was then up to each student to analyze the problem and recommend a solution. And one had better be well prepared, because at the start of each class the professor cold-called someone to present the case. And the solution. It was a big part of your final grade.

More learning by doing.

As *The Gospel's* writer, Peter Cohen, explained, "The difference between traditional learning and case learning is like that between eating a cream puff and having someone tell you about it. The difference is between an event and an experience. And because experiences are full and complex things, most schools and teachers never make an effort to create them...And two weeks afterward, you can't remember a thing.

"To be fair...even with the best case...a true experience in the classroom is an almost unattainable goal. So more often than not, case classes struggle along, reaching many little peaks, but no real climax. But at least they are little peaks, not the void, flat nothing of so many lectures."

The first couple days of classes, I read the cases, laid them aside, and then went out for a run. I was too naïve to realize I was supposed to analyze them too. Brilliant! Fortunately, I was not called upon, perhaps because I had wisely chosen to hunker down in the nosebleed seats. It would have been ugly!

Boy, I had a lot to learn.

There were eight sections of eighty students each in my Harvard MBA class, and every section had a different personality. Some sections were very serious and businesslike, attending class in coats and ties, others not so much. Our section, Section D, was pretty diverse and laid back, which helped me settle in more quickly than if I had landed in a straight-laced and uptight group. That would have been really intimidating.

One episode in particular was indicative of Section D's spirit.

In the fall of 1976, there was a TV show on the air called *The Gong Show,* hosted by Chuck Barris, who was also its producer. Amateur talent acts, sometimes notoriously bad ones, performed before a panel of three celebrity judges, any one of whom could halt the performance by striking an outsized Oriental gong. Barris would then ask that judge what was offensive enough to cause the gonging of the act.

Come one Saturday night, some of Section D's more notorious bachelors had a raucous—some said, alcohol-fueled—episode in Boston's Chinatown and returned to campus with a genuine Asian gong. The following Monday morning, there it was, mounted in the rear of our classroom, Aldrich 10, on a projector stand, ready for action. Since it happened to be right next to my seat, I was duly assigned to be the "keeper of the gong." Soon, with the advance nods of support of my other section-mates, I was silencing ill-prepared or overly verbose classmates with a single tap of the instrument.

The gong soon became a Section D institution. Amazingly, our professors put up with it.

Then, one day we were discussing the J.I. Case Tractor Corporation in Business Policy class with Professor Henderson. Deep into the discussion, he posed a question, "If you were an investor, what would it be about the Case Corporation that would *endear* that company to you?"

Now people have always said that my mind works in strange ways. Not only do I adore bad puns, but I make some extremely weird connections very quickly.

This was one such time.

The Professor's use of the word "endear," I too instantly concluded, was an intentional pun referring to one of Case's competitors, John *Deere* and Company. So, I gonged him for it. As classmate Phil Hunter later said, "Jim, I thought Henderson was going to come over the desks at you." It was not my finest hour.

The incident achieved such notoriety that my better half even heard about it as she walked through the b-school campus on her way home from work later that afternoon. "Hey, Denise," one of the other student wives tattled, "Did you hear what Jim did today? He gonged a professor!"

I didn't get any dinner that evening until, as the chastened schoolboy, I vowed to be much more conservative with the gong.

Miraculously, I nevertheless passed Professor Henderson's course.

Then, there were these things called WOCs, short for Written and Oral Communication.

Why the "Oral" appeared in the course title, I never quite got, because a WOC was a pressure-packed *written* exercise, with nothing oral about it. Maybe there was another part of the program involving an oral presentation that I've long since forgotten.

Anyhow, on a Thursday afternoon, right after the last class, everyone would be handed the same case study. We had until midnight Friday—all of thirty-three hours—to read the case, analyze it, write up a recommendation, and drop the recommendation into a slot carved into the side of Baker Library. At 12:00:01 Saturday morning, the slot locked up. If your paper wasn't in, you were out of luck. Docked a full grade for being late.

I guess the idea was to prepare us for those business situations when we would have to meet some impossible deadline.

When we were assigned the WOCs, I would delay hitting the road for my afternoon run long enough to read the case then spend the next ninety minutes ruminating on the facts as I pounded the pavement. That sufficiently de-stressed me such that I could logically and time-efficiently analyze the case and devise a recommendation that actually made some sense.

Quite remarkably, my WOC dissertations regularly hit the Baker chute around dinner time on those Fridays, freeing me up, after a few brews at the HBS Pub, to heckle other, less punctual classmates as they hurried to insert their works into the library slot before the clock struck midnight.

As for what role running would play in this grand business school adventure, Denise and I never had that conversation. Of course, she would be the breadwinner. She already had the job in Boston, to which she had been commuting from Duxbury.

On my end, studies would pretty much be 24/7. The workload was going to be tsunami-like, requiring my level best to keep from capsizing. Three cases a day, some of them fifty-plus pages of reading. Denise just assumed it would be impossible for me to study and run at the same time.

As she later reflected, "I never realized Jim was going to attend business school *and* continue running." But that's exactly what I did, as a pressure release valve for my anxiety and fear of failing. I would pop out of class at

2:40 p.m., listen to a couple of tracks from *Boston's* debut album while I stretched, and go out for a 10-miler into Watertown or along the Charles.

During that first fall at b-school, I ran 250 miles in September and 219 in October, actually finding time for races in Manchester (9.3 miles) and Hanover, New Hampshire (12 miles). November mileage slipped to around 100 as I fervently prepared for my first round of exams just before Thanksgiving.

Incredibly, I passed all my exams. For the first time, after some significant FUD (fear, uncertainty, and doubt), I knew I was going to make it at HBS.

And a couple of additional notes for the record...

While I was furiously dog-paddling my way through my first term at HBS, GBTC teammate Scott Graham demonstrated the wisdom of skipping the 100-degree "Run for the Hoses" Boston Marathon back in April by finishing twentieth in the inaugural five-borough New York City Marathon in 2 hours, 25 minutes, and 18 seconds. The winner? Bill Rodgers, of course.

And one other thing.

That professor who was quoted in *The Gospel* about one in three first-year HBS students imploding by Thanksgiving must have just been going for the intimidation factor.

Only two of our eighty Section D-ers ended up not returning for the second year.

STUDIES AND "STURDLEYS"

"Marketing takes a day to learn and a lifetime to master."

—Philip Kotler, Marketing Professor, Author and Consultant

CELEBRATED TURKEY DAY, MY TRIUMPHANT EXAMS, AND A BREAK FROM CLASS-
es with a long, slow morning run along the Charles River.

Now that I had established that graduate business studies and running could successfully coexist, it was time to establish that graduate business studies and marathoning could also successfully coexist.

So, I began training for the 1977 Boston Marathon. But there were other priorities to be considered. Like getting a summer internship. Obtaining some sort of meaningful business experience in between the two years of graduate school was critical, in that it set one up for the permanent job hunt at the end of the second year, upon graduation with the coveted MBA degree. And I was a bit behind the eight ball in that regard because (a) I had no real business experience, (b) I didn't know what I wanted to do when I grew up, and (c) I was at a huge competitive disadvantage with all my classmates who did.

Other than that, I was perfect!

As far as addressing issue (a), Harvard turned out to be the ideal place for me, since I was a total mercantile novice. In the first year, it required everyone, regardless of how extensive their business chops, to take the same basic business curriculum. Accounting. Finance. Production and Operations Management. Marketing. Managerial Economics. Real fundamental stuff.

Which was good for me, because I got a sampling of all the functional areas in business. I ended up being attracted most to marketing (or maybe advertising) because it seemed analytical and creative at the same time. I thought it might actually be fun.

So, (b) I now knew what I wanted to do when I grew up. Marketing.

Next, I had to find someplace to do it over the coming summer. As already noted, despite my stellar junior high teaching (and pupil disciplining) credentials, I was not exactly the strongest marketing intern candidate. I probably wasn't going to wow the interviewers when the big guns— General Foods, Procter & Gamble, and PepsiCo—came to campus to recruit for their prized summer slots.

So, with Denise's encouragement, I decided to try to create my own internship.

Over Christmas break, I jumped on a Greyhound and headed for New York City. I started knocking plaintively on the doors of the Madison Avenue advertising agencies, which traditionally did not recruit summer interns or hire Harvard Business School graduates. Did I also mention that entry-level advertising jobs were among the lowest paying marketing jobs around?

Brilliant strategy, huh?

Well, it may not have been brilliant, but it was mine. And as I continued to pursue it in the winter of 1977, I began gearing up for Boston.

With the amount of time that my studies demanded, I couldn't go over to Tufts and run indoor workouts with GBTC anymore. Instead, I ran my intervals on the 11-lap-to-the-mile track inside Carey Cage right next to Harvard Stadium, which was conveniently right across North Harvard Street from the business school. Remembering the other component of Coach Squires's marathon training success formula—long, hilly distance runs—I mapped out a 17-mile loop from Allston into Brighton, Watertown, Newton, and Brookline, then back to our apartment.

After the first seven miles out Western Avenue and Arsenal Street, my course turned east at Auburndale and picked up the marathon course at Route 30, Beacon Street, right in front of the Newton Fire Department. I was at the base of the 5-mile stretch of four slopes that culminated in Heartbreak Hill. After powering up those inclines, it was an easy five miles back to the business school.

By my count, I ran those hills fifteen times as I prepared for the marathon. I was also establishing my training pattern of 100-plus miles a week for eight to ten weeks before the race, with a 20- to 22-miler ten days out and then tapering back after that. In March, I recorded a monthly high of 528 miles, my highest month ever.

With the internship hunt clogging my calendar, I only logged a couple of local road races, one in Brighton (9.3 miles) and one in Wellesley (9.7 miles). My per-mile pace was respectable—under my customary six minutes a mile.

Not only was my training regimen getting more sophisticated, but things were getting more technical on the equipment and dietary fronts as well.

In the world of sneakers, when last we checked in, I was running the roads in Adidas product. But with our move to Boston, I had switched to a locally produced shoe, the New Balance 320, for training purposes. And having hung around the GBTC "sturdleys," I realized they trained in heavier, more cushioned shoes and competed in lighter shoes they called "racing flats."

Always the impressionable youth, I had to have some racing flats of my own, just like the big boys. And it just so happened that Nike—Bill Bowerman and Phil Knight's new company—was introducing a model called the Elite just weeks before the marathon. Electric blue uppers and a neon green swoosh with black waffle soles. Light as a feather. Really cool looking.

But the Elites were in really short supply and consequently really hard to find. I finally found the Nike factory store out in Wellesley that carried them, but each time I drove there, the inventory was sold out. Finally, on my third try, I got my shoe. Anxious not to repeat my blistering blunder of 1974, I made sure the Elites were broken in before race day.

Over on the dietary front, nutritionists had begun to teach endurance athletes about the virtues of "carbohydrate loading" or, in the vernacular, "carbo-loading." Carbohydrates are the sugars, starches, and fibers found in fruits, grains, vegetables, and milk products that are the body's main source of energy. Without penning a scientific treatise on the topic, the gist of carbo-loading is that, if before an endurance event, one fasts from carbohydrates for three days then feasts on them for three days, they will have more energy in the later stages of the event and be less likely to hit the proverbial "wall."

Well, for anyone who has run a marathon—in particular, Boston—this is indeed an immensely appealing proposition. "Hitting the wall" in the parlance of distance running can occur at about the 20-mile mark, coincidentally at the foot of Heartbreak Hill, when the typical body has exhausted its store of carbohydrates. Sapped of energy with six miles to go is no way run a railroad, I assure you.

Seeking to avoid derailment, I enthusiastically signed up for the program right away, and the week before the 1977 Boston was my initial carbo-loading experience. The three-day depletion stage was not pleasant.

I felt listless and cranky, and to this day, Denise and my fellow MBA class-mates can vouch for the fact that I was not pleasant to be around.

But the three-day loading stage. Truly nirvana. Pasta. Cake. Beer. My favorite was Kellogg Pop Tarts. Twenty grams of carbohydrates stuffed into each one of those sugary, frosted slabs of dough. I loved them so much I even snarfed them down untoasted.

My secret fear, though, having practiced extreme carbo-loading, was that 500 yards into the marathon, I would fall or twist an ankle and be unable to continue. Pulling to the side of the road, my weight would instantly balloon by fifty pounds. Providentially, such a course of events never occurred.

At long last it was April 18. Race day. And thanks to a combination of Coach Squires's training techniques, my racing flats, and carbo-loading, I decisively shattered the three-hour mark, finishing in 2:51:53, good for 521st place. I had sliced a whopping 16 minutes off my previous best time at Boston in the day's seventy-seven-degree heat.

In an odd coincidence, one Richard Bender finished in 520th place with the exact same finishing time as me, while I finished 521st. Richard was also from Valparaiso, where my parents still lived. Technically, we should have finished in a tie for 520th; instead, I think he placed higher than I did because, alphabetically, his last name trumped mine. However, I wasn't about to call Jock Semple to ask him to reconsider.

Anyhow, what were the odds we would finish as two peas in a pod? Thanks to my mom and occasional PR agent, that warranted an article in Valpo's *Vidette Messenger* a few days later.

Bill Rodgers dropped out in the Newton hills as Canadian Jerome Drayton captured the laurel wreath in 2:14:46, afterward complaining, "The race disappointed me because it was not that competitive."

HOT TOWN, SUMMER IN THE CITY

**"New York is an ugly city, a dirty city. Its climate is a
scandal, its politics are used to frighten children, its
traffic is madness, its competition is murderous."**

—John Steinbeck, American Author

HAVING RUN TWO MARATHONS IN 1975 AND TWO IN 1976, ALBEIT A BIT TOO
close together, I cogitated, why should 1977 be any different?

So, having proven that business school studies and marathoning could successfully coexist by setting a new personal record at Boston, I set my sights on
a fall race, hoping the cooler weather might allow me to further lower my PR.
A logical choice quickly became the New York Marathon, which on October 23,
for just the second year, would be contested throughout all five of the city's
boroughs. But more on that later.

In the meantime, my marketing internship strategy, flawed as it was,
nevertheless had borne fruit. I had landed an advertising account management internship at the Benton & Bowles Agency at 909 Third Avenue in
Manhattan, working on the Standard Brands Planters® Nuts account. And
it actually paid all of $250 a week. I guess you could say I was working for
peanuts. Or for Mr. Peanut.

But this was in the days long before working remotely was an option. If
I wanted this gig on my resume, it would be necessary for me to summer
in Gotham City. By happy chance, my aunt and uncle, "Mark" and Jack

Markell, had an apartment in Stuyvesant Town at 1st Avenue and 14th Street and offered me their lumpy guest room hide-a-bed. Another example of things working out for the best.

And what a summer it was to be residing in New York City.

The Yankees and Red Sox were bitterly battling for the lead in the American League East, with Mark and Jack backing the Bronx Bombers and me cheering on the Crimson Hose. It was more of a friendly rivalry than anything else; we were all equally amused when Billy Martin and Reggie Jackson engaged in fisticuffs in their Yankee Stadium dugout. By the time later that fall, when the Yankees won the AL East, the AL pennant, and the World Series over the Los Angeles Dodgers, I was preparing to return to New York City for the marathon.

Then, on July 13, New York City was enduring the first day of a nine-day heat wave, with a high temperature of ninety-three degrees. At 8:37 EDT that evening, there was a lightning strike at Buchanan South, a power substation on the Hudson River. By 9:38 p.m., a resulting power grid collapse plunged all of New York City except parts of Queens into total darkness, resulting in widespread arson, looting, and rioting.

Jack was on a business trip, and Mark and I watched, incredulous, as uptown, block-by- block, including the Empire State Building, the lights went out. Everything was still out the next morning at 5:30 a.m. when I got up to go for my 10-mile run. With the apartment on the eleventh floor, there was no elevator, so I had to descend the windowless stairwell in the dark. After my run, I washed up at the fire hydrant because there were no electric pumps to move water to the roof tank; hence, no shower. Then it was back up the stairs to the apartment in the darkened stairwell.

Soon came the call from Denise, tending the home fires in Boston, who was indignant when I declared that I was taking the day off from my internship.

"But, Jimmy," she wailed, "You can't! We need a job offer from these guys next year."

"Look," I explained patiently, "there's no electricity anywhere in New York City. It's already eighty degrees out, going up to over 100 this afternoon. First, the apartment elevator isn't running, so I could walk down eleven flights in the dark. Then, the buses and subways aren't running, so I could walk forty-six blocks uptown to my office building. Then, the building elevator isn't running, so I could walk up thirty flights in the dark. Then I could enter my office, only to work in the dark because it has no windows, and sweat my brains out because there is no air conditioning."

"Okay," Denise relented.

The power didn't come back on that day until 10:39 p.m.

Also, that summer, the "Son of Sam," also known as "The 44 Caliber Killer" was terrorizing the city. A year earlier, he had begun his nocturnal prowling, shooting people at close range with a .44 pistol, tallying six dead and seven wounded in attacks in the Bronx, Brooklyn, Queens, and Yonkers. He left letters mocking the police, promising future crimes and claiming to follow the instructions of a demon embodied in his neighbor's dog. Lurid details of his killing spree appeared daily in the media, which only fanned the public hysteria. Ultimately, the murderer, one David Berkowitz, was captured on August 10.

Meanwhile, my summer internship, as an introduction to the world of marketing and advertising, was proving to be quite educational, to say the least.

As the "agency of record" for the Planters brand, Benton & Bowles was responsible for all of the Planters nuts and Planters peanut butter advertising. That meant B & B created the advertising, produced the advertising, bought the media, and then placed the advertising in the media, whatever the media vehicle was—television, radio, magazine or newspaper.

To accomplish all that, Benton & Bowles hired writers and other creative types, media planners and buyers, and account managers. The B & B account managers handled the relationship with Planters—in this case the Planters product managers—and tried to prevent them from firing the agency, which happened more frequently in those days than B & B would have liked.

My internship was mostly doing the scut work that those above me—the Assistant Account Executive and the Account Executive—didn't want to do and therefore could assign to me. Things like market research analysis and advertising spending reviews. Long days in the office. But still good experience.

Learning by doing...from the bottom up.

Some faint writing on the wall, however, was beginning to appear to me.

The wall said, "Jim, once you graduate from business school, how are you going to find the time maintain this kind of a work schedule, have a family, and continue your running?" Perhaps imagining the Verrazzano-Narrows span at the start of the New York City Marathon, I just thought to myself, "I'll cross that bridge when I come to it."

The highlight of the summer was definitely the day my boss let me out of the office to go to a television commercial production shoot. He promised me I would get to meet Mr. Peanut and the Planters spokesman, retired New York Football Giants player and sports broadcaster, Frank Gifford.

He was kidding about Mr. Peanut.

ESCAPING NEW YORK

**It's been a great adventure. Everything I hoped for. But
it's time to go home. I miss my family. I miss the Earth.**

—John Phillips, American Musician, *The Mamas and The Papas*

A VERAGING 300 MILES A MONTH AROUND MANHATTAN IN JUNE AND IN JULY,
I did my interval workouts by myself on a cinder track in a New York
City park next to the East River. Denise came down from Boston many
weekends; when she didn't, we escaped, usually finding a road race wherever we were headed.

On July 2, in the Windy City for my sister Laurie's wedding, it was the
12.4-mile Chicago Distance Classic, followed later that month by races in
Marshfield and Duxbury. In August, it was consecutive weekly races in
Falmouth and Gloucester to wrap up the summer. Have race, will travel.

In particular, the 7-mile Falmouth Road Race was fast becoming a "must
run" event. Held the third week of August, its origins traced back to 1972,
when its fun-loving, bartending founder Tommy Leonard watched Frank
Shorter win the Olympic marathon on TV.

As Shorter crossed that 1972 Olympic marathon finish line, Tommy was
said to have uttered, "Wouldn't it be fantastic if we could get Frank Shorter
to run in a race on Cape Cod?" In the following year, 1973, those words
launched 100 runners in the inaugural Falmouth Road Race, 445 the year
after that, and 851 the year after that, including Shorter himself.

Tommy was also the proprietor of the Eliot Lounge,* the runner's bar at the intersection of Massachusetts and Commonwealth Avenues in Boston. A runner himself and quite a personality, Tommy would serve a free beer to any Boston Marathon finisher who brought their race number into the bar. Bill Rodgers brought some notoriety to the establishment when he said, after he won Boston in 1975, "I'm going to the Eliot Lounge to have a Blue Whale."

It was also reported in the 1970's that eccentric Red Sox pitcher Bill "Spaceman" Lee would occasionally sneak across the street from Fenway Park during rain delays to share a pint with Tommy. In fact, when he heard that Cincinnati Reds manager Don Gullett had been inducted into the Hall of Fame, the Spaceman said to some journalists in the vicinity, "Don may be going to the Hall of Fame, but I'm going to the Eliot Lounge."

By 1977, Falmouth was ready to be legitimized by my presence, although quite honestly, I am mystified, looking back, that living locally, I wasn't a regular participant starting in 1974. However, that was water under the bridge.

It was race time. And it was warm.

We started on the main drag in Woods Hole, a couple of blocks from the Martha's Vineyard/Nantucket Steamship Authority terminal. Seven miles later, at Falmouth Heights Beach, Bill Rodgers was victorious in a course record of 32:23, nineteen-year-old Alberto Salazar was second, and Frank Shorter was fifth. I finished 205th of 3,500 starters, with a time of 41:39, or 5:57 a mile, and then I rode back to New York City with my sister Laurie and her husband for the final week of my internship.

---

*   Remarkably and somewhat sadly, despite two years' incredibly close proximity to the Eliot Lounge while at HBS, I never set foot inside that sacred establishment. Perhaps yet another instance of things working out for the best.

And a colorful final week it was. In the mornings before work, I would typically be up at 5:15 and out the door by 5:30. I would run east on 14th Street to the East River and then south along the river, around the Battery, and back north along the West Side Highway before cutting back to the east side on 34th Street or 60th Street. Depending on how many miles I wanted to get in.

On Tuesday morning, as I rounded the Battery, I saw an NYPD patrol boat closing in on a dark object bobbing in the waters of New York Harbor. A blue-clad officer, grappling hook in hand, was reaching out for the object. It was a corpse. A somewhat bloated corpse.

Then, on Friday, my last day at the agency, I was running up 10th Avenue, approaching the old, abandoned West Side Highway trestle that hadn't been torn down yet. There was a woman on the curb—a hooker, by the looks of her—perhaps under the influence of some controlled substance. As I got nearer, she started screaming and tried to block my path. Once I moved around her, she started running after me.

The acceleration I employed to escape was one of the previously unarticulated benefits of Coach Squires's track regimen.

Moving up the west side, I interrupted my run, stopping at the Port Authority Terminal at 8th Avenue and 34th Street to buy a bus ticket back to Boston.

It truly **was** time to go home.

THE COMPLEAT RUNNER

"It's a treat, being a long-distance runner..."

—Alan Sillitoe, Author, *The Loneliness of the Long-Distance Runner*

CONTRARY TO WHAT MOST THEOLOGIANS WILL TELL YOU, THE BIBLE WAS PUB-lished on September 12, 1977. That's when *The Complete Runner*, authored by James E. Fixx, hit the shelves in bookstores and libraries. It was official.

The US running boom was underway.

Ultimately selling over one million copies, this volume and Fixx held court on anything and everything having to do with running. It was an over-night *New York Times* best-seller. I even received a copy of it for Christmas that year but didn't bother to open it.

After all, this was something I'd already been doing for six years, for heaven's sake!

To paraphrase the immortal Pee Wee Herman from the flick *Pee Wee's Big Adventure*, "I don't need to read it, Dottie. I already lived it."

Fixx, a former smoker who shed sixty pounds once he started running, tragically died a few years later of a heart attack at age fifty-two while out on a run. His father had likewise succumbed of cardiac complications at forty-three.

The math majors among us might conclude that Jim's pavement pounding added nine years to his life.

SEE YOU IN SEPTEMBER... AND OCTOBER

**"They come by the millions,
The hipster, the prince and the clown.
They come 'cause they know that
Something's going down
On the streets of New York."**

—Willie Nile, American Singer and Songwriter

UPON MY RETURN FROM NEW YORK CITY TO SOLDIERS FIELD PARK, I WAS greeted by one effervescent Denise, who had some exciting news. She had been running herself over the summer, one or two miles at a pop, and she looked tanned and nothing short of great.

"Guess what?" she exclaimed. "I signed up for a 10K run sponsored by Bonne Bell!"

"Fabulous!" I replied. "I had no idea you could run that far."

"What do you mean?" she asked, a bit confused.

"Well, 10K is 6.2 miles," I explained.

Now it was her turn to say, "I have no idea whether I can run that far."

But, a few weeks later, along Storrow Drive and the Charles River, she did just that.

CHASING DOWN A DREAM

Meanwhile, classes were back in session, and I was beginning my stretch training with about seven weeks to go to the New York City Marathon. From the pre-race hype that was already starting to appear in the media, it was shaping up as a pretty stupendous event.

Perhaps a bit of background is in order...

As previously reported in these pages, the first New York City Marathon, held in 1970 and founded by Fred Lebow, President of the New York Road Runners Club, consisted of four loops around Central Park. Emerging from a pack of 127 harriers that year, Gary Muhrcke won the race in 2 hours and 31 minutes.

Six years later, in 1976, after some serious arm twisting of municipal officials by Manhattan Borough President Percy Sutton and City Auditor George Spitz, the course was changed to its current format, encompassing all five boroughs of Gotham City.

Beginning at Fort Wadsworth on Staten Island, it crossed the Verrazzano-Narrows Bridge into Brooklyn, cruising up Fourth Avenue and then Bedford Avenue. The route then covered the Pulaski Bridge into Queens at the 13.1-mile halfway point, moved over the East River into Manhattan on the Queensboro Bridge, and dumped the racers onto First Avenue for a 5-mile run north to the Willis Avenue Bridge. After a mere mile in the Bronx, it wound back into Manhattan, down Fifth Avenue, and into Central Park for the finish.

Stupendous indeed! I was really getting excited.

My training had been going pretty well. I had racked up 370 miles in August, 425 miles in September, and over 200 in the first half of October. Nine track interval workouts in the five weeks before the marathon. On October 2, at the 8-mile Freedom Trail Road Race in Boston, I ran 47:30, or 5:56 a mile, for 121st place out of roughly 3,000 runners. I even ran into

Frank Shorter before the race, and he acknowledged my earthly existence with a quick, "Hi." Things really were going pretty well.

Then, the Sunday before the marathon, I went for a 15-miler in the Newton hills.

It had been a bit of a wild weekend, with the Harvard-Dartmouth football contest held the day before at Harvard Stadium about three blocks from our apartment. To celebrate the occasion, Denise and I had sponsored a keg party Friday night for those Big Greeners who happened to be in town. Initially, we commandeered the study room on the top floor of our apartment building for the festivities, but we were soon routed from the site by the Harvard campus police. Probably at the behest of some uptight b-school book jock who refused to take a break from studying.

Anyhow, the keg was moved to our apartment, which, if you remember, contained only one bedroom and virtually no space. By Saturday morning, the apartment—and the weather—were pretty much in shambles. The apartment was in shambles thanks to extreme partying, and the weather was in shambles thanks to extreme raining.

I mean, it was precipitation city! And it was cold. In the low forties. But we couldn't miss the game—which Dartmouth lost 31–25, by the way—could we? Denise and I trekked back to our place soaked, chilled to the bone, muscles tight and shivering. Probably not the best conditions to subject oneself to a week before a marathon. Apartment party damage control would have to wait while we thawed out.

Sunday dawned. No more rain, but still chilly and windy. During my run, I felt a twinge in my right hamstring. Not enough to make me stop, but all the same, something sure didn't feel quite right.

IN A NEW YORK STATE OF MIND

**"The city seen from the Queensboro Bridge is always
the city seen for the first time, in its first wild promise
of all the mystery and the beauty in the world."**

—F. Scott Fitzgerald, *The Great Gatsby*

AFTER THAT SUNDAY RUN, OVER THE NEXT THREE DAYS, I RAN A GRAND TOTAL of 25 miles, and that was it. Nothing out of the ordinary there. I normally cut way back before a marathon. But this was my first experience with any kind of an injury. As I think back, it was probably a mild hamstring strain. Nevertheless, I was concerned. After I had worked so damn hard.

Did I ever consider not running? Not really. My hamstring didn't feel right, but it didn't hurt so much that I felt impaired. Powering through injuries was the marathoner mindset, anyway. Macho. "ARR-ARR!" as Tim "The Toolman" Taylor of TV's *Home Improvement* might have expressed it.

So, I soaked in the bathtub, lathered on the Ben Gay, wrapped my right thigh in an Ace bandage, and packed up the VW for New York City.

Denise and I stayed with my summer landlords, Mark and Jack Markell, at their apartment in Stuyvesant Town. They were saintly people for continually putting up with these wayward running groupies. Also bunking there with us were Alan and Debbie Knobel, who had voyaged east from Ohio for Alan's very first marathon.

And Alan wasn't alone in that regard. An estimated 5,000 runners would respond to the starter's cannon at Fort Wadsworth on Sunday, not only first-timers, but a veritable "who's who" of marathoning mavens. Bill Rodgers, Jerome Drayton, Randy Thomas, Don Kardong, Tom Fleming, and Lasse Viren would lead the way, followed by the rest of us, each in search of some form of personal vindication.

The day before the race, while Denise showed Debbie and Alan around Manhattan, I tried to lay low, not wanting to further aggravate my malady. There would be plenty of time for that on Sunday.

The next morning, Alan and I rose early, walked over to Union Square, and took the subway downtown to South Ferry before walking over to the Staten Island Ferry terminal for the twenty-five-cent seaborne trip to Fort Wadsworth. Alan wasn't feeling tip-top, no appetite and up most of the night in the bathroom with what he speculated might be early flu symptoms. A less-than-providential beginning for his initial marathon.

Upon landing in Staten Island, we took a taxi to the starting line, and suddenly, we were there, and it was all about to happen.

It was a partly cloudy day, temperature in the low fifties, slight wind out of the north, a headwind for the first twenty miles, but not strong enough to be a problem. Perfect weather.

I shed my warm-up gear, threw it in a bag, and tossed it onto the truck that would carry it to the finish line. Hopefully, my "Greater Boston" singlet would not earn me epithets from the many Yankee fans and Beantown-phobes sure to be in the throng that day. With my right hammy swaddled and reeking of Atomic Balm, I would need every ounce of encouragement the spectators could throw my way to successfully complete this enterprise.

Then I made my way to the starting pen, where the 500 fastest qualifiers would start the race. The Verrazzano-Narrows Bridge stretched before us, and to our left, out in New York Harbor, NYFD fire boats were spouting streams of colorful water, celebrating this second annual five-borough marathon.

It was time to go.

At 10:30 a.m. sharp, the starter's cannon boomed, and we took off. Unlike the cramped roads of Boston, we had all three lanes of the Brooklyn-bound bridge to ourselves and, relatively speaking, I was at the front of the pack, so I was rolling at race pace right away.

The first half mile was a slight uphill and the second half mile, still on the bridge, a slight downhill. An amazing and little-known factoid: the Verrazzano-Narrows was so long that its design necessarily had to consider the curvature of the earth. As the pack descended into Brooklyn, I was feeling pretty good; ditto still at the 10-mile mark motoring past the Brooklyn Savings Bank.

Over the Pulaski Bridge, into Queens, and halfway home.

Now at 15 miles in 1:34. Still on pace for a PR. I was approaching the only real hill in the marathon, the Queensboro Bridge, also known as the 59th Street Bridge, made famous in the Paul Simon song subtitled "Feelin' Groovy." I wasn't sure I was feeling as groovy as I had earlier, but that comes with the territory.

Queensboro was the singular part of the course where the road's surface was not concrete or blacktop. Rather, the span was covered in steel grating that allowed rain or snow to pass right through it. It was slick and a difficult surface on which to get traction.

But Race Director Fred Lebow—bless his heart! He had thought of everything, actually talking a rug company into donating a three-foot-wide swath of carpeting to cover the entire length of the trestle! So, no worries about that steel grating as I climbed the incline, only worries about the slower folks I was overtaking in front of me.

And that was when disaster nearly struck.

Chugging up the bridge, head down, I pulled off the carpet to pass a fader. Suddenly, through the steel decking, I could see the ground about 100 feet below, and I almost lost it. Vertigo City. My stomach popped up into my throat, and for a split-second, I was completely disoriented. I might very easily have stumbled and fallen.

Slowing my pace, I stepped back onto the rug and regained my bearings. Taking stock, I was still in it, still moving, albeit not at the PR pace I had been a moment ago. Maybe between my tweaked hammy and this little steel decking episode, Queensboro had been for me, quite literally, with apologies, the proverbial "bridge too far."

By now, we were emptying onto Manhattan's First Avenue, where the bacchanalian brunches fueled what was a huge and enthusiastic crowd, reminiscent of those that line the Newton hills on Patriots' Day. After the span's relative solitude crossing the East River, the raucous cheering provided a shot of adrenaline that got me rolling again, propelling me over the Willis Avenue Bridge, through the brief tour of the south Bronx, and back into Manhattan.

As the course passed Harlem's Marcus Garvey Park before joining Fifth Avenue for the approach to Central Park, I heard one youthful spectator remark to his companion, "Hey, man. I'm just waitin' to see one of these dudes fall!" After my earlier experience on the bridge, I could only think, "But for the grace of God…"

Bill Rodgers, with a time of 2:11:28, had been declared the winner some 35 minutes previously by the time I crossed the finish line at Central Park West. The big digital clock emblazoned "Manufacturers Hanover" read

2:46:59—6:22 per mile. I was 279th out of an estimated 5,000 starters. I had knocked another 5 minutes off my PR.

As a race worker wrapped me in a shiny foil warming blanket, I got a medal and a metal serving tray embellished with a map of the course for my effort. Mark Markell and Denise met me at the finish line. Mark was always very frugal. She walked everywhere or took the subway. But today she must have been impressed or sympathetic or both, because she commandeered a cab to take us back to the Stuyvesant Town apartment.

My pal Alan wasn't as fortunate. He labored, severely cramping and alternatively running and walking after the halfway point. Later, he confessed to contracting a ravenous hunger around mile 18, stopping frequently thereafter to consume proffered victuals from the spectators.

However, to his eternal credit, he persisted and completed the New York City Marathon in 4 hours and 50 minutes.

A CONSUMER PACKAGE DEAL

"Life is short. Stay awake for it."

—Anonymous

A LTHOUGH I ACHIEVED MY PR, SOLDIERING THROUGH THE NEW YORK CITY Marathon that fall probably was not my wisest course of action. The hamstring injury had been a bellwether. I didn't know it at the time, but after six years of running, I was at my peak. My body was starting to break down.

A cryptic entry in my running log immediately after the October 23 marathon read "Right Thigh Problems." An early December notation was "Right Hip Problems." By the end of the month, it was "Hip Discomfort, Running Off and On."

After running 3,747 miles in 1977, I ran all of 17 in January of 1978. That was not exactly the way to prepare for April's Boston Marathon, and by the middle of February, I had pretty much decided not to run it, even though by virtue of both my '77 Boston and New York runs, I was qualified. No, way more than qualified.

But maybe that was another instance of things working out for the best. Graduation was coming up fast and it was time to leverage that pending Harvard MBA degree into a source of livelihood. Finding the right job needed to be Job #1. But how?

Back in the fall, I had taken a course called "Self-Assessment and Career Development." Who would have ever guessed they would have such a touchy, feely program at this, the bastion of capitalism, **the** Harvard Business School? But, most bodaciously, there it was in the syllabus, and I saw it as the insurance policy I needed to assure that I didn't screw up my job search.

After taking a psychological personality test and a personal interest inventory,* I then had to logically apply that information to justify the type of work I wanted to do and the specific companies at which I wanted to interview. The idea was, I guess, that if your job search plan was aligned with your inner being, you couldn't go wrong.

That is, until I came along.

So, somewhat predictably, after the summer internship Benton & Bowles, my thirty-page search blueprint pointed me toward the advertising account management ranks of nineteen agencies in New York and two in Chicago. Places like Young & Rubicam, Ogilvy & Mather, and J. Walter Thompson.

Obviously, I hadn't gotten enough of low-paying scut work the preceding summer.

In retrospect, I used the course to rationalize my one and only foray into the world of marketing to date, not to investigate what the other opportunities in that field might be out there.

---

*   Interestingly, the Strong Interest Inventory suggested a serious lack of calibration between my chosen career--advertising--and the career it found most suitable for me... that of a commercial printer. It also revealed that at age twenty-five, I had the interest level of a seventeen-year-old juvenile. Perhaps I should have taken this test **before** I entered HBS...

In contrast, on page thirteen of my plan, opining about what my career might look like in fifteen to twenty-five years, I wrote of the prospect of joining or founding a running-related business. Somewhat ironically, the New Balance corporate headquarters weren't more than a mile away from the business school campus in Allston, right across the Mass Pike. Why didn't I just pick up the phone? Or what about Oregon-based Nike, maker of my Elite racing flats, which at that point, was approaching $100 million in annual sales?

How different things might have been!

In addition to the "Self-Assessment" class, there was another course that I took the second year that was kind of interesting.

I should mention another course that "we" took, because Denise took it too. It was called "The Executive Family," taught by Dr. William Breitt. The program's premise was to prepare all of us future C-suiters and spouses for the stresses our presumed business success would exert upon our domestic lives. One of the required readings was an inspiring volume entitled *Corporate Wives, Corporate Casualties*.

Now Dr. Breitt, as a highly esteemed Harvard academician, took himself pretty seriously, and in the initial class session, he made it abundantly clear that our very first priority as his students was to learn to pronounce his surname properly.

"Good evening," he intoned. "My name is Dr. William Breitt. Breitt is a German name, so the 'e-i' spelling means it is pronounced 'Brite,' not 'Breet,' understand?"

We all nodded as one, obediently.

Dr. Breitt then went around the room, asking each of the married couples in the class to introduce themselves. Eventually, he got to us.

"Denise and Jim Rile?" he queried.

"No, Dr. Breitt," I replied. "Riehl is a German name, so the 'i-e' spelling means it is pronounced 'Reel,' not 'Rile,' understand?"

That sassy remark brought the house down.

Somehow, Denise and I passed that course too.

Well, even as I made the rounds, interviewing at the advertising agencies, most of which did not bother to come to HBS, I did have a Plan B.

I was talking to whichever consumer package goods companies I could about brand management positions when they came to campus to interrogate the inmates. I think I was beginning to have second thoughts about the whole idea of moving to New York, working for an advertising agency, and working for peanuts, if not for Mr. Peanut.

One of the things I had observed during my summer in advertising was that the agency account management guys made the **recommendations**, but the client brand management guys made the **decisions**. That was an important distinction to me. I wanted to be the one making the **decisions**.

Perhaps my "Self-Assessment and Career Development" job search blueprint wasn't really aligned with my inner being.

As I think back on it, the way I conducted job search later in my career and the way I did it then were two completely different animals. Much lighter on research and preparation then. Maybe HBS figured that by osmosis, we would apply the analytical case study approach to our hunt for gainful employment. I know I didn't. Incredibly, I didn't get much coaching from HBS, but then again, I didn't seek much coaching from HBS. Maybe I was too busy running.

Anyhow, at HBS, the brand management companies, if not the ad agencies, came to us.

Procter & Gamble. General Foods. General Mills. Quaker Oats. Kraft. I interviewed with 'em all.

Well, not Procter & Gamble. I overslept that interview. Oops.

In addition to an advertising agency I was invited to in New York, J. Walter Thompson, I did well enough in my on-campus interrogations with General Mills and Quaker Oats to be asked to their corporate headquarters—in Minneapolis and Chicago, respectively—for day-long follow ups. Time was getting short.

These were great trips. After a couple years of scrounging around, stretching to make ends meet, and wondering at times if I had the smarts to survive, it was downright gratifying to receive first-class air travel, a pricey dinner at a white tablecloth restaurant, and a room at the Waldorf-Astoria in New York or The Whitehall in Chicago. HBS had certainly opened some doors for this junior high Social Studies teacher.

The road show began with a visit to J. Walter Thompson. I had been cultivating a relationship with their head of recruiting, Rebecca Hadley, since a year and a half earlier, when I had come to the Big Apple in search of a summer internship.

In preparation for my day at JWT, Rebecca had asked me to complete a little exercise that she sent me in advance. It was a magazine advertisement for Close-Up, which had been launched in 1967 by Unilever as the first-ever brand of gel toothpaste. My assignment, simply stated, was to decipher the brand's advertising strategy. Another case study. And by this time, with something like 500-plus HBS cases dissected, I crushed it.

The ad was pretty basic. Boy sees girl. Boy is attracted to girl. Boy goes home. Boy brushes with Close-Up. Boy gets girl. Who writes this stuff anyway?

So after a day of niceties at JWT, there it was, my first offer on the table. Assistant Account Executive, paying all of $18,000 a year.

"But," Rebecca added conditionally, "I'm going to need your answer within forty-eight hours."

"I'm looking at a couple of brand management opportunities," I replied. "So I don't know if that's going to be possible."

"Oh, you don't want to go into brand management," she opined, now having assumed the role of my career advisor.

"As I said," I repeated, "I'm not sure I can meet your timeline."

"Well, I'm going to need your answer within forty-eight hours," she insisted.

"Then," I concluded, rising to leave, "I guess the answer is thanks but no thanks."

From JWT's offices in midtown Manhattan, I flew directly to the General Mills offices in Minneapolis, where on an uncharacteristically warm, ninety-degree March day, I got my second offer. As an entry-level Marketing Assistant at a slightly more bankable $23,000 annual salary.

Ultimately, offers also came in from Quaker and Drackett, the company in Cincinnati that used to own the Windex brand, but we decided to accept the Mills position. It was pretty much consistent with previous decisions because General Mills, Procter & Gamble, and General Foods were at the time the foremost consumer marketing companies in the country.

Just another chance to learn from the best...but a little bit more about that later.

In another two months, Denise and I would once again pack up the VW Super Beetle and depart for Minneapolis, where I would strive for what I was ultimately to call my "Second MBA," an MBA in marketing.

THERE'S SNOW BUSINESS

"Many people ended up trapped in their workplaces, living off vending machine food during the 1978 blizzard. Hockey fans who came to watch the Beanpot college tournament got stranded at Boston Garden. For several days they ate hot dogs, slept in the bleachers and, as *Boston Globe* writer Dan Shaughnessey pointed out, used 'combs and deodorant left behind by Boston Bruins Terry O'Reilly and Wayne Cashman.'"

—"15 Facts About the 1978 Blizzard,"
New England Historical Society

IN THE MIDST OF ALL THIS JOB HUNTING OCCURRED THE FAMOUS BOSTON Blizzard of February 1978.

When a lesser storm a few weeks earlier failed to close down graduate classes in January, Dean Lawrence Fouraker had declared in all his wisdom, "God himself cannot close down the Harvard Business School."

Well, God decided to take Dean Fouraker up on that challenge, dumping 27.1 inches of snow on Greater Boston on February 5, 6 and 7, for the next several days, shutting down the university (and the rest of New England, for that matter).

This in turn ignited a multitude of spontaneous student celebrations involving potent potables and various acts of licentious debauchery.

An idle mind...remember?

Later that week, the b-school's newspaper, *The Harbus*, published a front-page story detailing the storm. Its headline blared "God Himself...," reprising the Dean's arrogant assertion.

A CONCRETE CONCLUSION

**"I did not trip and fall. I attacked the floor
and I believe I am winning."**

—Anonymous

MEANWHILE, THE OMINOUS TRAINING LOG ENTRIES CONTINUED AS THE CALendar flipped from February to March. "Right Hamstring Problems. Saw Doctor. Calcium Problems Causing Hip Pain; Aggravate Hamstring." I was still out on the roads, but only to the tune of around 45 miles a week, with no track workouts or road races. And not the slightest thought of being out there on Patriots' Day.

By early April I began to feel better, and I put together three 20-milers, the last a week before the marathon. I knew I had the base, if not the speed work, to finish the race—if not to finish the race fast. I had qualified. I was moving to Minneapolis. I was about to become a responsible, full-time working stiff. Hell, I might never get the chance to run Boston again.

I had to run.

April 17, 1978 was a perfect day for a marathon. West-southwest wind— at the runners' backs at ten to fifteen miles per hour all the way into the Hub. Overcast, temperatures in the low fifties with an occasional drizzle. As I lined up, I wished I were in a lot better shape.

Boston Billy Rodgers won for the second time in 2:10:13. When he crossed the finish line at the Pru, I was still well back up the course, climbing the Newton hills. And while I clearly had the endurance to complete the marathon, I was fatiguing sooner than normal due to my much lighter training load the past several months.

As I commented earlier in this account, my running stride could never be described as picturesque, fluid, or graceful, like that of Shorter or Rodgers. Rather, it was more of a shuffle, back and forth, choppy and short to begin with. And as I got tired, my stride got choppier and shorter. And not as in Frank.

So, as I cleared Heartbreak Hill, I was laboring a bit. Shuffling through Cleveland Circle, I tripped on something—a manhole cover or some trolley tracks—and went down like a sack of bricks. Very briefly, after sliding along the pavement and incurring a couple asphalt-induced abrasions, I considered staying down for the mandatory ten-count that the Massachusetts State Athletic Commission would surely be coming along to administer.

But then, discretion being the better part of valor, I sprung to my feet and continued, much to the delight of the patrons in attendance.

I clocked in at the Pru 3:02:49.

Three minutes faster, and I would have qualified for next year.

That evening, as I painfully limped into one of our final "Executive Family" seminars with Denise, rehydrating with open container in hand, Dr. Breitt and the entire class saluted me with a round of applause.

135

GO WEST YOUNG MAN: EPISODE 2

"If the world has not come to its end, it has approached
a major turn in history... The ascension will be similar
to climbing onto the next anthropologic stage. No one
on earth has any other way left but upward."

**Alexandr Solzhenitsyn, Russian Novelist,
Philosopher and Political Prisoner
1978 Harvard University Commencement Speech**

DENISE AND I DECIDED TO TAKE A PASS ON THE JUNE HARVARD GRADUATION, missing out on Solzhenitsyn's commencement address that criticized both socialism and capitalism. Instead, I would receive my Harvard MBA sheepskin from a crimson mailing tube, which disgorged its contents on my parents' dining room table in Valparaiso. Not exactly Harvard Yard. So much for pomp and circumstance. More like fork and tablecloth.

After all, our Soldiers Field Park apartment lease was up May 31, Denise had resigned from her job, and we had absolutely no money. Other than that, things were perfect! However, Denise had been right about one thing. The roaches hadn't made it up to the second floor yet.

But as newly minted graduates, everyone in Section D was excited to be moving on to the next great adventure and the prospect of raising their standard of living above the bare subsistence level. One of my classmates, Phil Hunter, went out and bought a Chevy Chevette with his Visa card so he could drive out to sling Tater Tots in Idaho for Ore-Ida. Oh, the affluence of it all!

General Mills sent this humongous fifty-three-foot moving van to pick up our stuff. It clearly was going to be a mixed load, because our possessions couldn't possibly have taken up even a quarter of the van. The side of the trailer read, "North American Van Lines, Fargo, North Dakota." Uh oh. Where the hell was Fargo, North Dakota? There had to be some kind of mistake. I was going to be working in Minneapolis, wasn't I?

A quick call to Bill Newkirk , the head of recruiting at the Mills, cleared things up, but not without some major agita on my part. Our destination was indeed the Minneapple; the other portion of that mixed trailer load was in fact destined for Fargo.

It was time for this young man and his beautiful bride to head west— way the heck west—so without further ado Denise and I hopped on the Mass Pike, driving toward Springfield and Albany. To pass the miles, we were listening to WBZ AM's Bob Wilson announcing a Montreal Canadiens- Bruins Stanley Cup playoff game. Ken Dryden was the Habs' goaltender, and he was giving the Bs fits.

Somewhat symbolically, the signal faded away as we crossed over the Berkshires, severing our four-year love affair with Greater Boston.

Damn, I was gonna miss it.

ON THE BANKS OF THE WABASH... (REALLY) FAR AWAY

"I've learned that just because you're successful in one area doesn't necessarily mean you'll be successful in another."

—Jim Nabors, American Actor and Sometime Singer

AFTER B-SCHOOL, LIKE A LOT OF OTHER MBA GRADUATES, DENISE AND I FIGured we needed some downtime before I started work. So, we considered our options.

There weren't any.

Unlike some of my classmates, who had very lucrative internships in between years, I had been in New York working for, well, you know, goober peas. One woman had made thousands working for an investment bank. Another fellow had done some big-time consulting for some big-time jack. And then there was the guy who spent the summer in the Middle East working for Aramco, the Saudi Arabian Oil Company. He didn't get any home leave for three months but had to return by boat in order to bring all his money with him. Ka-ching!

Before assuming roles as captains of industry, these folks did their post-graduate downtime in truly royal fashion. European vacations. African safaris. National Geographic expeditions.

Not us.

Fortunately, for the six weeks before I was to report to General Mills in mid-July, our parents agreed to take us in—as they say on *The Price is Right*—"all expenses paid." Three luxurious weeks in Valparaiso and three in Lake Bluff, Illinois. It doesn't get any better than that.

Unless maybe it's a European vacation, an African safari, or a National Geographic expedition.

As we tooled along in the VW through New York, Pennsylvania, and Ohio en route to Valpo, I was struggling with more than just my building apprehension about my pending new job. It was, as Yogi Berra once said, "Déjà vu all over again."

Because I had run a 3:02 at Boston in April, here I was just like back in 1976, after "The Run For The Hoses," needing to complete another sub-3-hour marathon to requalify for Boston in 1979.

So, I did again what I did then, resorting to the nether pages of *Runner's World*. And there it was, this time on page 122. The redundantly named Marathon Marathon, sponsored by the oil company of the same name. It was scheduled for Saturday, June 17, in Terre Haute, Indiana, about a three-hour drive from Valpo.

Count me in.

With a 1978 population of about 61,000, Terre Haute was home to the Federal Correctional Complex, where Oklahoma City bomber Timothy McVeigh would later be executed by lethal injection, and Indiana State University, whose most famous alumnus is undoubtedly one Larry Bird. Larry's ISU Sycamores would be playing Magic Johnson's Michigan State Spartans for the NCAA hoops crown nine months later. The local topography was flat, and given the right conditions, the course might be fast.

Arriving in Terre Haute Friday afternoon, June 16, we caught up with Denise's mom and dad, who had come down for the spectacle. I had penuriously arranged overnight accommodations for next to nothing in a dormitory at ISU, and after the obligatory carbo-loading, it was time to bed down. Well, as the saying goes, you get what you pay for. The pallet was bumpy, and the room was stuffy. There were decidedly fewer than forty winks gotten that night.

As for the Marathon Marathon, suffice it to say, to use a Scottie Graham expression, "The clock is still running." Feeling flat and out of it on a very warm and sunny day and falling behind the required 6:52 per mile sub-3-hour pace, I dropped out at 17 miles. No point in continuing to the end just to log another "three-oh-something" clunker.

I resigned myself to waiting until sometime in the fall to qualify for Boston while simultaneously trying to master my challenging new job at a Fortune 500 company.

You think?

A GOLDEN OPPORTUNITY

**"If you're offered a seat on a rocket ship,
don't ask what seat! Just get on."**

—Sheryl Sandberg, Chief Operating Officer, Facebook

MY STARTING DATE AT GENERAL MILLS WAS JULY 17.

I assumed the lowly entry-level role that day of Marketing Assistant on Gold Medal® Kitchen Tested flour—or, as the locals called it, "GMKT." Nowadays the title would be something more politically correct, like Tactical Marketing Associate, but a grunt was a grunt, no matter what the job was called.

Let me assure you, GMKT was far from a plum assignment. General Mills, stock symbol GIS as listed on the New York Stock Exchange, made all sorts of consumer edibles and managed them out of its Minneapolis offices located in suburban Golden Valley. Brands like Cheerios®, Wheaties®, Trix®, Nature Valley® Granola Bars, SuperMoist® Cake Mix, Creamy Deluxe® Frosting and Bisquick.

In fact, a lot of the stuff that people don't buy quite as much anymore.

But back in the 1970s, these were big businesses with big advertising and promotion budgets.

That's where the action was. And, as an MBA just coming in the door, that's where you wanted to be. Not Gold Medal Kitchen Tested flour.

And, man, were there a lot of MBAs just coming in the door! Bluntly practicing an "up or out" approach, General Mills in those days annually recruited a thirty-plus member MBA "class" into its marketing program, fully cognizant that most of those recruits would be gone within a few years. No wonder they rolled the dice on this former junior high school Social Studies teacher!

By the time I left the company six years later, there were only five of my "class" left standing. Our incoming group represented a who's who of elite MBA programs—Harvard, Michigan, Northwestern, NYU, Stanford, Dartmouth's Tuck, Wharton—and, by inference, a bunch of very smart and very savvy competitors. People who knew how to angle for the best brand assignments. *Before* they arrived in Minneapolis. Maybe even *before* they signed on the dotted line.

But not me. And that's probably how I ended up on low budget, boring GMKT. It was reminiscent of the first couple of days at HBS, when I read the cases, set them aside, and went for a run. Once again, I realized I had a lot to learn.

I reported to an Assistant Product Manager, an ex-Marine named Sam McMahon, who reported to a Product Manager, George Fredericks, who reported to a Marketing Director, Bob Rice. In Medieval Feudal terms, as Marketing Assistant, I was the Serf, Sam was the Tenant, George was the Esquire, and Bob was the Lord. And at first, that's pretty much what it felt like. I was out working in the fields, and Bob was up in the castle, kind of overseeing things. Well, I exaggerate a bit. They did give me an ox with which to pull the plow.

And Bob did take me under his wing a bit. He was a good guy, an ex-baseball catcher and Ohio State University MBA who drove an American Motors

Gremlin. Calling me his "Double Ivy-Leaguer," he showed me the ropes, offering me advice like, "Never come into my office without your boss." And the priceless "Don't dip your pen in company ink," as if I would dare, knowing the catastrophic consequences that would await me at home when Denise inevitably found out about it.

But I signed up for this tour of duty knowing that, as in running, to get anything worth having, you have to pay your dues. And for me, General Mills was going to get me my "Second MBA," an MBA in marketing. That would set me up to do anything I wanted to do in marketing, anywhere I wanted to do it, with any company I wanted to do it with.

So, let's get to work.

A BOOKING IN BROOKINGS

"South Dakota...is like the world's first drive-through sensory deprivation chamber."

—Bill Bryson, American Author

B UT AS BOB, GEORGE, SAM, AND I BEGAN TO WHIP THE FEUDAL GMKT MAN-or into shape, I still had this other problem to address—qualifying for the 1979 Boston Marathon.

You know the drill by now. Grab *Runner's World*, rifle through to the dorsal section, and see what fall upper Midwestern regional marathons there were out there. Ahhh...page 115. The Longest Day Marathon. Sunday, November 5. In Brookings, South Dakota, four hours west of the Twin Cities.

West? Why were we always heading west for things? I was destined, I thought to myself, to be buried in California.

Rolling into August, I had just a couple of months to get ready. So, as Denise and I settled into our two-bedroom apartment in Wayzata, about twenty minutes from downtown Minneapolis, I resumed my Coach Squires-inspired training regimen of distance running, track intervals, and hilly road runs.

Well, actually, I resumed only two-thirds of my Squires-inspired training program, distance running and track intervals.

You see, I could find roads for distance running. And I could find a track. There was one right up the road at Wayzata High School. But hills? Those were a bit more difficult to find. It was just so damn flat out in Minnesota. So, I had to settle for a lot of long runs along the Loose Line, a gravel right-of-way that was an abandoned rail line. Just north of Lake Minnetonka, it ran from Wayzata out to Long Lake and Orono. From Orono, I could turn south to the lake and ramble back into town along the lake's shoreline, with nary a change in elevation.

But that was probably OK. I mean, how many hills could there be in Brookings, South Dakota? With the distance base I already had, a course without hills, and a cool November morning, I was pretty confident Denise and I would be headed back east the following April.

In the meantime, I was getting to know my immediate GMKT supervisor, Sam McMahon, the ex-Marine. For the most part, Sam was a reasonable boss, but if you screwed up, he justifiably let you know it. Like the time I failed to double check some numbers I had crunched for an analysis he was presenting to the brass. That piece of paper, with the errant calculation circled in red ink, remained taped to the wall of my cubicle for weeks.

When I joined the GMKT team, Sam was already a casual jogger, having learned the benefits of staying fit from his time in the Corps. Once he found out that Brookings was my strategic objective, he beseeched me to allow him to join the mission. Harking back to the archaic collapse-point theory, in order to test his resolve, I outlined to him the mileage commitment he would need to make to complete his first marathon.

Enthusiastically and without hesitation, right on the spot, he readily agreed.

Even before his affirmative response, I knew that Sam, a real "Semper Fi" guy, was going to be successful in his inaugural 26.2-mile outing.

GOLD MEDAL FEVER

"Life doesn't imitate art. It imitates bad television."

—Woody Allen

ABIG REASON I HAD DECIDED TO PURSUE THE DISCIPLINE OF MARKETING AT HBS was because I thought it could be simultaneously analytical, creative and fun.

One of my first assignments on GMKT reassured me in that regard.

The week following my July 17 arrival, Sam came into my office and said, "Partner, I need you to put together a Gold Medal related items sales brochure."

To which I, the uninitiated rookie, said, "What's that?"

"Jim," Sam replied, "flour is a very seasonal business. Fifty percent of annual sales occur between September and December because people are less active, celebrating the holidays and making more recipes. So during that time, our salespeople encourage retailers to promote Gold Medal—you know, put it in their newspaper ads, lower its price, display it in their store."

"OK," I said, following along so far.

"Well," Sam continued, "Every time a store sells a five-pound bag of GMKT, it also sells other ingredients—sugar, baking soda, baking powder,

146

vanilla extract, walnuts, whatever else—that go into the same recipe. So, your Gold Medal–related item sales brochure is going to convince the retailer to promote GMKT because of all the other recipe ingredients they will also sell—and the additional profit they will make as a result.

"Just don't make it boring," Sam concluded.

"Yes, sir." I solemnly saluted as he pivoted on his heel and exited my cubicle.

Yep, I guess this was truly learning by doing.

Fortunately, the muses were with me that day. The movie *Saturday Night Fever* had been released the previous December, and in the ensuing seven months it had become a cultural phenomenon. Much to the disappointment of rock music aficionados such as myself, we were living in a disco summer.

What better theme for my related item sales brochure?

The rest is Marketing Hall of Fame history.

On the brochure's front, an illustrator's John Travolta look-alike, clad in platinum white disco suit, arm pointed skyward, danced with a shopping cart piled high with bags of Gold Medal flour and related recipe ingredients. Beneath his platform shoes, blinked the disco-lighted dance floor. The headline screamed, "Gold Medal Fever...Catch It!" At the bottom, a subheadline read, "Bump Up Related Item Profits to the Tune of $30.69!"

On the brochure's back appeared the more mundane details about how to promote GMKT, what to promote it with, and when to promote it.

I still can't believe the corporate lawyers approved that one. I bet nowadays they wouldn't.

MY SECOND MBA

"The earliest origins of marketing...may have first
begun with the branding of farm animals in the
Middle East during the Neolithic period."

—Wikipedia

THUS FAR IN THIS ACCOUNT, I HAVE ALREADY MADE A COUPLE OF REFERENCES to the fact that I intended to get "my Second MBA" at General Mills, an MBA in marketing.

That comment deserves a bit more explanation. So, climb aboard.

Let's face it. When I arrived at General Mills in the summer of 1978, I knew virtually nothing about marketing. **NOTHING**. Oh, sure, I had taken a first-year Marketing course and a second-year Advertising course at HBS. And I'd worked as a summer account management slug at Benton & Bowles. But during those experiences, I had been lectured at and entombed in the deepest of trenches.

This was very contrary to my educational philosophy of *learning by doing*. Remember those junior high classes in which, at least on a simulated basis, the North fought the South and the world exploded prematurely?

General Mills was my chance to learn marketing by doing. And not only that. Like GBTC and HBS, General Mills was my chance to learn from the very best.

Time out for a bit of Marketing 101.

Whether it began in the Neolithic period or whenever, marketing has evolved over the ages as a discipline used to differentiate products or services from commodities, thereby ideally commanding increased customer loyalty, higher prices, and higher profits. It's pretty simple. If done properly, the better the marketing, the better the money.

Perhaps a bit crass, but true.

In managing a product or service, the marketer has many potential levers to push or pull. Advertising. Distribution. Formulation. Manufacturing. Packaging. Pricing. Promotion. It's a very complex tactical stew with lots of moving pieces.

Initially, at least as Wikipedia has it, one guy differentiated his farm animals from the other guy's by putting his logo on them. Did it bring him a higher price or more loyal customers when he took his beasties to auction? We'll never know, but that was his general objective. What we do know is his animals probably didn't care for the red-hot branding part of it.

By the twentieth century, of course, marketing and branding had gotten a lot more sophisticated. Advertising sprouted into new media like radio and television. Distribution found new channels beyond the traditional small mom-and-pop stores. Product formulations evolved far beyond the simple commodities of the past. Mass manufacturing became the norm, and unique new packaging materials became available to simplify shipment and entice customers. Price promotions via coupons and on-site discounting began to be commonplace.

And as marketing evolved over the ages, so did marketing management practices.

Fast forward to 1931, four years after Charles Lindbergh made the first successful air crossing of the Atlantic Ocean, when a twenty seven year-old Harvard graduate wrote a three-page memo that was to totally revolutionize marketing governance. His name was Neil McElroy, and he was a junior executive at Procter & Gamble, working on the Camay brand of soap. McElroy, who later served as President Dwight Eisenhower's Secretary of Defense, penned the principles of brand management.

Neil's theory was that P & G should assign a separate marketing team to each brand, as if that brand were a separate business. The brand's marketing team was then to assume responsibility for everything having to do with the brand's operation.

Everything. The brand's topline sales. The brand's bottom-line profits. And everything in between. Its advertising. Its distribution. Its formula. Its package. Its manufacturing. Its pricing. And its promotion.

Now Neil wasn't asking the brand team to be Superman incarnate. They would have plenty of support. An outside advertising agency. An internal distribution and logistics department. A lab to conduct product formulation research and testing. Packaging design and purchasing folks. A manufacturing and operations team. A group to assess the impact of pricing decisions and experts to help put together promotions and hire outside vendors to execute them.

But the marketing group would in effect be running their own mini-company. And that was the beauty of the concept. Learn to run a mini-company successfully, and you already had learned how to run a maxi-company successfully. A company's marketing managers of today could easily be its general managers—its leadership—of tomorrow.

But at the end of the day, it was up to the marketing team and, in particular, its captain, the Product Manager or Brand Manager, to use all these resources to simultaneously increase brand sales, profitability and market share, all within budget. Managers who failed to do so encountered their own personal career Kryptonite and were exiled back to Smallville, never to be heard from again.

Neil's bosses liked his organizational philosophy so much that they implemented it, and Cincinnati-based P & G became a renowned post-World War II marketing powerhouse, with Neil assuming command as President in 1948. Two of the first companies beyond

P & G to recognize the wisdom inherent in the brand management model were General Mills and General Foods, with both companies pivoting to the structure shortly thereafter.

By the mid-1970s, P & G, Mills and Foods were all among the most highly regarded institutions of brand management learning in the country, if not the world.

So, it stands to reason, as I jumped at the chance to learn by doing with the best at GBTC and HBS, that accepting a marketing position at General Mills meant that I would be matriculating there to get my "Second MBA," my MBA in marketing.

THE LONGEST DAY

"When you're going through hell, keep going."

—Winston Churchill

"I'VE NEVER BEEN MORE THAN ABOUT TWENTY MILES WEST OF MINNEAPOLIS," I remarked to Denise as we climbed into Sam McMahon's gold Chevy station wagon on Saturday morning, November 4.

"I'm not sure I ever want to go more than about twenty miles west of Minneapolis," she whispered in response.

It was the day before the Longest Day Marathon, and we were carpooling with my boss, Sam, and his wife, Katsuko, on the four-hour ride to Brookings, South Dakota. A few weeks earlier, Bill Rodgers had won his third consecutive New York City Marathon in 2:12:12, but for me, it was time to put up or shut up.

I needed a sub 3-hour marathon the next day in order to return to Boston the following spring. There was absolutely no question this would be my last shot. We had already seen our first snow flurries in the Twin Cities, and GMI's annual business planning season was about to begin, meaning sixty-plus hour weeks and not much time for anything else.

As we headed west, we were a colorful assemblage, seemingly suited for anywhere but the bowels of the South Dakotan grain belt. There was Sam, the macho ex-Marine, who had been all over the world. Then his

152

Japanese wife, Katsuko, whom Sam had met and married during one of his tours of duty. Dainty and beautiful, she spoke halting English, hardly mainstream Upper Midwest. And of course, Denise and me, with our mantra of "Have Race, Will Travel." But I had to admit, this was really pushing it.

This was quite the automotive excursion. Dr. Seuss wasn't kidding when he said, "Oh, The Places You'll Go!" En route, we rolled through rural bergs like Belle Plaine, Le Sueur, and Sleepy Eye, and we even detoured about twenty miles south on Route 75 to see the Pipestone National Monument because we knew there would be nothing to do when we finally got to Brookings.

And, boy, we were sure right about that. There wasn't much going on in this small town of 15,000, home to South Dakota State University and its Division I athletic squads, the Jackrabbits. To kill even more time, we prolonged our prerace check-in by chatting up the friendly locals with questions about the event.

"Why is it called the Longest Day Marathon?" Sam asked.

"Well," the race director replied, "we used to hold it around June 21, the first day of summer and the longest day of the year."

"Makes sense," I commented, looking at the commemorative race t-shirt, which bore the image of a jogger with a humongous sun at his back.

That made me curious. "Why did you move it to November?"

"June was the middle of growing season," he deadpanned. "Too many tractors on the roads."

"Then why didn't you change the name from the Longest Day?" queried Denise.

"We printed too many T-shirts."

Oh, the trials and tribulations of race management.

As I tried to get some sleep that night, I could hear the wind outside starting to pick up. Not a good sign. By the time we got up Sunday morning, there was a steady twenty miles-per-hour wind out of the northwest gusting to over thirty miles per hour. Definitely not a good sign. The temperature was downright cold, in the low forties, creating a wind chill of thirty degrees.

The course was out and back, the first 13.1 miles with the wind, the last 13.1 miles into the wind. Lovely. The strategy was simple. Try to put enough time in the bank during the first half that I could tough out the second half and still finish under 3 hours.

The first half strategy worked well enough along the flat farm roads as I was pushed by the gusting blasts. I turned back into the wind well under 1:30, and it was there that the trouble began. Perhaps I had underdressed, but as I battled the chill winds, I began to tighten up. At some point, my old nemesis surfaced, and I pulled- or tore- my right hamstring.

Why I didn't simply call it a day, pull to the side of the road, and wait for the Triple-A crash cart to gather me up, I have no idea. Maybe I still thought I had enough of a time reserve to qualify. Maybe I didn't want to quit in front of my boss, the Leatherneck. I don't know. But I insisted on being one of the Few. The Proud. The Knuckleheaded. Anyway, I pushed on to the finish, recording something like a 3:20. Quite honestly, I don't remember the time.

Sam, as I knew he would, finished strong, not long after I did. A very nice effort for his first marathon, especially under the conditions.

But clearly, I was quite badly hurt. By the time we stopped for a pizza in New Ulm on the way home, I had further tightened up and had to be helped to and from the car.

And I didn't go to work the next day. I couldn't walk, much less run.

Nor would I...run, that is...for quite some time.

FLOUR POWER

"And sure enough, even waiting will end...if
you can just wait long enough."

—William Faulkner, American Writer

MAYBE THIS WAS YET ANOTHER OF THOSE TIMES IN DISGUISE WHEN THINGS turn out for the best. I certainly didn't think so at the time.

But as I waited for my hamstring to heal, I had to focus on putting together GMKT's annual marketing plans. Annual marketing plans were a big deal at General Mills. They were the marketing team's blueprint for how they were going to grow sales, profits, and market share in the next year. The process began in December and extended into late February, at which time all efforts would culminate in a major dog-and-pony show in front of the divisional General Manager.

If I was initially disappointed by my Marketing Assistant assignment to boring, low budget GMKT, I was a bit more encouraged as we began to assemble the business plan.

Let me elaborate on the reason behind my optimism, beginning with a brief history lesson.

General Mills traced its history back to 1866, when a guy named Cadwallader Washburn built a six-story flour mill in Minneapolis, along the banks of the Mississippi River. Subsequently, his enterprise entered into a partnership with John Crosby, forming the collegially monikered Washburn-Crosby Company. Despite a major setback in 1878, when an accumulation of flour dust triggered a massive explosion that leveled the mill, the firm won gold, silver, and bronze at the 1880 Millers' International Exhibition in Cincinnati, spawning the launch of the Gold Medal brand.

As we sat down to hammer out GMKT's 1979–1980 marketing plan, it dawned on the historians among us that our little brand was turning 100 years old. Hey, how often does that happen?

It was the perfect opportunity to create a year-long mega-event, with a year-long mega-budget, just like the big-spending Cheerios and Wheaties brands that some of my MBA peers managed. Lots of TV and magazine advertising. Lots of consumer promotions. Lots of retail trade events. A new TV commercial. And a 112-page centennial cookbook with *The Best Gold Medal Recipes of 100 Years*.

So, we put it all in the marketing plan, and we sold it all to the divisional General Manager.

I was in the right place at the right time after all.

BOOK 'EM DANNO

"Remember, a gift you bake is a gift from the heart... They'll love you so much more for it."

—Betty Crocker

I WAS PUT IN CHARGE OF THE COOKBOOK.

Of course, I was involved in all the other Gold Medal flour centennial related marketing stuff—great exposure—but the cookbook was my baby. Recipe selection, recipe development, photography, proofreading, publication, advertising, distribution, everything.

Not that I was in any way remotely qualified for this assignment, but fortunately I had some help.

By way of background, the General Mills offices at the intersection of Highways 394 and 169 in suburban Golden Valley were also the home of the world-famous Betty Crocker Kitchens.

"Who was this Betty Crocker?" my Gen X readers might query.

Suffice to say, she was the figment of some advertising executive's imagination, born in 1921 to provide a personalized signature to those writing to request recipes from the Washburn-Crosby Company. But that was just the start.

Always the epitome of the intelligent and nurturing homemaker, the brunette Betty evolved throughout the rest of the twentieth century, first voiced by actresses over the radio and later portrayed by a plethora of divas on TV. But above all, she was recipe royalty; her face launched a thousand cookbooks and sold tons and tons of Gold Medal flour. So now we've come full circle.

In 1958, as a shrine to their popover priestess, General Mills built the Betty Crocker Kitchens on the first floor of their office tower. These were seven active kitchens used for product testing and recipe development, each paying homage to a separate area or subculture of the United States—as in the Arizona Desert, California, Cape Cod, Chinatown, Hawaiian, Pennsylvania Dutch, and Williamsburg galleys.

To further proselytize their recipe-driven religion, the company made daily facility tours available to the public.

Then I arrived on the scene.

"Jim," Sam reasoned, "in order to oversee the production of a cookbook, you need to understand the basics of baking. So, in much the way I did as a young Marine, you are going to boot camp."

There was no protesting. Apron in hand, I was trundled off for a week in the Cape Cod Kitchen. Well, at least I was in Massachusetts. Sort of.

I was working with a blonde home economist named Janis McCarthy, who was very sharp, had a good sense of humor, and would be leading recipe development on the cookbook. She showed me a whole lot of very basic things, like how to assemble ingredients for a recipe, how to measure them, and how to mix them without explosion. Then I made bread from scratch.

Like I said, very basic stuff. It was pretty clear that this kid was not destined for the Culinary Institute.

It was a long week. Kind of embarrassing in a way. Not what I saw myself doing when I came out of business school. But I tried to roll with the punches. One thing was for sure. It gave me a real appreciation for the home economists who would be developing, testing, and perfecting the recipes in our cookbook.

Toward the end of my week in Cape Cod, Janis was just taking some Irish soda bread out of the oven as the last visitor tour of the day shambled through the kitchens. Last in line, about fifty feet behind the group was a seven-year-old. As the kid passed our kitchen, he glanced in, saw Janis, and, aghast, went running down the hall, screaming, "Mom! Mom! Betty Crocker is a blonde!"

LET THEM EAT CAKE

"Mmm, this cake is too much, hon!"

"No, it's just the right size!"

—Stir'n Frost Television Commercial, Circa 1977

BILLY DID IT AGAIN. HE WON BOSTON IN APRIL 1979, LOWERING HIS RECORD by 28 seconds to 2:09:27. Our GBTC workout partners Bobby Hodge, Randy Thomas, and Dickie Mahoney were 3rd, 8th and 10th, respectively. Four out of the top 10. This certainly suggests Coach Squires was one of the best if not *the best* marathon coach of his time. And, oh yeah, a Minnesota runner, Garry Bjorklund, was 5th.

Bill would win again in the fall at the New York City Marathon, with Frank Shorter coming in 7th. Rodgers was really on a roll.

As for me, my string of five consecutive Bostons was broken, as I had crashed in flames while twice trying to qualify in Terre Haute and Brookings and was, thus, laid low while my hamstring recovered. By late spring, I was starting to run again, up to 8 to 10 miles on the road, but no track workouts or racing lest I reinjure myself. Taking it very slowly.

After all this, beginning a new job and a new life in a new place, did I ever consider hanging it up? Not for a second. I had found an athletic endeavor that was mine. Really mine. It made me unique, gave me a personality. It was something I enjoyed and was halfway good at. And I was very blessed to have a wife who got all that.

No, I didn't consider hanging it up.

What I considered was how to get healthy so I could get back to Boston. But I had to rebuild slowly. I had learned my lesson. It had been a very serious injury.

In the meantime, somewhat amazingly, in my first year, I had mastered Market Assistant-hood on GMKT.

Among my many storied accomplishments, the *Gold Medal Century of Success Cookbook* was published in early 1979 to rave reviews; used copies are still available on Amazon. How's that for making a mark? I had also figured out how to manage a multi-million-dollar advertising, promotion and trade spending budget without plunging the company into bankruptcy. And I forecast flour demand well enough to keep American supermarket aisles stocked and prevent food riots in the streets.

General Mills moved marketing people around a lot, on the average of once every year. I guess that was to see how adaptable they were and how quickly they could learn new businesses. Consequently, it was time for me to move on. So in July, I was among the first in my MBA "class" to be promoted to the exalted role of Assistant Product Manager, with two fully functioning human beings actually reporting to me.

My new assignment took the cake. Well, actually, two of them.

My new brand group managed two packaged cake mixes, Betty Crocker Stir'n Frost® and Betty Crocker Angel Food® Cake Mix. Again, we weren't talking Mills's crown jewels here.

Angel Food Cake Mix, introduced in 1953, was a mere twelve months shy of matching my age. In grocery product lingo, it was both a dinosaur and a commodity, sales driven by trade promotion, not consumer advertising. And it being 1979, the previous brand group had just missed the opportunity to celebrate the brand's twenty-fifth anniversary. Not much excitement there.

Stir'n Frost was a little more interesting. Launched in 1975, it was a four-flavor line of pure carbohydrates, each package containing a packet of cake mix, an envelope of ready-to-spread frosting, and a disposable five-by-seven-inch baking pan. Just tear open the mix pouch, dump it in the pan, add water, stir, and bake. Once out of the oven, let it cool and then smear the frosting over the top. Sold in the United States and also in Canada, where it was branded Tout En Un. All in one.

SNF, as we abbreviated it, actually had TV and magazine advertising and consumer coupon promotions. The advertising tag line was "When a big cake is more than you need," and the mixes, which were surprisingly tasty, frequently disappeared from the company product locker to fuel many of my training runs.

Sadly, the brand was to be discontinued eight years later, in 1988, probably the victim of healthier eating trends, more working moms, and less time for—and interest in—baking.

Or, to put it a bit more succinctly, by that time, Stir'n Frost no longer panned out.

OH YEAH, YOU BETCHA

"Uffda!"

—Scandinavian Expression of Surprise,
Exhaustion, Relief, or Dismay

BACK ON FEBRUARY 22, 1980, AS WE PUT THE FINISHING TOUCHES ON THE Stir'n Frost/Angel Food Cake Mix annual marketing plans, the US men's Olympic ice hockey team was in the process of triumphing by a score of 4–3 over the mighty Soviets in Lake Placid, New York.

I missed the Friday afternoon game that day because I was at some long-ago-forgotten General Mills company function.

One of the highlights of the American victory was the way Coach Herb Brooks, from the University of Minnesota, actually got bitter collegiate rivals from Massachusetts and the Gopher State to team up and play as one.

And after spending four years in metro Beantown, Denise and I could understand the deep underlying cultural basis for that rivalry, as we found Minnesota to be...well...different.

How so? Let me count the ways.

Somewhat in contrast to Bostonians, in Minnesota, the people were incredibly nice, overly courteous, and friendly. This pattern of behavior actually had a term: "Minnesota Nice." Not necessarily a bad thing.

Minnesotans were very non-confrontational in a passive-aggressive way. For those who can remember, think of Mary Richards of *The Mary Tyler Moore Show*. The locals also tended to maintain their own social circles and not admit outsiders, but we socialized with all the transplants from General Mills, so this wasn't a big deal.

Another difference we noticed was on the roads.

In Boston, driving had been a competitive sport. In Minnesota, not so much. Drivers made their way slowly, seemingly unconscious as to their ultimate destination. They were courteous to a fault. "You go first...No, you go first..." You might be at a four-way stop sign for hours. However, my pet peeve was the blue-haired sedan jockeys who would tool along in the left lane at fifty miles per hour, oblivious to the queue of impatient drivers stacked up in their rearview mirror.

The Gopher State also put a unique spin on certain culinary items.

What the other forty-nine states would call "casseroles" Minnesotans would call "hot dishes," often festooned with a plethora of Tater Tots. Then there was the immortal "Juicy Lucy," which was a burger made famous by Matt's Bar at 35th and Cedar in Minneapolis. Lucy wasn't your typical cheeseburger with a slab of cheddar on top. Rather she was *stuffed* with the gooey, runny dairy derivative! And the Minnesota State Fair, regularly attended by 40 percent of the state's 5.5 million residents, offered its own gustatory delicacies—Pronto Pups corn dogs, Mouth Trap cheese curds, alligator sausage on a stick, big fat bacon, and deep-fried scotch eggs. Yum.

In Boston, the Red Sox, Celtics, and Bruins, if not the Patriots (in contrast to more recent times), were all pretty regular post-season competitors. In Minnesota, it was quite literally a different ballgame. The MLB Twins, who had arrived in the Twin Cities as the ex-Washington Senators in 1961, wouldn't win a World Series until 1987. The most colorful thing about them during my tenure was a Puerto Rican outfielder named Bombo Rivera.

The NFL Vikings, who also played their first season in 1961 as an expansion team, have subsequently been to four Super Bowls without a win. And by 1978, the year we arrived, the NHL's North Stars, who began play in October 1967, had missed the Stanley Cup playoffs in five of the six preceding years. As for the Big Ten Golden Gophers at the "U," the University of Minnesota? Please. Don't get me started.

In New England, the expression was "If you don't like the weather, wait ten minutes, and it's likely it will change." Well, that wasn't quite the case in Minnesota, but as with many of the other things I've been discussing, the weather was indeed unlike any we had ever seen.

The summers were beautiful, blue skies with low humidity. "The land of sky-blue waters," as the Hamm's beer jingle described it. North as we were, heat waves were rare, and sunsets occurred after 9 p.m. But there was a downside.

Tornadoes were always a possibility, one once passing within two miles of our house. And the mosquito was the Minnesota state bird, traveling in swarms and occasionally carrying off a small animal or a newborn baby. Its companion, the black fly, bit with ferocity and was particularly adept at avoiding the swatter.

The winters were endless. No other way to describe them. Come the first of October, it was time to see the shrink. Winter is coming. Depression is setting in. Time for therapy. The first snowflakes normally flew by Halloween. Then months of snow and bone-chilling, bitter cold. Sometimes wind chills as low as seventy or eighty degrees below zero. You couldn't go outside. You had to plug your car into an electric heater or it wouldn't start. When, in mid-January, the temperature would go up into the twenties or thirties, it actually felt *warm*.

And I was going to run in this stuff?

166

The ice remained on the lakes until May. In fact, the locals liked to bet on the exact date when the ice would "go out," that is, sink beneath the water on Lake Minnetonka. You had best remove your fishing shelter from the ice by then. If you didn't, Minnesota state statute read that you were subject to fine, prosecution or both, and your shelter was subject to removal or destruction.

No, we weren't in Kansas anymore, Dorothy.

THE RUN FOR THE ROSIE

Rosie, what kind of training have you been doing?
Have you been doing a lot of heavy intervals?

—Katherine Switzer, Reporter and Marathon Runner

"Someone else asked me that. I'm not sure
what intervals are. What are they?"

—Rosie Ruiz, Unofficial Winner,
Women's Division, 1980 Boston Marathon

IT WAS APRIL 1980, AND SPRING WAS FINALLY APPROACHING IN MINNESOTA.

A few weeks earlier, President Carter had taken the extremely unpopular decision—at least among the running community—not to send the US Olympic Team to the Moscow Summer Olympics. His rationale in doing so was that the Soviets had not met his deadline for withdrawing their troops from Afghanistan.

Either that, or he thought beating the Russians at ice hockey was sufficient American athletic achievement for one year.

Back East, Patriots' Day had rolled around again, so it was time for Bill Rodgers to do what he was pretty predictably doing all the time—win another marathon. In fact, upon deciding to skip the meaningless US Olympic trial in Buffalo, Billy was free to shoot for his fourth Boston win. Which he did, crossing the finish line at the Prudential Center in 2:12:11, almost three minutes slower than his 2:09:27 record, set the previous year.

But that wasn't the big story coming out of Beantown that day. The headline grabber occurred in the women's division, where a total unknown, twenty-six-year-old Rosie Ruiz, won with a course record time of 2:31:56, logging the third fastest women's marathon time ever. Not just at Boston. The third fastest time run *anywhere*.

In a flashback to the 1972 Munich Olympic marathon, when our old buddy Norbert Sudhaus tried to steal gold from Frank Shorter, Rosie was crowned with the champion's laurel wreath, but certain things didn't seem quite right.

At the finish, Rosie seemed very fresh, not at all sweaty or fatigued after a long run. Her Boston time was a whopping 25-minute improvement over the 2:56 she had run at the New York City Marathon six months earlier to qualify. And no runners could recall seeing Rosie out on the course in the earlier stages of the marathon, nor did she appear in any of the race day videos. In fact, a couple of Harvard students recalled seeing her bursting out of a group of spectators on Commonwealth Avenue, about a half mile from the finish.

Hmmm.

As suspicions mounted regarding the authenticity of Ruiz's Boston victory, the New York Road Runners Club launched an investigation into her New York City Marathon performance. One freelance photographer remembered encountering Rosie on the subway and walking with her to the Central Park finishing area. Once there, Ruiz claimed she was an injured marathoner, and race workers recorded her as having completed the event, thereby punching her ticket to Boston.

As a result of their probe, the New York Road Runners retroactively disqualified Ruiz from the New York City Marathon, which technically would also have nullified her Boston victory, since that's how she had qualified for Boston.

But the Boston Athletic Association insisted on conducting its own investigation, which brought to light several other disturbing facts. Ruiz was not familiar with running terms, like "splits" and "intervals." Her thighs were not as muscular as those of other world-class female runners. And her resting pulse was in the mid-70s, not the mid-50s, as with many of her competitors.

A few days later, the B.A.A. disqualified Ruiz and declared Canadian Jacqueline Gareau the winner in a then course record time of 2:34:28. When Gareau returned to Boston to be properly acknowledged for her standard-shattering effort, Tommy Leonard organized an informal awards ceremony for her at the Eliot Lounge.

Hoisting their Blue Whales, the barroom patrons saluted her with a rousing chorus of "O Canada!"

MOVING THE GOALPOSTS, AGAIN

"With 7,927 entrants in the 1979 race
(an increase of 3,163 from 1978)
the standards were tightened for all potential competitors to curb
the dramatic growth that occurred during the preceding year."

—Boston Athletic Association

WHILE I HAD BEEN HEALING MY BADLY TORN HAMSTRING AND STARTING TO rebuild my distance base, the B.A.A.'s Jock Semple and Will Cloney did it to me again, just like back in 1976.

Effective starting in 1980, they lowered the Boston Marathon qualifying time for men ages twenty to thirty-nine from three hours to 2 hours and 50 minutes.

Sure, I had run better than that at the 1977 NYC Marathon, but I was coming off a pretty serious leg injury that had cost me all of 1979. I was starting all over again. And my margin of error based on my New York time—a measly 3 minutes or less than 7 seconds per mile—was very narrow.

Now it was New Year's Eve 1980, and Denise and I were headed to a celebration at the Lake Calhoun Beach Club to ring in the next twelve months. To pass the time until the stroke of midnight, I had penned a Jeopardy game of 1979 trivia, which as usual, was a huge hit. In a genuine surge of inventiveness, our hostess, Sara Weston, had required all guests to come dressed as their respective New Year's resolutions.

171

Somewhat predictably and unimaginatively, I came to the soiree clad in my "Greater Boston" singlet pinned with my 1978 Boston Marathon number—1139. My 1980 resolution was clairvoyantly predictable—qualify for the 1981 Boston Marathon by running a sub-2:50.

Somewhere. Anywhere.

OVER THE RIVER AND THROUGH THE WOODS: EPISODE 1

"Newcomers should comprehend that Duluth is at present a small place and hotel and boarding room accommodation is extremely limited. However, lumber is cheap and shanties can be built. Everyone should bring blankets and prepare to rough it at first."

—Duluth Minnesotan, August 24, 1869

I DIDN'T EVEN HAVE TO GO TO THE BACK OF THE JANUARY ISSUE OF *RUNNER'S World* to find my "somewhere, anywhere" marathon. Which is a good thing, because by then, I don't think I subscribed to that publication anymore.

With my post-injury return to the roads and our move from rural Wayzata to a small house in suburban St. Louis Park, I was gradually integrating myself into the local running community. And I was finding it pleasantly and surprisingly vibrant.

From our new home on Vernon Avenue South, it was an easy mile and a half past the southern shore of Cedar Lake over to Lake of the Isles, Lake Calhoun, and Lake Harriet. Fortuitously, these lakes were where all the Minneapolis runners hung out.

Most notable was the "Eleven O'Clock Club," a loose band of guys who met at the Lake Calhoun bath house at that appointed hour on Saturday and Sunday mornings for a long, slow tour of the paths around Calhoun, Isles and Harriet. For the most part, these were not elite guys, rather, plodders. So I, still recovering from my injury, fit right in.

A charter member of the club was Alan Page, who after an All-American career as a defensive tackle at Notre Dame, played eleven seasons for the Minnesota Vikings as one of their famed "Purple People Eaters." He was one of only eleven of the Norsemen to play in all four of their Super Bowl losses.

Originally, he took up running to help his wife, who coincidentally worked at General Mills, quit smoking. Becoming an avid practitioner, running as much as 55 miles a week, Alan apparently lost so much weight running that the Vikings cut him. No problem. He tootled on down to the Windy City, signed on with Da Bearz, and played four more seasons. He's now in the Pro Football Hall of Fame in Canton, Ohio, where he grew up, and as a teenage laborer, helped lay the foundation of the building in which he is now enshrined.

And when Alan hung up his cleats, he wasn't done. He had already received a law degree from the University of Minnesota and spent five years working as a lawyer before serving seven years in the state Attorney General's office. In 1992 he was elected to an open seat as Justice on the Minnesota Supreme Court, from which he eventually took mandatory retirement at the age of seventy in 2015.

Needless to say, I didn't brag too loudly to His Honor Alan about my three episodes of lawless banditry at the Boston Marathon. He might have locked me up.

In addition, to the Eleven O'Clock Club, I was finding out that there was a lot more to the Minnesota running scene.

One of the guys in the club, Chuck Allen, turned me on to *Raceline*, a recorded phone message that was updated weekly by another local running luminary, Charlie Bryant. *Raceline* carried announcements about local road races and other running news. And now that I was plugged in, I found a decent number of nearby competitions, where I could work on regaining my somewhat eroded speed and conditioning.

Also, I was discovering, with a certain degree of amazement, that Minnesota was not without its very own "sturdleys." Three of them were Steve Hoag, Garry Bjorklund, and Dick Beardsley.

Steve Hoag was an All-American runner out of the University of Minnesota, who competed in the 1968 and 1976 US Olympic marathon trials. He was runner-up to Bill Rodgers at the 1975 Boston with a time of 2:11:54, which was the fourth fastest in the world that year.

Another Golden Gopher from the "U," hailing from Twig, Minnesota, Garry Bjorklund went to the 1976 Olympics in Montreal and ran in the 10,000-meter final, finishing 13th. After that, he focused on the marathon, finishing fifth in the 1977 NYC Marathon and, as we have seen, fifth in the 1979 Boston Marathon. We'll hear more from Garry a little later.

And Dick Beardsley will show up again, too. For now, let's remember him as the shy kid from Excelsior, Minnesota, who was too small to play football but wanted a varsity letter to impress the girls—so he began to run. Completing his first marathon in 2 hours and 47 minutes, he improved his time in each one of his next twelve, a feat for which his name is in the Guinness Book of World Records.

So, net net, a bit to my initial surprise, running was alive and well in Frostbite Falls.

Consequently, I didn't need the *Runner's World* want ads to steer me to my next marathon. The skinny on the street, courtesy of the Eleven

O'Clock Club, was that I needed to go over the river and through the woods to Grandma's.

But not to Grandma's house. To Grandma's Marathon. In beautiful, if somewhat remote, Duluth, Minnesota.

The first Grandma's Marathon, sponsored by Grandma's Saloon and Deli, had been contested in 1977 by 150 hardy harriers and was won by Garry Bjorklund in 2:21:54. See, I told you we would hear more from him. In 1980, it was scheduled for June 21, which made me wonder—albeit only for a split second--why they didn't call it the Longest Day Marathon.

Because Grandma's Saloon and Deli had paid race organizers a $600 sponsorship fee, that's why.

And because that name had already been taken by some other marathon out in South Dakota. The one in November that had too many t-shirts.

Grandma's June 21 timing was perfect—five and a half full months for me to train, with the heaviest mileage and speed work happening after the winter lake ice "went out" and before the dog days of summer set in.

Duluth, for those unfamiliar with the Gopher State's geography, is situated practically due north of the Twin Cities, at the westernmost tip of Lake Superior. Along with its sister city, Superior, Wisconsin, Duluth constitutes the Twin Ports of Superior, through which pass coal, iron ore, and grain headed for steel and flour mills along the Great Lakes and St. Lawrence Seaway.

The marathon course begins 26.2 miles northeast of Duluth, just outside of Two Harbors, so named for its twin natural anchorages, at which ore boats dock to take on loads of taconite from the nearby iron ore fields. From there, the route proceeds southwest on US Highway 61—as immortalized in Bob Dylan's 1965 album *Highway 61 Revisited*—along the shore of Lake Superior through several tiny, unincorporated hamlets named Larsmont, Knife River, Palmers, and French River. Upon reentering civilization, the course circles around the Duluth waterfront before finishing in Canal Park, hard by the landmark Aerial Lift Bridge and, of course, Grandma's Saloon and Deli.

And the scheduling of Grandma's Marathon wasn't the only thing that was perfect. So was the elevation. It was flat, flat, flat. From start to finish, the elevation decreased from 740 feet to 600 feet. The steepest ascent, an incline benignly called "Lemon Drop Hill," occurred at mile 22 and was a climb of all of 45 feet.

No Heartbreak Hills. No Depressions.

Either topographical ones or mental ones.

So, I marked the calendar and laced up my shoes.

ASTRIDE THE COMEBACK TRAIL

"It's not whether you get knocked down. It's whether you get up."

—Vince Lombardi, Head Coach, Green Bay Packers

JANUARY 1, 1980.

It had been 425 days since I had finished any marathon. It had been 622 days since I had finished any marathon in a time approaching three hours. And it had been 799 days—two years, two months, and one week—since I had finished my one and only marathon under 2 hours and 50 minutes, the new Boston Marathon qualifying standard for my age group.

And now, hopefully fully healed from my badly torn right hamstring and assorted hip problems, I had just 171 days to get ready to repeat that last feat, which would earn me a return trip to Boston in 1981.

As I look back, that seemed like long odds, but I'm not sure I recognized it at the time.

January and February began slowly. I averaged about 55 miles a week, 225 miles each month. No road races. No track intervals. Hell, it was the dead of winter in Minnesota. The St. Louis Park High School track was buried under two feet of snow.

Running in the Minnesota winter was a very different animal. Since I was working a fifty- to sixty-hour workweek during the General's

marketing plans season, workouts had to happen first thing in the morning, while the rooster was still asleep. Three days a week, there would
be a second workout after work, on the roads. I would climb out of bed
around 5:20 a.m. and sleepily shamble down to the kitchen, where I would
pick up the wall-mounted telephone receiver and dial the Northwestern
National Bank Weatherball Weatherline.

What?

The Weatherball itself was this huge neon sphere mounted atop the
Northwestern National Bank tower in downtown Minneapolis, 367 feet
above the street. From its mighty perch, said to be visible from fifteen
miles away, the colorful Weatherball would predict the weather according
to this clever little verse:

> *When the Weatherball is glowing red, warmer weather is ahead.*
> *When the Weatherball is shining white, colder weather is in sight.*
> *When the Weatherball is wearing green, no weather changes*
> *are foreseen.*
> *Colors blinking by night and day say, precipitation's on the way.*

But, alas, I couldn't see the Weatherball from my St. Louis Park kitchen,
and since it didn't have a thermometer on it anyhow, I was forced to dial up
its meteorological sister, the Weatherline, which would tell me the current
air temperature, wind direction, and wind chill.

I needed to know what I was about to let myself in for, since the average
January overnight low in Minneapolis was seven degrees Fahrenheit.

Forewarned and thusly forearmed, I would descend into the basement, where I would stretch and then don running shorts, t-shirt, long
johns, turtleneck shell, nylon warm-up pants, suspenders, running shoes,
nylon warm-up jacket, pull-over balaclava, and stocking cap. Eleven pieces of apparel in all. Three layers on the upper body and three layers on

the lower body. Two layers on the head, from which the greatest amount of body heat would otherwise escape. And mittens, of course, industrial-strength mittens.

Then I would head out into the crisp elements, where naturally it was still dark, and the snow in the streets would crunch underfoot. When it was exceptionally clear, one could actually see the aurora borealis to the north, and by run's end, the vapor created by exhaling actually crystallized into an icicle flowing from mouth to breastbone.

When the mercury or wind chill dipped below zero, I would add Vaseline to the mix, covering exposed facial flesh to prevent it from freezing. And once, when the wind chills exceeded eighty degrees below zero, I asked Denise to drive me ten miles out *into* the wind so I could run back *with* the wind.

I had to be committed. Or perhaps I should have been committed.

Training-wise, the gloves started to come off in March, figuratively and literally. The weekly mileage average crept up to 85, and a couple of road races appeared on the docket, a 25-kilometer run in Hopkins and the St. Patrick's Day 5-miler in St. Paul. The latter was a mostly downhill course that I covered in 31:58, or 6:24 per mile. Not too impressive for such a short race.

In April, time was beginning to get short, so I began to get serious. I ran 106 miles a week for a monthly total of 456. My second highest month ever since March of 1977. Not only that. The high school track had thawed out enough for me to start running my first three interval workouts in two years. And in three road races, my per-mile pace approached its former luster, at 6:09, 5:59, and 6:02, respectively. So far, so good.

Focusing more on speed than mileage in May, I booked eight interval ladder workouts with the longest repeats at 1 mile, and three road races.

In two shorter races, the per-mile pace continued to improve, at 6:02 and 5:47. But in the other, a 16.3 miler in Grantsburg, Wisconsin, my 6:50 pace translated to a 2:59 marathon. Not necessarily a confidence builder. Monthly mileage was 440.

Entering June, I was twenty-one days away and beginning to taper, since whatever I did now wasn't going to help me much anyway. Weekly mileage averaged 53. I ran a couple of final interval workouts, and in one last tune-up, the Do-It-Downtown 10-kilometer run on June 14, I ran a terrapin-like 6:42 per-mile pace. I was clearly saving myself for Duluth's big day.

At least that's what I told myself.

TICKED OFF

"One must work with time and not against it."

—Ursula Le Guin, American Author

YOU MAY HAVE NOTICED, IN THE COURSE OF THIS ACCOUNT, MY OBSESSION with my minutes per mile pace. Minutes per mile, to me, was the coin of the realm. It was the yardstick by which I measured my fitness as a runner, and my progress in preparing for a marathon.

Problem was, I couldn't calculate my average minutes per mile in a road race or a marathon until *after* the event. Until *after* my official time had been posted and I could divide the total minutes and seconds by the total mileage. By then, minutes per mile was much less helpful to me than in real time, *during* the event, to help me manage my racing strategy.

Until then, I might as well use an abacus.

My prayers were about to be answered. Enter Casio, the company that manufactured the very hand-held, battery-powered calculator that got me through all my pressure-packed exams at HBS. In fact, for exactly that reason, I already had a certain reverence for the company.

Headquartered in Tokyo, Casio had been founded in 1946 and was a pioneer in the manufacture of compact electric calculators, digital cameras, and home electronic musical keyboards. But it was their global leadership in the mass production of chronograph wristwatches that piqued my interest.

For under $20, you could purchase a digital watch that not only told the time of day but also had a stopwatch function and an elapsed time function. And it was waterproof to boot. So now, real time minutes per mile splits were, literally, at my fingertips.

I couldn't unlimber my credit card quickly enough to order one.

SOUTH BY SOUTHWEST

"An athlete cannot run with money in his pockets. He must run with hope in his heart and dreams in his head."

—Emil Zatopek, Czechoslovakian Distance Runner

THE PREPARATION WAS OVER.

So, reminiscent of the old days, Denise and I packed up the intrepid VW Super Beetle, still running but rusting, and jumped on I-35 north, headed for Duluth.

We rolled into town, obscurely nicknamed the "Zenith City of the Unsalted Seas," late Friday morning and decided to tool up to Two Harbors to check out the course. The complete lack of elevational undulation did not disappoint, and to ensure an uninterrupted carbo load, we stopped at a Two Harbors institution since 1957, Betty's Pies, for lunch. The Lemon Angel pie did not disappoint either.

That evening, at the Olympic Stadium in Montreal, two undefeated welterweight boxers, Roberto Duran and Sugar Ray Leonard, squared off in the ring, with Duran prevailing in a fifteen-round unanimous decision. At that time, it was the highest grossing fight in boxing history, with the two pugilists raking in a combined purse of $10.5 million.

As I read about the fight in the next morning's first edition, over my ritual pre-race black coffee and REO Speedwagon, I ruefully observed that those assembled for today's marathon would be competing for a significantly smaller pecuniary reward.

But admittedly, that wasn't really why most of us were here. It was about setting a goal. Working hard to get better. Feeling good about yourself. Testing yourself. And achieving that goal. Or in failing, knowing that you gave it your very best—and because of that, you were a better person now than you were a couple of months ago.

At least, that's why I was here.

Up in Two Harbors for the 9 a.m. start, the weather wasn't perfect, but it was close. The temperature hovered around sixty degrees, with a high cloud cover. There was a slight headwind out of the southwest of between seven and fifteen miles per hour, right in our faces. Later in the day, the sun would break through, and the mercury would climb to almost eighty, but, God willing, I would be done by then.

Clad in my "Greater Boston" singlet, red shorts, and Nike Elite racing flats, I was ready to go. Despite the fact that I was half a continent away, I was still a member of GBTC and proud to be associated with such a well-known crew, even though many of the original "sturdleys," including Rodgers and Salazar, had gone their separate ways.

Billy had a couple of running stores in the Boston area and his own line of running gear. Alberto had gone on to run at the University of Oregon and, after that, for the Nike Athletics West team that Phil Knight and Bill Bowerman sponsored for post-collegiate runners. Sad to say, I had lost track of Scottie Graham, who at last report was teaching down in the Dallas area.

As had been the case at my last sub-2:50 marathon in New York all those many days ago, I was right at the front when the gun popped. And that was a good thing, because Grandma's was getting to be a big deal in its fourth year of existence, with over 2,400 starters. The two-laned Highway

61 was bound to be pretty jammed up farther back in the pack, but for me, it was a clean getaway.

To digress for a second and talk race strategy, marathon running is very different between the "racers" and the "pacers."

"Racers" are the runners who actually have a shot at winning the event. This day, in the men's division, that would be our old friend Garry Bjorklund, who would win with a time of 2:10:19, and in the women's division, Lorraine Moeller of New Zealand, who ran 2:38:35.

Racers cruise along in a lead pack, constantly surveying the competition, searching each other for signs of fatigue or physical distress, ready at a moment's notice to throw in a speed surge to drop a competitor, not unlike a Wild-West gunslinger going for the kill, in order to claim victory.

"Pacers" are runners like me, who have a very specific time goal and know what the per-mile pace is required to achieve it. So, applying all my finely honed HBS analytical skills, I could calculate that, in order to run under a 2:50 marathon, I would have to average 6:29 per mile. Now if you think back to the road races I was running in April and May, most of them were around a 6-minute pace, as were my track workouts.

Consequently, as I motored out of Two Harbors and hit the first mile split in 6:25, I could almost hear Billy Squires saying to me in his classic high-pitched Beantown accent, "Be comfortable, Guppy. Be *comfortable!*"

And so, I was comfortable along that flat course, in those fast conditions, finishing in 2:47:10, 153rd overall of 2,375 finishers, at an average pace per mile of 6 minutes and 23 seconds.

Jock and Will had moved the goalposts--again--but the football sailed through the uprights anyway.

LETTUCE PRAY

"I have yet to see anyone in this business do what I would consider to be a professional job of marketing. General Mills had quite a marketing plan but they never put it into action."

—Noel Davis, Founder and President, PhytoFarms of America

I WAS CHANGING KITCHENS, SO TO SPEAK.

From the Betty Crocker Kitchens...to Kitchen Harvest.

Let me explain.

After two years in the humdrum world of flour and cake mixes, admittedly all good rookie marketing learning, I was assigned in the summer of 1980 to the Kitchen Harvest brand.

To use an automotive analogy, it was like going from a couple of Model T Fords to a Tesla.

You've already gotten the flour and cake mix dossier. Stale tales, pun intended.

Kitchen Harvest was, by contrast, nothing short of revolutionary.

The concept was this. In the northern US states during the summer, consumers enjoyed delicious lettuce and salad greens sourced locally from regional farmers. In the winter, not so much. Greens imported from points south and west... California and Mexico... did not arrive fresh, given their lengthy over-the-road trip by eighteen-wheeler.

In order to address this problem, General Mills bought some technology in 1973 and constructed in 1978 the very first "phytofarm." The term "phyto" comes from Greek, meaning "of a biological plant, or related to plants."

So, we're talking a "plant farm" here.

Something right out of a bad science fiction movie.

The windowless phytofarm, located in DeKalb, Illinois, west of Chicago, hard by the East-West Tollway, was designed to grow four kinds of specialty lettuce—Boston, Bibb, Romaine, and Spinach—***indoors*** in a purified-water and nutrient-rich solution under intense electric lights in 28 days.

Each lettuce plant began life as a seedling in a square white plastic clip and, during its four weeks on the farm, sprouted roots, stem, and leaves, all highly delicate, tender, tasty, and ***highly*** perishable. Upon reaching maturity, the product, having never encountered either soil or the light of day, was packed in nitrogen-flushed, polyethylene pillow-shaped package and shipped to the local grocery store.

The marketing strategy—here's finally where I came in—was that GMI could build one of these phytofarms on the outskirts of each northern US city and, in the winter, when local produce wasn't available, sell its product locally for roughly ***nine times*** the price of the field-grown stuff. Consumer tests suggested that folks would in fact pay that kind of a price premium, which had the C-suiters back in Golden Valley licking their chops, anxious to put their very best marketing talent (meaning me) on the project.

And the magic of the brand name, Kitchen Harvest? Once home from the supermarket, Mr. or Ms. Consumer had only to remove the four-ounce lettuce plant from its pillow pack and snap off its roots, which were still in their square white plastic clip, before tossing it into a salad bowl. In effect, they were "harvesting" the product in their kitchen.

Pretty clever, huh? Wish I could take credit for that one, but the brand name was already set when I arrived.

And the longer-term vision for this so-called "hydroponic" technology was even more intriguing. What if General Mills could execute a similar strategy with other produce staples, like tomatoes? The sky could be the limit.

So why don't we see Kitchen Harvest in the Whole Foods and Costcos of today?

In his chapter-opening comment above, Noel Davis implied that it was because a full marketing program was never implemented.

Rather, it was more likely because of the project's financials.

General Mills had made a multi-million-dollar investment in the technology, in the construction of the DeKalb facility, and in the subsequent preparations to launch a test market. Naturally, the company expected a certain return on investment (ROI) against those dollars, probably in the 15 percent range, over the anticipated life of the investment.

The financial projections General Mills used to justify its initial investment assumed certain costs and a certain amount of production that may not have materialized as operating experience with the phytofarm increased. Consequently, when adjusted projections using more realistic numbers might have yielded an unacceptable ROI, the company probably decided to cut its losses.

No amount of increased marketing would have improved the project's return. In fact, more marketing spending would have been throwing good money after bad, making the ROI even worse.

In 1982, Davis proverbially "bought the farm" from General Mills, most likely at a deeply discounted price. When last heard from in the late 1980s, Noel was selling its produce to Chicago area grocers at what must have been a sustainable profit.

A LITTLE TOMFOOLERY

"It is much more secure to be feared than loved."

—Niccolo Machiavelli, Italian Renaissance Diplomat, Philosopher, and Writer

MY BOSS ON THE KITCHEN HARVEST ASSIGNMENT WAS A PRODUCT MANAGER named Peter Thomas, who for some totally incomprehensible reason, resented Harvard MBAs and wouldn't have minded facilitating a shorter stay for me at General Mills.

Thomas, a University of Virginia Darden School MBA, was sharp as a tack, irreverent, and incredibly quick of wit.

To illustrate, one day, as we queued up at the corporate cashier's office to cash a check for lunch money, the teller limited the number of checks Peter could cash, saying, "Only one check today."

Without missing a beat, he replied, "Make mine a procto." Think about it.

He was also famous, when we traveled together on business, for assigning me the role of the bagman. I would pay all meal, beverage, and entertainment expenses, which on occasion could be somewhat excessive. As my supervisor, Peter would delay and delay but, eventually and fortunately, sign off on them all. Otherwise, I would still be in debtor's prison.

When Peter left GMI for another job, he even organized his own going away party.

A true Renaissance man.

JOIN THE CLUB

"I refuse to join any club that would have me as a member."

—Groucho Marx, American Comedian

MY RUNNING WAS GETTING ME NOTICED AT GENERAL MILLS.

And not always in a good way.

On weekdays, sometimes I would duck out of the office a little too early for a track session. Or run into the office in my sweats for a Saturday marketing plans meeting, leaving the conference room atmosphere a bit savory. I'd even been known to nod off in a business review or two because of the predawn runs and the mileage I was putting in.

So, I decided to try to make lemonade out of the lemon. I would create a General Mills Runner's Club where none existed previously. And it actually worked.

I sold it to the company, skilled marketeer that I was, based on the premise that it would, in the short term, improve employee fitness and productivity and, in the long term, reduce health insurance premiums. The fact that the running boom was in full swing and that I had just run Grandma's and qualified for Boston didn't hurt. Anyway, the powers that were bought it and gave the club a budget of a couple of thousand dollars.

I started recruiting employees to participate on our corporate team in local road races, and before I knew it, we had more than 100 members. It was time for my next funds requisition. I asked the company for running singlets, emblazoned with "General Mills" and the "Big G," and running shorts.

"Those uniforms will be excellent for getting the company exposure and creating positive public relations at community running events," I told Ralph Mineta of the Corporate Communications department.

"I couldn't agree more," Ralph replied, nodding.

We got our uniforms.

In addition to the road races, we put together company fun runs, conducted social events, and brought in lunchtime speakers like the "Running Doctor," Alex Ratelle, to discuss other topics of interest. The Mills even thrice sponsored a team of our runners to the Corporate Cup, a California corporate running competition held by none other than *Runner's World* magazine. But much more about that later.

Over time, the club became more of a brotherhood and a sisterhood. We attracted a lot of newbies to the sport, but we also brought out of retirement a fair share of former high school and college tracksters and harriers. And the skill levels were all over the map. From "Turbo" Tony Benthin, who could run a 34-minute 10-kilometer, to ex-rugby player Jim Bird, whose 10-K pace was close to two minutes per mile slower.

But like GBTC, we didn't discriminate between the Sharks and the Guppies. We were all just looking to improve.

We had our share of characters, too.

Perhaps first and foremost was Dave "Bubba" Gelly, the Director of Corporate Security, who had taken up running several years earlier after he quit smoking. Despite his Clydesdalian dimensions, Dave ultimately ran a marathon under 3 hours using Squires's training methods.

Another was Dick "Amos" Shaw, a gentle soul. We convinced him he could complete a marathon, and I think he pleasantly surprised himself when he did.

And then there was "Treadmill Tommy" Rohn, who did ferocious, world-class indoor treadmill workouts that projected to phenomenal race day times. But when the moment of truth came, for some reason, Tommy more than once crashed and burned.

For me, this was really the first time I had a group of guys to run with, to hang out with. Sure, I had done the workouts with GBTC, but I never had the time to know those runners as well as I might have liked, and besides, they were world class—or bordering on it. And there were the weekend sessions with the Eleven O'Clock Club down by Lake Calhoun, but maybe with the exception of Alan Page, one never knew who might show up week to week.

And even Alan was unaccountably absent between the months of August and December.

Due to schedule, school, location, or whatever, I had mostly run by myself ever since I started. Bonding with guys like Bubba Gelly, Tony Benthin, Dick Shaw, and Tommy Rohn over a long Sunday morning run, trading insults and laughs all along the way, created a special kind of fellowship I hadn't experienced before.

An old Nike magazine advertisement expressed it best. The photograph showed a group of runners, having just finished a spirited road workout together, bent over, each catching his breath.

The headline read, "The Harder You Push, The More You Are Pulled."

THE RUNNERS ON THE TRACK
GO ROUND AND ROUND

"I think I proved something to the people who said I couldn't do
it, who think running a marathon is some mystical thing. But
to me, a marathon is just another race, and under the right
conditions I can run a lot faster. I think I can go 2:08 or 2:07."

—Alberto Salazar

THE SUMMER AND FALL AFTER MY SUCCESSFUL GRANDMA'S RUN PASSED
quickly.

There were assorted road races and interval workouts to maintain my
base, but no fall marathon in the cards. Lord knows, I wasn't going back to
South Dakota. Once burned, twice shy.

In August, a number of us in the General Mills Runner's Club were introduced to a totally new phenomenon called the Steve Smith Memorial
10-Mile Track Race. It was exactly as advertised, a 10-mile race on a quar-
ter-mile high school track. Doing the math, that adds up to 40 laps. Now
I don't quite recall who this Steve Smith was, but I do seem to remember
that he succumbed to a terminal case of dizziness.

In order to enter this event, each contestant had to supply their own lap
counter, so I cajoled Denise into coming along. The starter's pistol sounded,
and there we were, going around and around on this track. In the early

going, I was locked in a duel with Bubba Gelly, matching him stride for stride. It was the first of several memorable encounters I would have with the big fella. Around the five-mile mark, I threw in a surge, and on this day, Bubba unfortunately couldn't respond. After the race, over a post-event pilsner, he christened me "Doctor Oval"—or "Dr. O" for short—a nickname that I retain to this day.

With the United States not fielding a team at the Moscow Olympics, that was about as much track action, inferior in quality as it was, as we were going to get that summer.

Come fall, it was time for my two geographical running worlds to intersect at the New York City Marathon, where Alberto Salazar lined up for his first shot at the event alongside perennial winner Bill Rodgers and Minnesotan Dick Beardsley.

Before the race, Alberto offered two brash predictions.

"I will beat Bill Rodgers," he proclaimed, "and I will run under 2 hours and 10 minutes."

Trailing the lead pack at 14 miles, Beardsley stumbled over a pothole, and Rodgers fell over him, bruising both knees and losing 100 yards. By the 17-mile mark on First Avenue, Beardsley was back in it, challenging Salazar for the lead while Billy gamely tried to claw his way back into contention.

At 21 miles, Alberto had dropped Beardsley and was running with Mexican Rodolfo Gomez, who had finished sixth in the Olympic marathon three months earlier. A mile later, Salazar, who to that point in the race was averaging 4:57 per mile, threw in a speed surge to which Gomez could not respond.

A little more than 4 miles later, all of 22 years old, Alberto had done it.

Fulfilling both of his pre-race prognostications, he ran 2:09:41 and beat Bill Rodgers, who finished fifth.

And this was only his first marathon. What might lie ahead?

SHIPPING UP TO BOSTON

"I call Boston home because it's where I started coming into my own."

—Sasha Banks, American Professional Wrestler

IT WAS DECEMBER 31, 1980, AND AS AMERICANS PREPARED TO INAUGURATE A new President, Ronald Reagan, I took a pass on going to any stupid parties dressed as my New Year's resolution. And I wasn't writing any Jeopardy games for any of those parties either.

I had more important business to attend to, namely one Boston Athletic Association Marathon, to be held April 20, 1981. After a long and at sometimes seemingly improbable climb, I was headed back there after a two-year absence. And, boy, was I psyched.

As we waited for the DeKalb phytofarm to produce enough lettuce so we could launch our Kitchen Harvest test market, I was planning the launch of my training regimen in January.

But how could one best recreate Coach Squires's peak marathon performance three-legged training stool—100-mile plus weeks, interval workouts on the track, and repeat hill workouts—in the dead of winter in Minnesota?

The 100-mile plus weeks, I think, I had figured out while preparing for Grandma's the previous year. The repeat hill workouts? A little more challenging. Yes, Minnesota was flat, but if one covered the right courses around the lakes and in South Minneapolis, some hills could be found.

That left interval workouts on the track. If I wanted to do speedwork in January, February, and March, before the outdoor tracks were clear of snow and ice, I had to go inside. Problem was, the options were limited.

There were the local colleges, and there was the Metrodome.

The local colleges were plentiful and had indoor tracks. The University of Minnesota, the University of St. Thomas, Hamline University, Macalester College, and Augsburg University, among many others. The catch was that one had to be enrolled as a student to use the facilities, and I didn't have the time, the inclination, or the coin to embark upon that journey. Heck, we were still paying off my student loan to Harvard.

Over to the Hubert H. Humphrey Metrodome. You know, the home of the Minnesota Vikings from the early 1980s until 2013 and the site of the December 2010 roof collapse, which necessitated the relocation of the Vikings-New York Giants game two days later to Ford Field in Detroit.

On Tuesday and Thursday evenings during the frigid months, the Metropolitan Sports Facilities Commission admitted area runners to "The Hump Dome" to gambol along the stadium's concourse in its delightful sixty-eight-degree atmosphere. However, this venue unfortunately proved itself unsuitable for interval workouts for a couple of reasons.

First, it attracted hordes of unruly harriers anxious to escape the chill while putting in their miles at speeds ranging from 5 to 12 miles per hour. Second, the concourse was not clearly demarcated into one-eighth or one-quarter-mile segments. Ergo, in such a chaotic, undisciplined environment, it was impossible to sprint consistently timed, consistently measured ladders.

Jewish Community Center to the rescue. The JCC was an easy 1-mile jog east of my house in St. Louis Park, and it had all sorts of athletic facilities, including a swimming pool, basketball courts, squash courts, and…yes, an indoor track.

The track was nothing to write home about. It was wooden, narrow, steeply banked and 125 yards around, which meant it was 14 laps to the mile. Yes, this track would have killed Steve Smith much sooner than the conventional four laps to the mile track did. As it was, we had to alternate running direction daily or risk the elongation of one gam at the expense of the other.

In any event, beggars can't be choosers, and soon, for a slight fee, Denise and I were full-fledged members of the JCC, and I was rocketing around the oval three times a week, yelling, "Track!" at anyone who dared to obstruct my path.

I logged 390 miles in January and 353 miles in February, so I was a bit below my sought after 100-mile per week average. However, there were eleven interval workouts at the JCC and two road races in the same time frame. In March, I went slightly berserk, running 481 miles for my second highest month ever, with eleven track sessions and two road races, both paced at about 6 minutes per mile.

Then it was April and time to go to Boston.

WITH THE WIND IN OUR SAILS

"A wild pony must run free."

—Rob Harkel, American Philosopher and Comedian

DENISE AND I DECIDED TO MAKE A VACATION OF THE TRIP BACK EAST, PLAN-ning to fly out the Wednesday before the marathon and return twelve days later. My running gear came aboard the plane as an over-the-shoulder carry on. For obvious reasons, I wouldn't let that bag out of my sight until the starter's gun went off in Hopkinton the following Monday.

By this time, I had pretty much become a total convert to New Balance and their 220, 420, 660, and 770 training shoes and recently introduced red, white, and blue racing flats. There was a good reason, and no, it certainly wasn't because I was under a lucrative contract with them.

Unlike Adidas and Nike, their shoes were sold in different widths, which meant that, after a couple of hundred miles, my D-width foot wouldn't pop through the outside of the shoe. So, no more Abebe Bikila comparisons.

Upon landing at Logan Airport in Boston, we rented a car and drove down to a bed and breakfast on Cape Cod to chill out for a couple of days before the madness began.

Mercenary non-amateur that I was, I had negotiated a deal with General Mills that, in exchange for wearing the company colors in the marathon, they would cover my expenses. Since fellow Runner's Club member "Turbo"

Tony Benthin was running too, we got the same package for him. We were careful to make sure that Jock Semple and Will Cloney didn't catch wind of this nefarious under-the-table arrangement.

Checking out of the Cape Cod inn on Saturday morning, it was west on Route 6, across the Sagamore Bridge, then north on Route 3 to Duxbury, where we would stay with my sister Nicky and her husband, Dave. My parents, who hadn't seen me accomplish anything athletically since sixth grade youth football some seventeen years previous, were coming in from Syracuse for the marathon. It would be a full house.

The next day, we headed into the Runners Expo at Hynes Auditorium in the Prudential Center to pick up my race number. It was good to be back. It was always a festive scene in Boston on marathon weekend, but there seemed to be a special buzz in the air this year, because Johnny "The Elder" Kelley would be running his fiftieth Boston Marathon.

To clarify, there are two John Kelleys in Boston Marathon lore. And that has always confused me. We met one of them back at the "Where's Boston?" slide show before the 1976 "Run for the Hoses," if you remember correctly.

But lest you be confused by the twin Johns, let me help. Age before beauty.

John A. Kelley (aka Johnny "The Elder" Kelley), who was celebrating his fiftieth marathon in 1981, won the race in 1935 and 1945 and competed in sixty-one of them before his passing in 2004 at the age of ninety-seven. He was a member of the 1936 US Olympic Team, along with Jesse Owens, finishing eighteenth in the marathon, and he completed his final Boston in 1992 at age eighty-four. Johnny at age sixty-five was quoted as saying, "For me, the race these days is to try to beat the girls to the finish line and to wave to all my old friends along the course."

The other John, John J. Kelley (aka Johnny "The Younger" Kelley), winner of the 1957 Boston Marathon, ran in thirty-two of the Patriots' Day Classics and made the 1956 and 1960 US Olympic marathon teams. Winner of the Yonkers, New York Marathon eight years in a row, he coached the 1968 Boston champion Amby Burfoot. Three years after his death, in September 2014, a bronze statue of Kelley and his dog Brutus was dedicated in downtown Mystic, Connecticut.

Between the two of them, they ran in ninety-three Boston Marathons. Incredible.

Patriots' Day dawned cool and cloudy. It was about fifty degrees with a ten-mile-an-hour wind out of the northwest. Minor crosswind for the runners, I concluded as I settled in with a cup of black coffee and some inspirational AC/DC on the headphones to review the cast of characters I would be sharing the asphalt with a little later in the day.

Some of the usual suspects, but not the all-star cast seen in New York last fall. Boston Billy Rodgers. GBTC's Randy Thomas and a newer club acolyte, Greg Meyer. The 1974 Boston winner from Ireland, Neil Cusack. And Minnesotan Barney Klecker, who was also a very good snowshoe racer. That comes with the territory in the Gopher State. But Alberto Salazar and Dick Beardsley decided to take a pass.

It was the usual zoo out in Hopkinton. Actually, more so. There were almost 7,000 entrants, or about 2,000 more than the last time I ran three years ago. The Porta Potties were mobbed. So much for ratcheting down those qualifying times, Jock and Will!

As the noon starting time approached, race officials herded us all into separate pens, according to our anticipated pace per mile. Ostensibly, to make for a smoother, less congested start.

"Reminiscent of cattle headed for the slaughter," I mused to myself.

At this point, everything's in the tank. The preparation's all done. The waiting is over. This is what I worked months and months for. Got up and ran in the cold and the dark for. Ran as hard as I could on the track for. To be here. On marathoning's grandest stage. To run with some of the world's best. In front of an estimated two million plus spectators. At the Boston Marathon.

This was the dream I was chasing down.

And, as long as I live, it's an experience I wouldn't trade for anything in the world.

If you have trained well—and not over trained—the first miles always go by easily. That certainly was the case today. Through Ashland, past the train station in Framingham, I was feeling good coming into Natick with 10 miles already behind me. On this, my sixth Boston tour, the course landmarks felt like old friends, welcoming me back after a two-year absence.

And my splits were good, too. I reached the B.A.A. Framingham 6.72-mile checkpoint in around 43 minutes, meaning I was running 6:20 miles, on pace for a 2:46 marathon. By the halfway point, just past the screaming Wellesley College women, I had put the hammer down a bit, with average 6:15 miles projecting to a 2:44 finish. Remember, the first 16 miles of the race are mostly downhill, so you have to make hay while the sun shines.

Meanwhile, a real battle was unfolding three miles up ahead, among the lead pack consisting of Rodgers, Meyer, Craig Virgin, Gary Fanelli, and Toshihiko Seko, a Japanese Olympic marathoner. Meyer took the lead from Fanelli as the group thundered past the fire station in Newton Lower Falls and began the ascent.

"It felt like *The Magnificent Seven* and who was going to get gunned down next," Virgin later said of the unfolding attrition rate in the Newton hills.

Rodgers was the first to fall off the pace with a side ache at mile 17, at which point Meyer, Virgin, and Seko continued digging into the hills. By mile 19, Meyer could no longer sustain the tempo, and Virgin and Seko continued on, side by side, until the Japanese dropped the American with a 4:40 mile at the 23-mile mark.

Seko won in a new course record time of 2:09:26, one second faster than Rodgers's previous course record, run in 1979. Virgin finished second, a minute back, and Boston Billy, recovered from his side ache, rallied for third, crossing the line only 8 seconds later. Winning the women's division was Allison Roe, a twenty-four-year-old New Zealander, who set another course record time of 2:26:46.

Obviously, I didn't know it at the time, but with all these records being broken, the pressure was on me to break my existing PR, which was the 2:46:59 I had run at the New York City Marathon back in 1977. And halfway through this Boston, I was poised to do it.

I had the perfect weather in that it had remained cool and cloudy, with a very slight drizzle, and the crosswind had become a tailwind. And I was on 2:44 pace through the first half, running very methodically and under control.

The big question mark, of course, was the Newton hills, which occupied miles 16 through 21. I was four years removed from my repeat hill workouts with Bill, Scottie, and the GBTC, and, in Minnesota, I had to scrounge to find any hills on which to train. Would I be up to the task?

Well, I was about to find out.

I'm not sure I thundered past the fire station in Newton Lower Falls quite as authoritatively as the lead pack had, but I entered the hills with grit and determination. This was what I had worked for. Sure, it had been a while, but still, I knew these hills.

206

Starting to climb, I certainly was no longer fresh, but I knew what to expect, and there was no fear of the unknown. It was all out there in front of me, and I was in the zone. Others dropped off the pace as we ascended, but I felt like I was in control, and this was going to be a day I would remember for the rest of my life.

I crested Heartbreak Hill at 2 hours and 13 minutes into the race, meaning I had slowed somewhat over the last 5 miles, but I was still on pace for a 2:46 and a new PR if I could hold it all together.

The crowds all day had been crazy. And with *The New York Times* suggesting that there had been threats of local cop interference to protest police job cutbacks, perhaps the spectators were more poorly controlled than in previous years. In any event, an estimated two million strong, they had been pushing far out from the curb onto the course ever since Hopkinton. The racket was deafening.

Denise, Nicky, Dave, and my parents were along the right side of Commonwealth Avenue as I came off the hills and headed down into Boston, with five miles to go. They almost missed me as I went by, so I had to shout out to them. There were so many runners going by that I think they were hypnotized by all the motion. It was either that, or I was blazing by them so incredibly fast. Probably the former.

The final miles dragged by—or so they seemed to. I really hadn't slowed dramatically; it's just the way things feel after you have put in 20-plus miles at maximum effort.

The finish line at the Prudential Center welcomed me home at 2:46:38, a new PR by only 21 seconds, but a new PR nonetheless, on a much tougher course than New York. I had smashed my previous best at Boston by more than 5 minutes. As an indication of the quality of the competition, I finished way back at 1,401st out of 6,881 official entrants.

And let me add a couple of happy postscripts.

"Turbo" Tony Benthin, my General Mills teammate, finished a minute and 10 seconds and 106 places ahead of me.

And Johnny "The Elder" Kelley completed his fiftieth Boston in 4:01:57, commenting to reporters afterward, "It was my easiest race in years."

Then, grinning, he added, "I'm part of the furniture."

OVER THE RIVER AND THROUGH THE WOODS: EPISODE 2

"There is nothing noble in being superior to your fellow man. True nobility is being superior to your former self."

—Ernest Hemingway, American Novelist

I T WAS INEVITABLE.

Coming off my marathon PR at Boston and having had such a positive run at Grandma's Marathon the previous year, there was never even a speck of doubt. I was headed back to the "Zenith City of the Unsalted Seas" for a return engagement. Two PRs within two months was a real possibility.

But I had to be careful. This year's edition of the Twin Ports extravaganza was slated for June 20, two months to the day after Boston. And we all remember what happened the last time I ran two spring marathons too close together. I fought "The Depression," "The Depression" won, and I ended up in the medical tent after Cleveland's Western Reserve Marathon, listening to some guy talk about making love to his wife.

It was the Harvard-educated writer and philosopher George Santayana who opined, "Those who do not learn history are doomed to repeat it." So, as an astute history major and scholar of lost causes—including my high school athletic career—I tried to take Dr. Santayana's advice, despite his dubious educational pedigree.

Accordingly, in the intervening month of May, I ran a paltry 310 miles—or 70 miles a week and only four track workouts. However, my racing in the weeks leading up to the Duluth dust-up was among my best ever. Plymouth, Minnesota, 4 miles—23:59 (6:00 per mile); Lake Harriet, Minnesota, 5.6 miles—32:34 (5:49); Chicago, Illinois, 6.2 miles—36:30 (5:53—a 10K PR); and Excelsior, Minnesota, 13.1 miles—1:21:00 (6:11). That last one, a half marathon, projected to a 2:42 marathon, if my slide rule was correct.

Shades of things to come?

There were a couple of troubling notations in my training log a few days before and after the Chicago 10K PR regarding a "sore right hip," but I was too absorbed in my Grandma's Marathon crusade to think too much about them.

And then, all of a sudden, it was June, and caught up in the enthusiasm of the General Mills Runner's Club, I forgot Dr. Santayana's wise counsel.

One weekend, two weeks before the marathon, the club had teams entered into two events. The first one, on Saturday, was the *Runner's World* Corporate Cup Minneapolis Regional Meet, pitting ten or twelve major Twin Cities Fortune 500 companies against each other in a sweat suit-clad struggle to the death. Lots more about this shortly. The second one, on Sunday, was the First National Bank of Minneapolis "Do It Downtown" 10 Kilometer Run.

Since I was President and Chairman Emeritus for Life of the Runner's Club, non-participation in these events was not an option, as it would have surely led to my impeachment. So, on Saturday I ran 3,000 meters and 3 miles on the track at respective 5:42 and 5:50 per mile paces. Then on Sunday, I polished off the 10K at a 6:01 per-mile pace.

Not necessarily something one does after a marathon PR and four hard road races, right before gunning for another marathon PR. Sorry, Dr. Santayana.

Fast forward to Grandma's race day in Two Harbors.

The weather was perfect. Temperature in the fifties, where it would remain for the duration of the run. Wind out of the southeast at six miles per hour. Coming off Lake Superior to provide an even more cooling effect. Mostly cloudy. Really, they ought to package this weather up and sell it to marathons around the world, especially that one in South Dakota.

If I was ever going to go under 2:45, with this weather on this course, today was the day.

But it's a balancing act. Go too fast, and you crash and burn. Go too slow, and you have too much time to make up toward the end, when fatigue is setting in.

That's where Casio's digital electronic wizardry stepped in to save the day.

The previous evening, harnessing analytical powers seldom engaged since business school, I settled in after a huge spaghetti repast to plot my race strategy. On the desktop to assist me in this task were my twin Tokyoite tools—the well-worn HBS Casio calculator and my $19.99 Casio chronograph wristwatch.

My thought process went something like this. Two months ago, I averaged 6:22 per mile on a much more difficult Boston Marathon course. More recently, I was running under 6 minutes per mile in shorter road races and 6:11 in a half marathon. Reasonably well rested, in this weather, on this course, to use Squires's logic, why shouldn't I be **comfortable** at a 6:15 pace? And that translated to a 2:43:45.

Made sense to me.

So, using the calculator, I crunched my split times at 1, 2, 5, 10, 15, 20, and 25 miles. I then programmed them into my watch, such that it would chime at each split. Once I engaged the elapsed time function at the start, the watch would beep at 6:15, and I would know I should be at or slightly past the 1-mile marker. It would beep again at 12:30, and I would know I should be at 2 miles, and so on.

The evil professor had diabolically devised an arcane methodology to lead him to the promised land. But would it work?

By this time, I couldn't tell what was smoking more—my ancient, well-worn calculator or my aching head. So, I went to bed.

In the men's division, the contest was a battle between the past and the future of Minnesota distance running, as aces of the asphalt Garry Bjorklund and Dick Beardsley battled for the lead much of the way before Beardsley won in a course record 2:09:36 that was to stand for thirty-three years, until 2014.

As for me, my strategy was an absolute, utter, and abject failure.

I finished in 2:43:46.9, two minutes and 49 seconds *faster* than two months ago at Boston. It was another PR.

But it was 1.9 seconds *slower* than my projection.

Sometimes in life, you have to live with a little bit of imperfection.

CORPORATE CLASH ON THE CINDERS

"I thought it would be a good idea to get companies more involved in running on a national competitive basis for the fun of it."

—Bob Anderson, Publisher, *Runner's World*

J UST WHAT THE CUTTHROAT BUSINESS WORLD NEEDED. A LITTLE MORE COMPE-tition.

It's not enough that corporations battled relentlessly Monday through Friday over customers, markets, and market share, ruthlessly slashing costs, profits, and jobs. In 1979, thanks to *Runner's World* magazine, corporate conflict spread beyond the boardroom to Saturdays and Sundays on the running tracks of America.

That's when *RW* publisher Bob Anderson founded the Corporate Cup Relays, a competition dedicated to proving that, in the corporate world, splits didn't just happen to stocks anymore. They could occur on the track as well.

The relays were a series of fourteen track events. ***All*** the events were multiple runner relays—ostensibly to encourage ***espirit de corporation***—and they ranged from the Women's 800-Meter Race, to the Men's Mile Team Race, to the Master's Relay (for folks over forty), to the President's Relay (for C-suiters). All corporate team members were required to be card-carrying employees, having worked at least thirty-two hours a week for at least three months before competing.

That **should** keep out any ringers, right?

Contested every summer, the Relays hosted seven regional meets around the United States. The best and brightest teams from each region advanced to the national finals, which were held at Stanford University in Palo Alto, California, right next door to *Runner's World's* headquarters in Mountain View.

Well, if I couldn't get to Stanford by gaining admission to their graduate business school, maybe I could get there by the semi-fleetness of my feet.

But first, we had to find some tracksters. As many as possible.

I mean, the General Mills Runner's Club was built around roadies, road runners. Very few of us had spent any time on the track. And those of us who did—well, we did it to make ourselves faster on the roads. We had to be honest with ourselves. We weren't exactly 400-meter or 800-meter speed merchants, and for the most part, we didn't know the difference between a relay baton and a pipe bomb.

Fortunately, a few of our members had been ovalists in high school or college. Lynn Brown. Wendy Nelson. Andy Johnson. John Newman. We plugged them into the relay slots where we thought they might do the most damage. For the rest of the events, we decided we were just going to have to wing it. This was supposed to be fun after all. Bob Anderson said so.

That brings us to the aforementioned Minneapolis Regional, contested a fortnight prior to Grandma's Marathon. Held at suburban Richfield High School, the meet attracted a virtual "who's who" of Twin Cities corporate giants in addition to General Mills—3M, Best Buy, Cargill, Dayton Hudson, Honeywell, Medtronic, and Pillsbury, among others. You name the company, and they were there. Along with reporters from *The Wall Street Journal*, *The Economist*, *Financial Times*, and *Barron's*.

When all the laps had been run and the smoke of battle had cleared, General Mills stood alone atop the victory podium. In second place.

At a joyous post-meet reception, as Runner's Club President, I addressed the team.

"Because you have all represented General Mills so honorably on this field of mighty endeavor, your individual employment status, perhaps probationary as recently as this morning, is no longer in question," I declared.

Then, after a long pause, I added, "Just kidding."

CALIFORNIA,
HERE WE COME... MAYBE

"Finally, it happened. Corporations had come together to reveal that they indeed rule the world. Or so it seemed."

—The New York Times

COULDN'T RESIST.

On the heels of our surprisingly strong finish in the Minneapolis Regional, I just had to pitch our management on a company-funded trip to California for the Corporate Cup Finals. I can't remember the rationale I used, but it must have been powerful, because astonishingly, it worked, and they bought it, agreeing to send eighteen of us on an all-expenses paid junket to Palo Alto.

Be careful what you ask for. You just might get it.

The Finals were held the weekend of July 18 and 19, which left less than two weeks to plan once we got the green light on funding. The logistics were murder. I had the rare privilege of coordinating all the travel arrangements, and my teammates chose this as their opportunity to get back at me for my facetious comment about their tenuous individual job security after the Minneapolis Regional.

Everyone wanted a different flight, a disparate rental car, a special meal, a divergent airport. Yep, they didn't get mad; they got even.

However, once these cats had been successfully herded and queued up for their Friday afternoon departure, it looked like, miraculously, everyone and every detail was aligned for our adventure.

Except for me. I got caught up in a marketing meeting and missed the flight. By the time I got out to the airport, there was a 5:55 p.m. Northwest Airlines flight to San Francisco that was jam-packed. The best I could do was stand by, which meant the only way I would get a seat was if someone who already had a reserved seat didn't show up.

Good grief. I was going to miss my own rodeo.

Fortunately, the flight was late in boarding, and the gate attendants, let's just say, were not acting in a very operationally precise manner. They needed to get our plane, a DC-10, off the gate quickly to accommodate an incoming flight. So, they rushed us into line to board, tickets in hand.

Stapled to my coupon was a little tag that denoted my stand-by status.

Necessity being the mother of invention, I subtly and with great sleight of hand removed that tag. But I wasn't home free yet. My ticket was for the earlier flight that afternoon. If the gate attendant had read the stub as she took it, she would have booted me back into the boarding area and probably issued me a game misconduct. Instead, she was in a hurry, and I was on my way to SFO. Some poor soul with a reserved seat on that aircraft would be spending the night in the Twin Cities.

The next morning, as I caught up with the rest of the team, it was…

Welcome to the 1981 *Runner's World* Corporate Cup National Relay Championships.

This is how *The New York Times* described it a couple of days later:

"Here, in Stanford Stadium, in an atmosphere mildly redolent of the Olympics, the opening ceremonies consisted of teams parading behind standard bearers whose upraised flags read not France or England or United States or Somalia, but General Electric and Texas Instruments and Ford. In the infield, among the $30,000 worth of small trees brought in especially for the competition, bright-colored company flags waved, songs by Chuck Mangione and Pat Benatar were played, and a young torch-bearer lit the flame that began the one-day finals of 14 races."

That about sums it up. One thing was for sure. We weren't at the Minneapolis Regional anymore. And, consequently, the General Mills Runner's Club got smoked like a cheap cigar.

Our team's comparative paucity of tracksters came back to bite us big time, as we finished twenty-ninth out of 130 corporations who had made the pilgrimage to the finals.

Texas Instruments dominated for the second year in a row, with Hewlett-Packard second, General Electric third, and Montgomery Securities and Pacific Gas & Electric locked in a tie for fourth.

As an example of our complete futility, Bubba Gelly and I offered ourselves up as the sacrificial lambs in one of the Men's Mile Team Race preliminary heats on Saturday. Bubba ran a 5:11 mile, and I came in at 5:22. These times were *lifetime bests* for Bubba and me. Running against three other teams, Bubba was second to last, and I was dead last. The winner completed his four-lap tour of the oval in four minutes and change. We were totally outclassed.

Many of these companies, unlike General Mills, as the results certainly indicated, actively recruited quality runners.

Texas Instruments brought to California a summer intern named Thomas Marino, who it just so happened, could run 10 kilometers within a minute or two of the world record. Another TI employee based in England, Cliff Stebbings, also an excellent runner, very coincidentally was in Dallas for software training, so he came to Palo Alto too.

Then there was Montgomery Securities, which openly advertised for runners to fill various openings in its San Francisco office. Contributing to its strong performance in the Finals were two recent hires, Alice Trumbley, a national class miler, and Vicki Randall, an Olympic hopeful in distance running.

"I checked out both of their qualifications because I was suspicious," said meet director and grand poohbah, Bob Anderson. "But both women fulfilled the requirements."

We came, we saw, we were conquered.

But fortunately, upon our return to the Twin Cities, despite our dismal showing in Fruit and Nut Land, we were all welcomed back to our day jobs.

LIGHTS, CAMERA, ACTION!

"Chariots of Fire is one of the best films of recent years, a
memory of a time when men still believed you could
win a race if only you wanted to badly enough."

—Roger Ebert

O<small>N</small> O<small>CTOBER</small> 9, 1981, <small>THE BEST RUNNING MOVIE</small> *EVER* <small>WAS RELEASED.</small>

That day, *Chariots of Fire*, the tale of two British Olympic sprinters
preparing for the 1924 Paris games, hit the silver screen. The film ultimately netted $59 million at the box office and four Oscars from the Academy of
Motion Picture Arts and Sciences, including Best Picture and Best Original
Music Score by Vangelis.

In the film, two 100-meter trackmen, Harold Abrahams and Eric Liddell,
dream of winning gold in the City of Lights. But that's where the similarity
between them ends.

Abrahams is the son of a Lithuanian Jew studying at esteemed Cambridge
University. He leverages his quickness afoot in an attempt to overcome the
pervasive anti-Semitism in British society. Liddell, on the other hand, is a de-
vout Christian born to Scottish missionaries in China who runs to glorify God.

En route to the Paris games, the British Olympic team learns that a preliminary heat of the 100-meter race will be contested on a Sunday. Liddell refuses to
compete on the Sabbath and is disqualified from the event. Ultimately, although

my summary does absolutely no justice to the quality of this cinematic classic, Abrahams wins the gold in the 100-meter, and Liddell instead runs the 400-meter and triumphs in that event.

The running community, including yours truly, ate this movie up with a fork and spoon. It immediately became de rigueur personal inspirational viewing before any competitive event.

In fact, subsequently, Bob Anderson renamed his *Runners World* Corporate Cup National Relay Championships, christening it the *Chariot Cup*. And instead of Chuck Mangione and Pat Benatar playing over the sound system at Stanford Stadium, it was Vangelis.

JUST FOR THE RECORDS... SORT OF

"I did notice the roads were fairly uneven."

—Allison Roe, Official Winner, Women's
Division, 1981 New York City Marathon

"Yes, we build them that way."

—Ed Koch, Mayor of New York City

SUCH WAS THE PRESS CONFERENCE BANTER IN THE AFTERMATH OF THAT FALL'S New York City Marathon, a contest on a wind-blown fifty-five-degree day that saw both the men's and the women's world mark in that event shattered.

In the men's division, once again it was twenty-three-year-old Alberto Salazar, in his red and white Nike Athletics West singlet, fulfilling his prerace prediction: "I really think I should be able to run 2:08." He slightly trailed the lead pack on world record pace through 10 miles, later descending from the Queensboro Bridge onto First Avenue to challenge the frontrunning but unrelated Mexicans Rodolfo Gomez and Jose Gomez.

Between miles 16 and 19, Alberto threw successive 4:33, 4:46, and 4:49 miles at the pair, who consequently were avocado toast. The rest was history, as he crossed the Central Park finish line in 2:08:18. A new world record by 21 seconds over Derek Clayton's mark, which had stood for 12 years.*

"It was very satisfying," Alberto told reporters after his record run, "because a lot of people thought it was a fluke or I just got lucky last year."

Over on the women's side, Allison Roe followed up her spring victory at Boston by touring the five boroughs in 2:25:28, also a new world record. In doing so, she bested Grete Waitz, three-time defending champion and NYC Marathon institution, who dropped out at 15 miles with shin splints.

Also in attendance at the Gotham City distance classic was one Frank Shorter, who, using the race as a training exercise, muddled home in, for him, a glacial 2:25. Bill Rodgers chose not to run when he couldn't work out the terms of his remuneration with the various companies sponsoring him.

"If you guys can't come up with the scratch, then I will," unverified reports quoted Boston Billy as saying. "Scratch, that is."

And so he did.

---

*   Salazar's world record was subsequently de-certified in 1985 when the New York course was found to be 170 yards short when it was remeasured along the tangents of every curve, not from the middle of the road, which was the previous standard.

MY SECOND MBA REVISITED: PART (A)

"When you're a little kid, you want the ball. You
don't want to play defense. When you get the ball
basically you can do whatever you want."

—Champ Bailey, Cornerback, Denver Broncos

GENERAL MILLS ALWAYS MADE ITS MARKETING PERSONNEL ANNOUNCEMENTS
on Fridays at 4:00 p.m.

I guess that was so that the winners had the weekend to celebrate and the losers had the weekend to get over it.

Remember, the company recruited lots and lots of MBAs from the most elite schools, moved them around to different positions kind of like pieces on a chess board, and promoted only the best of the best into its senior management ranks.

The thirty-plus MBAs who matriculated with me in the summer of 1978 mostly realized that the odds weren't great that any of us were ultimately headed to **the** corner office.

But what each of us minimally wanted was to ascend from entry-level Marketing Assistant to Assistant Product Manager and ultimately be promoted to Product Manager running a major brand. If we could (A) earn the title of Product Manager and (B) successfully run a well-known national brand at a vaunted consumer marketing company like General Mills, then the world would be our oyster.

I would then have captured what I have previously termed my "Second MBA."

If at that point, the upward career path still remained an option at Mills, wonderful. If not, we could polish up the resume and leverage our "Big G" experience to go wherever, do whatever, with whoever.

In the world of marketing, it was Willie Wonka's golden ticket.

And at 4:00 p.m. on December 11, 1981, when the announcements were made, I fulfilled Part (A). I had earned the title of Product Manager.

I had the whole weekend to celebrate.

NINTH AVENUE FREEZE OUT

"Nine out of ten new consumer products are destined to fail."

—Advertising Age

MY NEW PRODUCT MANAGER ASSIGNMENT WAS NEW FROZEN PRODUCTS in the Northstar Division.

To provide prospective, a quick primer, if you don't mind, on business strategy.

Every business, whether it deals in products or services, needs new products. That's because of something called the "Product Life Cycle." Every product or service is introduced, it grows, it matures, and it declines.

Take, for example, General Mills's product Bisquick baking mix. When it was introduced in 1931 as a shelf-stable biscuit mix, it was truly revolutionary, allowing homemakers to whip up delicious biscuits at home in minutes. It went through a several-decade growth trajectory, supported by advertising and promotion. Then, in the 1970s and 1980s, it entered a mature phase, its sales beginning to be cannibalized by other baking mixes and ready-to-eat grocery alternatives. At some point, due to lifestyle changes and reduced at-home food preparation, the brand most likely has entered decline, with overall 2015 baking mix category sales off over 6 percent, as reported by syndicated data tracker IRI.

The Product Life Cycle. Introduce. Grow. Mature. Decline.

With each of its core flour and baking mix businesses ultimately destined to die, Mills got the new product religion. Big time. It started out by doing line extensions. These were simply new flavors of existing brands. Gold Medal Whole Wheat Flour. Honey Nut Cheerios. Chocolate Chip SuperMoist Cake Mix. These were the no brainers.

Then it branched out into snacks. Some were healthy, like Nature Valley Granola Bars and Betty Crocker Fruit Roll-Ups®, appetizingly christened "fruit leather" by product insiders. Some, not so much, like Bugles®, Daisys®, and Whistles®, which were the company's attempt to see if it could compete with Frito-Lay using its cereal production lines. The answer for Daisys and Whistles, at least, was a resounding, "No!"

In the '60s and '70s, General Mills also experimented with diversification, acquiring a portfolio of disparate brands including Eddie Bauer ® clothing, Olive Garden ® restaurants, Parker Brothers ® games, Pennsylvania House ® furniture, Red Lobster ® restaurants, Talbot's ® women's apparel, and York ® Steak Houses. What selling clothing, furniture, and Monopoly®, or serving diners cooked pasta, seafood and rib-eyes had to do stocking America's grocery stores, who knew?

But then again, in the 1940s, the company had established an Aeronautical Research Division, which developed high altitude balloons, and an Electronics Division, which created the *DSV Alvin* submersible, investigator of the wreck of the *Titanic*.

Doesn't make our Kitchen Harvest lettuce-growing phytofarm sound quite so far out there.

Ultimately, however, the General recognized packaged food as its core competency and over time divested the retail, restaurant, and toy divisions. The exact fate of the weather balloon and submarine operations, however, has been lost to succeeding generations.

From there, the firm looked at new grocery store categories to penetrate, namely produce, dairy, and frozen. We've already witnessed the innovative but unsuccessful campaign to enter the produce section. On to the dairy category, where GMI said, "Oui!" by licensing the French yogurt brand Yoplait® in 1977, over time building a very successful business.

So, what about frozen? That brings us back around to my inaugural Product Manager assignment. New Frozen Products in the Northstar Division.

I suppose it's like when your sixteen-year-old comes home from the DMV clutching her new driver's license. You probably don't give her the keys to the 1961 Ferrari 250 GT that is sitting in your garage.*

In the same way, you don't assign a newly promoted Product Manager to a Cheerios or a Wheaties, or even a Bisquick.

Instead, it's New Frozen Products, where one's relative inexperience in a leadership position cannot result in financial disaster or public embarrassment to the corporation. Makes perfect sense.

To digress for a moment, new product development at General Mills was a very disciplined process. Let me count the ways...

It began with idea generation. First, we gathered in a brainstorming session, prior to which we were told, "There's no such thing as a bad idea." Then the ideas we came up with were subjected to concept testing, through which we learned that there were, in fact, lots of bad ideas.

On a sheet of paper, each concept was sketched out in black and white and described in a few sentences, including flavor, serving size, package size, and price. Purchase intent was gauged among a panel of 200-plus

---

* For the uninitiated, the 1961 Ferrari 250 GT is the automobile that Ferris Buhler, Sloan Peterson, and Cameron Frye drove into Chicago on *Ferris Buhler's Day Off*.

consumers. If purchase interest was sufficiently high, product prototypes were developed and refined via focus groups and in-home testing.

The final product was subject to something called a BASES test, which integrated consumer response data with the manufacturer's marketing plan to provide a new product sales projection. Given favorable results, the product could then be rolled out nationally, or as a final test, it might be introduced into a couple of regional test markets to assure its consumer acceptance.

In my new role as Product Manager in the Northstar Division, I was challenged with breathing life into four pretty marginal projects, which from my perspective, weren't all that likely to resurrect General Mills as its flour and baking mix businesses slowly and inevitably declined.

The first was perhaps the most promising. Chef Saluto® brand Pizza Crescents. These were actually a potential line extension of the Chef Saluto® frozen pizza brand that the firm had introduced a couple years earlier. The concept was a frozen crescent roll filled with pizza toppings that one heated in the oven. Like a miniature calzone. Delicious!

The hand-rolled prototypes made up by the technicians in the lab were very well received in focus groups, and at one point, we thought we had something. But when the operations team tried to automate the production process, the prototypes came back looking less like crescent rolls and more like blobs of vegetable shortening. And at the retail price we needed to charge, we couldn't afford to hand roll the product.

So, we Saluto-ed the project good-bye.

The second highest potential project was a frozen dessert bar. We envisioned putting the General's Nature Valley® brand on this post-meal delicacy, which was granola-wrapped and filled with cream cheese and strawberry jam. Boy, it was plenty tasty too!

This one did even better than the Chef in focus groups but, like him, foundered on the rocks of mass-production operational reality. How the hell do you inject frozen cream cheese and strawberry jam into a granola shell? The answer is you don't.

The other two projects were a good deal more nebulous. Freezer fruit jam and frozen cheese spread. Freezer fruit jam was supposed to taste fresher than its shelf-stable cousins from the grocery store. As I recall, it actually did, but only to the most discerning of palates. And the frozen cheese spread? To be completely honest, its consumer reason for being and why we worked on it totally escape me.

New Frozen Products in the Northstar Division.

Yes, I had fulfilled Part (A) of my Second MBA, earning the title of Product Manager. But I sure wouldn't be fulfilling Part (B), successfully running a well-known national brand, anytime soon.

THE DUEL IN THE SUN

"Dick Beardsley made me run harder than I ever have before."

—Alberto Salazar

N ATURALLY I WAS GOING TO RUN THE 1982 BOSTON MARATHON.

I had run two of my three best marathons, including my PR, in 1981, and I had qualified to go back east in April. Why wouldn't I?

Entering the new year with a couple of 100-mile weeks and multiple indoor track workouts, I was nicely positioned to begin my training ramp-up to Patriots' Day. Then, during a 10-mile predawn outing on January 26, I pulled my right hamstring. Again. I would end up being on the shelf until March 20.

Turns out Denise and I missed the closest, most exciting Boston Marathon in history.

Lining up in sunny, seventy-degree Hopkinton on April 19 were Bill Rodgers, Alberto Salazar, and Dick Beardsley. They wore, respectively, the numbers 1, 2, and 3 because the 1981 champion, Toshihiko Seko, chose not to return to defend his crown.

In addition to their ordinal racing bib numbers, one other common thread united the trio. As we have already reviewed, both Rodgers and Salazar, along with yours truly (albeit briefly), trained at the knee of GBTC coach Bill Squires back in the mid-1970s. Some would say that was the key to their success in the marathon.

In the meantime, after Beardsley ran in the 1980 Olympic marathon trial and in the Falmouth Road Race, New Balance offered him a $500 per month stipend and the opportunity to also work with Squires, who coincidentally now was a consultant for the shoe company. After Dick won the 1981 Grandma's Marathon where I ran my PR, New Balance increased his stipend to a whopping $1,000.

Salazar didn't seem at all concerned that his former coach was guiding one of his top rivals. Quoth Alberto, "Bill Squires has done a lot for me and gotten very little in return. He received no payment, just headaches for working with a high school runner. He deserves all the respect I could give him."

At Squires's suggestion, Beardsley spent January, February, and March before the marathon in Atlanta: "I went there so I could get out of Minnesota's harsh winter, but I also wanted to train on hills to get ready for Boston," remarked Dick. Seems he was having some difficulty finding elevation in his home state of Minnesota. Imagine that.

As Beardsley awaited the crack of the starter's pistol with Rodgers, Salazar, and a cast of thousands, he felt a tap on his shoulder. He turned around and saw fellow Minnesotan, Barney Klecker, our marathoner and snowshoe guy, standing behind him.

"Dick," Barney said, "good luck. Did you double-knot your shoes?"

Beardsley, jolted from his game face, was confused, "What?"

"Your shoes. It's important."

Dick didn't like this distraction right before the start. He thanked Barney but turned his attention back to the road ahead.

But Barney wouldn't give up, "Dick, it's important to double-knot your shoes."

"Barney, leave me alone!" Dick wailed.

Instantly regretting his sharp retort, Beardsley turned to offer his apologies, but Barney was nowhere to be seen. Then Dick looked down.

Klecker was kneeling at his feet, double-knotting Dick's shoes.

Now *that's* Minnesota Nice.

After the gun, Salazar and Beardsley stayed at the rear of the lead pack—made up of Bill Rodgers, Dean Matthews, Doug Kurtis, Ed Mendoza, and Ron Tabb—for the first 10 miles.

Recognizing that it was hot and sunny, Beardsley was grabbing water at every opportunity. Salazar not so much; in fact, he later estimated he had only consumed two and a half cups of water throughout the entire race. At least twice, he declined bottles of water offered him by Beardsley.

More Minnesota Nice.

By mile 15, only Rodgers and Mendoza remained with Salazar and Beardsley, and both of them were gone shortly thereafter.

Squires had counseled Dick before the race to focus only on Alberto, and in an attempt to break him in the Newton hills, Dick picked up the pace. The strategy was to blow Alberto out of the water on the ascent, because if he was able to stay close to Dick until the summit of Heartbreak Hill,

Alberto could crush Dick with his superior foot speed over the final five miles en route to the Pru.

Squires, succinct for perhaps the first time in his life, put it this way: "Dick, Alberto doesn't have a great kick, but it's better than yours."

For his part, Alberto certainly wasn't enjoying his finest day. He was used to dictating the terms, controlling the race. As we've seen, he was the one who threw in the sub-5-minute miles, the surges at his opponents at mile 17, 18, 19, whatever, blowing their doors off, and finishing alone. For him, this was a new and different experience.

But, doggedly, he hung on, running slightly behind Beardsley, just off his left shoulder. "It was frustrating for me to be behind him," Salazar later admitted. "It was a point of pride with me that I didn't want anybody to be that close to me at that point in a marathon."

And that was exactly how the pair crested Heartbreak, primed for their descent into Boston. Neither had broken the other. Beardsley's pace slowed slightly, almost imperceptibly, but Alberto remained anchored to his left shoulder, unable at least for the moment to go any faster. And that's how things remained for the next four miles, to mile 25, as the exuberant, raucous, and poorly controlled spectators pressed in on Dick, Alberto, and the eight motorcycle cops accompanying them.

As Beardsley initiated a surge in the final mile to the finish line, his right hamstring cramped. Whether or not Alberto detected Dick's momentary distress is a point of historic debate, but at that precise moment, Salazar grabbed the lead, quickly opening up a 20-yard advantage as they turned onto Hereford Street. Simultaneously, a couple of the Metropolitan Police Harleys moved into the gap between Alberto and Dick.

His hamstring cramp subsiding as quickly as it took hold, Dick had some catching up to do—and not much time or distance to do it. He moved around the motorcycles, later recounting, "Al's lead started shrinking. It seemed like every 10 feet he went, I'd go 20. I remember him glancing back, and I don't think he expected to see me that close."

Alberto, in fact, ***didn't*** expect to see Dick that close. As he later recalled, "I was thinking, 'There's more than a half mile to go.' Then, all of a sudden, Dick was on top of me. I looked ahead and realized, less than 200 meters! That was the exact nightmare situation I wanted to avoid."

But Squires had been right. About both Alberto's and Dick's kicks.

Salazar outkicked Beardsley over the last 200 meters to finish in 2:08:52, a new course record.

Dick finished two seconds back, in 2:08:54, the closest 1-2 finish in Boston Marathon history.

After a brief awards ceremony, Beardsley went to the media room to meet with reporters. Salazar was ushered to the medical tent in the parking garage at the Pru, where the dehydrated marathoner was administered six liters of intravenous fluid in thirty minutes.

Yes, we truly missed one for the ages.

THE FUTURE IS BECOMING APPARENT: EPISODE 1

"History repeats itself, first as tragedy, second as farce."

**—Karl Marx, German Philosopher, Economist
and Socialist Revolutionary**

A S I WAS RECOVERING FROM MY JANUARY HAMSTRING INJURY, DENISE AND I discovered we were going to become parents. Maybe that was *because* I was recovering from my hamstring injury.

Anyway, we were excited. We had enjoyed eight years together as a couple, we had gotten through graduate school as planned, and I was, at least according to my performance appraisals, establishing a somewhat successful career in product management. It was time to start a family. We looked forward to the November due date.

Awaiting our own new product and still working on General Mills' frozen ones, I started running again in March. Having built up to 60 miles a week in mid-April, I tweaked the hammy again and had to start all over after a couple of weeks of downtime.

My training log notes that "Comeback Number 2" began May 2, and this time there was a successful progression over the summer toward my now standard 100-mile weeks, track interval workouts, and road races. The company again fielded a squad for the re-named *Runner's World* Chariot's

Cup, and it was a chronological replay as we soared in the Regionals and were waxed in the Finals. This year, however, I didn't miss the team flight to California.

As my fitness improved, I got into full training mode and remained healthy, and I realized a fall marathon might yet be in the cards. And no, the folks in Brookings were not offering me any personal appearance money.

Instead, there was a new kid in town. Or should I say, in **towns**. Plural.

Between 1976 and 1981, the Twin Cities hosted two autumn marathons—the City of Lakes Marathon and the St. Paul Marathon. The former consisted of four loops around Lakes Calhoun and Harriet in Minneapolis. The latter was a 26.2-mile tour-de-pied of Minnesota's capital city, St. Paul.

Perhaps taking a cue from the five-borough New York City Marathon, but allowing six years to elapse before acting on it--contemporary trends can take a while to make it to the Midwest-- the race directors of these two events decided to combine them into one. Thus was born the 1982 Twin Cities Marathon, with the boastful promotional tagline "The Most Beautiful Urban Marathon in America."

I've often wondered if Boston's Will Cloney or New York's Fred Lebow took that personally.

The marathon's course started in metropolitan Minneapolis and wound around Lake of the Isles, Lake Calhoun, Lake Harriet, and Lake Nokomis before cutting over to the Mississippi River, crossing it, and picking up Summit Avenue for the long trek into St. Paul, where the runners finished adjacent to the state capital.

With General Mills' prominence in the Twin Cities corporate running scene, Jack Moran, the inaugural marathon's race director, approached me looking for a major sponsor. When I queried him regarding the race budget, he floated the rather astronomical figure of $125,000. Senior Mills management, who usually said "yes" when I came around asking for running rubles, said "no" this time, citing the herculean hoard requested.

Our archrival in the baking wars, Pillsbury, subsequently snarfed up the sponsorship for $75,000, garnering compelling positive corporate public relations. I could hear their advertising mascot, the legendary Dough Boy, cackling at General Mills from high atop his downtown office tower.

Despite the failed sponsorship gambit, the junket looked like it might be fun.

At least from the warped perspective of a marathoner.

But because I had been up and down with my hamstring, I wasn't really sure what to expect from myself. Then came the Airport Half Marathon, contested on frontage roads adjacent to Minneapolis-St. Paul International. Held on a sixty-eight-degree day about five weeks before the marathon, the course was flat and fast. Inspired by all the aeronautical acceleration action around me, I scored a half marathon PR of 1:19:31, or 6:04 per mile. A total and pleasant surprise.

I registered for "The Most Beautiful Urban Marathon in America."

Marathon morning, Sunday, October 3, was downright cold. Clear, with the mercury in the mid-forties, it was not the kind of day you wanted to be waiting around outside for an extended period of time before the race. Especially with my history. Muscles tighten, and bad things can happen.

Fortunately, Denise, by this time very pregnant, was working for a downtown Minneapolis law firm in the same Pillsbury office tower frequented by the Dough Boy, which was conveniently contiguous to the starting line. So, after rising at 4:30 a.m. and imbibing in my pre-race caffeine and carbs with a motivational dose of the Canadian rock band Rush, I jumped into the car with her and Bubba Gelly and headed into town. Upon arrival, Denise flashed her creds and building security admitted us to her eleventh-floor law office suite, where we luxuriated with access to warmth, comfort, coffee and, most importantly, bathrooms, awaiting the 7:30 start.

Once the marathon launched, the conditions were just about perfect for the 4,563 entrants, who set a record for the number of participants in a first-time race in the United States. The course, actually, was as beautiful as its promoters promised, with the fall foliage at its peak, and I finished up over in St. Paul by the state capital in 230th place with a time of 2:48:18, my fifth fastest marathon.

One day short of six weeks later, Denise and I welcomed into the world our firstborn, James H. Riehl, III. Ever the supportive spouse, Denise had waited to go into labor until I returned from my Saturday morning run with the guys.

Our bouncing baby boy was born eight hours later, at 6:53 p.m., on November 13, weighing seven pounds and eleven ounces. He was nicknamed "Pete" after his grandfather, James H. Riehl, Sr. who had been similarly monikered by *his* parents.

As we explained it, the baby was our own little "Re-Pete."

Given the fact that Denise and I had six sisters between us, we were thrilled to have a little boy and to become a new family. Among the baby gifts the lad received were a pair of New Balance running shoes I had bought when back in Boston for the '81 Marathon and a Cleveland Browns warm-up suit from his godfather, John Larson.

Not exactly a silver spoon, but not chopped liver either.

Pretty much lost in all the shouting was the fact that Alberto Salazar won his third consecutive New York City Marathon by a mere 6 seconds over Mexican Rodolfo Gomez in a time of 2:09:29. Not quite the dominant showing of his first two victories in Gotham, but a win's a win.

Comeback Number 2 had been a success.

In all respects.

MY SECOND MBA REVISITED: PART (B)

"My first big break was getting into the Beatles.
My second was getting out of the Beatles."

—George Harrison

DENISE, BLESS HER HEART, COVERED MOST OF PETE'S 2:00 A.M. FEEDINGS.

For two reasons. One, she was still on maternity leave. And two, all of a sudden, I needed all the sleep I could get. Because with absolutely zero successful Northstar Division new frozen product launches to my credit, the powers that were at General Mills felt it was time for me to show what I could do. Up or out, remember?

So, along came another of those 4:00 p.m. Friday announcements. And I wasn't sure if I was a knight, a rook, a bishop, or in reality, maybe a pawn on the Big G chessboard. All I knew from the subterranean pre-blurb rumblings was that I was on the move.

The rumblings were accurate, the pizza crescents and granola cream cheese bars were orphaned, and I was the new Product Manager of Bisquick baking mix, replacing Michelle Harrison. Michelle had graduated from HBS the year before me and had piloted the brand to unprecedented heights.

I needed the whole weekend to get over it.

Don't get me wrong. Bisquick was one of the biggest brands at General Mills, racking up tens of millions of dollars in sales annually. It was my chance to complete that two-pronged "Second MBA" that keeps reappearing in these pages like a bad penny. Part (A): Earn the title of Product Manager. Part (B): Successfully run a well-known national brand.

But Michelle was a tough act to follow. I felt like Phil Bengtson must have felt when he was appointed as head coach of the Packers to replace Vince Lombardi. That, plus I was back in the world of baking mixes again, and, well, compared to cereal, granola bars, and yogurt, baking mixes just weren't sexy.

But, as previously noted, you get what you get, and you don't get upset.

Dead ahead, coming up in only eight weeks, were the annual marketing plans presentations. I had two months to learn the business, put together the annual business blueprint, and pitch it at our advertising agency down in Chicago like I actually knew what the hell I was talking about.

The thought crossed my mind that this would be the first of many tests of my future General Mills management potential.

I had to make this work, or our years in the Twin Cities might be numbered.

IN THE ICEBOX OF THE NATION

**"Rocky and Bullwinkle, your bravery and friendship
has been an inspiration to Frostbite Falls. We would
like to honor you with the key to our city."**

—The Mayor of Frostbite Falls

A S I REVELED IN MY NEWLY BESTOWED FATHERHOOD AND BURNED THE MID-
night oil to absorb the intricacies of the biscuit mix business, there
wasn't much room for running. This was evidenced by only occasional entries in my training log and a road race here and there at the end of 1982
into 1983.

However, by mid-January, with administrative alligators up to my lower
extremities, I needed a break, and my buddies in the General Mills Runner's
Club came up with a doozy of a diversion.

It was called the "Freeze Your Gizzard Blizzard Run," a 10K held in
International Falls, "The Icebox of the Nation," about four and a half hours
north of the Twin Cities up on the Canadian border. The event, first held in
1981, continues to this day. Its organizers take pride in the fact that runners
might, on any given day, face seventy- to eighty-degree-below-zero wind
chill factors.

You couldn't run without signing a "hold harmless" waiver. You shouldn't
be allowed to run without being held mindless.

The run is one of a plethora of local events creatively called "The Icebox Days" that punctuate the two weeks before the Super Bowl and are intended to sweep away the midwinter malaise that threatens to otherwise overcome the residents of the Northern Plains.

In reality, the whole thing is merely an excuse to party like it's 1999.

Anyhow, after receiving Denise's blessing, an intrepid band of GMI runners, including Bubba Gelly, Tony Benthin, Steve Chesebrough, and Dick Shaw, kidnapped me after a marketing planning meeting just after noon on Friday and bundled me into a rented RV for the trek north.

En route, we violated at least one state statute forbidding open containers in a moving vehicle. Then, to assure a unified team presence once we landed in the Falls, Bubba broke out our nom de guerre, baseball caps complete with military "scrambled eggs" on the visors, branding us as the "Bombardiers."

On north the RV rolled, traversing such notable landmarks as Eveleth (the home of the US Ice Hockey Hall of Fame), Virginia (the heart of the Mesabi iron range) and the alliteratively named Rat Root River. We arrived in the Icebox just in time for cocktail hour. How appropriate.

We were bivouacked at the local Holiday Inn, which somewhat fortuitously, was the epicenter for all the Icebox Days festivities. In fact, the headquarters for the entire two-week celebration was the inn's Bronko Nagurski Room, so named for the NFL great who had lived in International Falls before moving on to the University of Minnesota and the Chicago Bears.

Among our cellmates was a running club which had bused in from Winnipeg, Manitoba, the Meter Eaters, with whom, over drinks at the hotel bar, we quickly developed quite a heated rivalry.

Now these guys from Winnipeg were a bit strange. They had this weird Canadian accent, and they were saying "eh" like every other word. What's more, their team warm-up suits, emblazoned with "Winnipeg Meter Eaters" across the back, were red and black polyester, right out of the '70s. But what really took the cake was their club mascot. It was a log.

A North American white ash log, for God's sake, appropriately named "Blanche."

You can't make this stuff up.

As the beverages accumulated, so did the trash talk. When the Meter Eaters started calling us "hosers," that was the last straw. Bubba challenged them to a duel to the death. Sort of.

Before Friday evening became Saturday morning, the terms of engagement for the inaugural *IF Cup* had been tersely negotiated. There would be four theaters of competition—the 10-kilometer run, a pizza-eating contest, and a dance contest, all on Saturday, as well as a cross-country ski race on Sunday. The first event and the last event were official parts of the Icebox Days agenda, while the other two were improvised by the two warring factions.

The 10K would be scored like a cross-country meet with each team's first five runners counting and would be worth 40 percent of the total. Each of the other three events would contribute 20 percent of the final score.

As for the so-called *IF Cup* itself, the "IF" obviously stood for "International Falls," and it remained to be seen **IF** the Bombardiers or the Meter Eaters would win it.

And did I mention that, while the Bombardiers and Eaters were haggling over the specifics of the weekend's matchup, I clandestinely kidnapped Blanche out of one of the Winnipegger's backpacks and spirited her up to my room?

THE CUP RUNNETH OVER

"The harder the conflict, the more glorious the triumph."

—Thomas Paine, Founding Father of the United States

THE LOCALS DIDN'T QUITE KNOW WHAT TO MAKE OF EITHER THE BOMBARDIERS or the Meter Eaters.

Come to think of it, we didn't quite know what to make of the locals. How could they possibly live that far north, in a place that cold, that snowy, that dark, for so many months of the year? Yet, predictably, they were Minnesota Nice and welcomed us into their village like the prodigal sons we were.

Saturday, predictably, dawned cold. Ten degrees below zero. Some canned beers and sodas we had left in our rented RV had exploded all over the interior.

Dick Shaw wasn't happy about that, complaining, "We'll have to pay more to have this thing cleaned when we turn it in."

"Relax, Dick," I consoled him. "Now you won't be lying when tell people you had a blast in International Falls."

Dick's response was not recorded.

By the time we encountered some of the Meter Eaters at Rainy River Junior College before the 10K run, they were missing Blanche and grilled us regarding her whereabouts. Of course, we had no idea where the absent mascot might be, but I opined that perhaps she had mistakenly happened into a roaring hearth somewhere. My attempt at levity was not appreciated. In fact, the Winnipeggers took it out on us on the road, soundly topping us in the 10K and taking a solid lead in the chase for the International Falls Cup. They needed only to win one of the next three events, and the trophy, along with its perpetual bragging rights, would be theirs.

Uh oh.

Next up was the pizza-eating contest, which pitted yours truly, "The Minneapolis Pig," as my teammates had christened me, against Claude "The Animal" Snow at the Pizza Hut adjacent to the Holiday Inn. This was a winner-take-all tilt for whoever could eat a large, one-topping pie the fastest.

And there was a science to this about which The Animal did not have a clue.

The first consideration was which topping to choose. Claude chose pineapple. Poor choice. Grainy and difficult to swallow. I chose mushrooms because they are small, smooth, and slide down the gullet.

The second consideration was how does one eat the pizza? Claude ate it one bite at a time. Bad idea. I employed my patented, manual "rip-and-tear" methodology, which involved the ripping and tearing of the pie by hand into bite size pieces before ingesting.

Finally, what does one drink to wash the pizza down? Claude chose cold soda. Another lousy selection. I chose warm water. Chilled carbonated beverage contracts the throat and makes one want to burp.

The Animal burped, all right. In technicolor, out in the Pizza Hut parking lot, and the Bombardiers were back in the game.

International Falls Cup event number three was the dance contest, which was to be held in conjunction with the Icebox Days Beach Party at the Holiday Inn Saturday night. The local Chamber of Commerce, which sponsored Icebox Days, went all out for this one, even dumping a load of sand in the hotel ballroom and encouraging everyone to wear their bathing suits to the soiree.

It was here that Bubba and I again crossed swords with Claude "The Animal" Snow. We were dressed not in our bathing suits, but as Jake and Elwood Blues, The Blues Brothers. We had been nominated to represent our club in the dance dust-up, more for sheer comedic effect than for our twinkle-toed talent. The Animal, fronting the Meter Eaters, had ostensibly recovered from his afternoon's gastrointestinal gaffe. He made a grand entrance into the ballroom, comely female companion in tow and girded for battle in a loosely fitting Speedo.

Our juking joust was to be judged by an impartial local who had refused attempted bribes by both the Meter Eaters and the Bombardiers. A winner would be subjectively declared after the first three dances based on gracefulness, athleticism, and creativity.

However, once the music started and our bodies started gyrating, the competition was abruptly terminated by the judge, and The Animal was disqualified for "lewd and lascivious behavior unbefitting a public venue." The authorities stopped just short of summoning the local constabulary.

It seems The Animal's Speedo was just a bit *too* loosely fitting.

As we filed out of the Holiday Inn ballroom at the conclusion of the beach party, one of our local friends, Mary Beth, offered these wise words of caution regarding the exiting female pulchritude: "Careful, boys. About this time of night, the 2's are starting to look like 10's."

So, rolling into Sunday's cross-country ski race, the Bombardiers and Meter Eaters were tied for the International Falls Cup at 40 points each. The hardware would belong to whichever team waxed the other on the snow-covered surface of Rainy Lake, which doubles as the international boundary between the United States and Canada.

Due in part to the excesses of the preceding evening, neither team had more than a couple of skiers in the contest, and the rest of us waited nervously in the lake lodge for the results. Ultimately, the Bombardiers' own Andrew Ward and Steve Chesebrough prevailed over the Meter Eaters, and after defiantly waving our newly claimed trophy in their faces, we piled into the RV, triumphant, and set off for Minneapolis.

In the ensuing year, every couple of months, our anonymous kidnapper would send a postcard addressed to the Meter Eaters in Winnipeg. On the front of the postcard was a photo of Blanche the Log in the foreground of some famous global landmark. The Eiffel Towel. The Taj Mahal. The Great Wall of China. The Empire State Building.

On the back of the postcard, a barely legible comment, scrawled in black Sharpie, confirmed that Blanche surely was "a sweet piece of ash."

THE PLAN, BOSS, THE PLAN: EPISODE 2

"A formal, written marketing plan is essential, in that it provides an unambiguous reference point for activities throughout the planning period. However, perhaps the most important benefit of these plans is the planning process itself. This typically offers a unique opportunity, a forum, for information-rich and productively focused discussions between the various managers involved."

—Wikipedia

EANING THAT, IF I WASN'T PREPARED, THE PLANNING PROCESS JUST MIGHT be open season on the new guy.

The time for fun and games was over.

I was back from International Falls, and my four-person brand group and I had a measly five weeks to put together the best marketing plan in the universe. On a business I was still getting to know.

Well, actually, we had a measly five weeks to put together three of the best marketing plans in the universe. You see, I was actually responsible for not one but three brands. Bisquick, the biscuit mix standard-bearer, of course. But also, Bugles, the remaining General Mills snack survivor from the Bugles / Daisys / Whistles imbroglio of the mid '60s, and Bacos®, the bacon-flavored soy bits that came in a jar.

We called them "The Killer Bs." And nutritionally, that may have been somewhat accurate. Anyhow, despite my skill at creatively rationalizing any status quo after the fact, the logic behind the consolidation of these three disparate products into one brand group totally escaped me.

Neither Bugles nor Bacos was a very big business, relative to Bisquick, so the powder that came in the yellow box with the big bright blue letters on the front got the lion's share of our efforts.

And when it came to that brand, my predecessor, Michelle, as previously noted, had done a bang-up job embracing the lifestyle trends that were changing how consumers used the product. With more women than ever headed into the workforce, they were using the product less and less to make traditional recipes like biscuits, pancakes, and muffins. To counter that drift, she had introduced, over the course of her tenure, a series of Bisquick recipes called the "Impossible Pies."

These were main meal recipes that could be pre-assembled using typical on-hand household ingredients, refrigerated in advance, and baked in a matter of thirty-five to forty-five minutes. They were perfect for the family coming home for dinner and seeking to serve up a hearty meal in a hurry. So, Michelle had pivoted the majority of the brand's recipe emphasis behind the "Impossible Pie." And the sales revenue and market share had responded, heading north, way north.

It didn't take a rocket scientist to conclude that the 1983 marketing plan should continue down the same road. And since no one ever accused me of being a rocket scientist, by and large, we replicated the previous year's blueprint. We also made a list of every conceivable question we thought we might be asked during the planning session and actually drafted and memorized the responses.

By the time we got on the plane to go to Chicago to present the dog-and-pony show to senior General Mills management, we had one three-inch three-ring binder containing all the transparencies for the presentation it-self, and two three-inch three-ring binders with transparencies addressing all of the backup questions.

Remember, this is in the days before PowerPoint. And, fortunately, also before airport metal detectors.

FEVER PITCH

"Luck is when preparation meets opportunity."

—Seneca, Roman Philosopher

AS I HEADED INTO THE CONFERENCE ROOM AT OUR ADVERTISING agency Needham, Harper & Steers's Chicago headquarters, it was confirmed.

All the big guns were there.

Jared Robinson, the Marketing Director, my new boss. Norm Cooper, the General Manager, his boss. And from the agency, my counterpart, Account Executive, Bob Klein, and various and sundry other folks who were way above both of our pay grades. All assembled to witness my coming-out party as Bisquick Product Manager.

We had scheduled four hours, 1:00 to 5:00 p.m. Leading off and batting first, I had the privilege of presenting the Bisquick plan until 4:00 p.m. Once I was escorted to the medical tent, Bugles and Bacos, each presented by one of my Assistant Product Managers, would receive their obligatory thirty minutes apiece.

Time to stand and deliver.

I was sufficiently new to my Product Manager position that I thought I would begin the presentation on a humorous, perhaps slightly cheeky note. Of course, it had often been pointed out that what might seem funny to me, to others, was, well, not so much.

"Good afternoon," I began. "Welcome to the annual Bisquick marketing plans presentation."

"Allow me to introduce myself," I continued, "My name is Jim Riehl."

And with that, I put a copy of my resume up on the screen.

Fortunately, this attempt at humor did not rank among my many miscalculations in that regard, and if the truth be known, broke some of the ice floating out in Lake Michigan that day. We flew through the plan quite effortlessly, nimbly handling every challenging query tossed our way. We showed management that in eight weeks, we had thoroughly learned the business and we were well on the way to being *in control*.

The hours of preparation had paid off big time, just like they had in a marathon.

I had passed my first big test of Part (B): successfully running a well-known national brand.

Or, at least creating the perception of it.

MISSION "IMPOSSIBLE PIE": EPISODE 1

"Your mission, Jim, should you decide to accept it..."

—*Mission Impossible* TV Introduction

U NFORTUNATELY, THE NOTION THAT WE WERE IN CONTROL OF THE BISQUICK business turned out to be a fairly short-lived phenomenon.

About ten weeks after the Chicago marketing plans presentation, both Bisquick's monthly sales revenue and market share began to decline, according to the syndicated market research data General Mills purchased from Nielsen.

"What's going on?" I asked Marian O'Neill, the Assistant Product Manager. "What's changed? Our marketing and sales tactics certainly haven't."

"I'm not sure," she replied, puzzled. Marian was bright, always on top of her business. If she didn't know what was happening, that wasn't good news.

As Product Manager, I was the CEO of my brand. When sales revenue and market share started shrinking, so did profits. It was my job to figure out what the problem was and fix it. Fast. In fact, someone over in the corner office was probably already saying it was my job to have seen this downturn coming and address it proactively, before it arrived.

As Bisquick's skid continued, I was not in a good place.

It was all hands on deck.

Marian, Bob Klein, my agency Account Executive, and I left no stone unturned. We tried to pinpoint the weakness. Where was it centered? On a particular package size? In a certain region? In a certain distribution channel? What was happening to Bisquick's shelf pricing? Its promotional pricing? Was the brand being promoted less frequently by the trade? What brands were gaining market share at Bisquick's expense? What advertising and promotional tactics were they using? And yadda yadda yadda.

But nada, nada, nada.

All this extensive analysis by some incredibly bright people, and we had no answers.

Bisquick, an American institution, was bleeding to death and we...no, scratch that, *I*...couldn't figure out how to stop it.

THE LAST ROUND UP

"In our ever-more-mechanized, programmed society, marathoners want to assert their independence and affirm their individuality...call it humanism, call it health, call it folly. Some are Lancelots, most are Don Quixotes. All are noble. Whatever it is, our ailing world could use a whole lot more of it."

—Erich Segal, American Author, Educator and Classicist

THE BRAND'S REVENUE AND SHARE DECLINES CONTINUED ACROSS THE BOARD.

Sales were tanking on all package sizes, in all areas of the country, across all classes of trade. Our shelf and promotional pricing, relative to competition and year ago, was steady. Bisquick was getting as many in-store displays and grocer newspaper ads as it usually did.

And market share losses were proportionate to each of our regional competitors. Not a single rival stood out as doing anything differently. Not Jiffy in the Midwest, Krusteaz in the Pacific Northwest, or Martha White in the South.

Things were getting tense at the office, and I'm sure I was a little testy to be around at home. After all, I had worked hard for four-plus years to get a crack at Part (B) of my "Second MBA," successfully running a well-known national brand. The entire proposition was turning to dust—or, should I say, rancid biscuit mix—right before my eyes.

It was mid-September when Denise, in her infinite wisdom, decided to take "Portable Pete" on a road trip to visit his grandparents in Montana. Smart move. The second annual Twin Cities Marathon was a couple of weeks away.

No wonder I wasn't doing much running or, for that matter, recording it in my training journal. As I had searched furiously night and day for the solution to my biscuit mix quandary, I was unable to mount any semblance of a pre-marathon preparation program. And I think that just magnified the stress.

I longed for the simpler times when I could drop everything, go for a long run, and come back refreshed and renewed, feeling really good about myself and the positive things I was accomplishing. Even for just a day, I needed an escape.

That escape became the second annual Twin Cities Marathon.

A single day in the Democracy of Distance Running, where everyone was equal until the starter's gun sounded, everyone gave it their best shot out on the course, and everyone became best friends over a beer beyond the finish line.

Given life on the "Killer Bs" as of late, that was a very appealing prospect.

It was like my decision to run Boston in 1978. I knew I had the base conditioning to finish the race, but my time would be anyone's guess. Given a reasonably flat course and cool weather, I decided to shoot for three hours.

Appropriately enough, to reflect my somewhat diminished level of conditioning, I was assigned the racing bib "747."

Sunday morning, October 2, dawned warmer than a year ago, sixty degrees, cloudy, and humid, with a slight ten-mile-per-hour breeze out of the east that would become a headwind after the 10-mile mark. Still decent running weather.

As I idled my four Rolls Royce RB 211 engines prior to the 7:30 a.m. takeoff on Minneapolis' 3rd Street runway, my plan was to run very conservatively, assess what I had left at the half marathon, and see if I could bring it in before 10:30.

If there was one thing at which I had become proficient after all these miles and marathons, admittedly with significant help from Mr. Casio, it was pacing myself, and this day was no exception. Hitting the half at 1:32, I was still relatively fresh and able to ratchet down my terrapin-like 7 minute per-mile pace to a pretty astonishing 6:36 for the duration.

That's called a "negative split," covering the second half faster than the first, and it speaks to the incredible strength and endurance base I had built over the years, in the absence of a disciplined and consistent training program prior to this particular marathon.

Making my way up St. Paul's Summit Avenue, approaching the State Capitol and the finish, I heard the "clop, clop, clop, clop" of size 13 Nike hoofbeats approaching from the rear. Never one to look back, I pressed ahead, intent on maintaining my pace. Soon came a tap on my butt and an ebullient "Hello, Doctor O!" as Clydesdale Bubba Gelly powered past me on my right, laughing heartily as he disappeared down the road ahead.

Bubba finished in 2:58:17, a PR for him, and I followed shortly afterward in 2:58:43.

As I crossed the finish line, Bubba, paraphrasing George C. Scott as he triumphed over Field Marshal Erwin Rommel in the classic movie *Patton*, exclaimed at the top of his lungs, "Riehl, you magnificent bastard! I ran Squires's training program!"

He was the better man that day.

And it was a good day.

MISSION "IMPOSSIBLE PIE": EPISODE 2

"As always, should you be caught or killed, we will disavow any knowledge of your actions. This tape will self-destruct in five seconds. Good luck, Jim."

—*Mission Impossible* TV Introduction

AFTER THE MARATHON, IT WAS BACK TO THE ROCK PILE TO BREAK MORE ROCKS.

We had analyzed everything having to do with Bisquick—the advertising, the competition, the distribution, the pricing, the product, the consumer promotion, the trade promotion—everything.

But there simply was no smoking gun.

As with a marathon, I was trying to overcome a tremendous obstacle, but unlike a marathon, I'd not yet found the tools—the long-distance runs, the hill workouts, the track intervals—to successfully attack it.

Things were getting more and more uncomfortable.

But the discomfort became exponential one Friday afternoon at 4:00 p.m., when Michelle Harrison was announced as my new boss. My predecessor on Bisquick, she had reams more experience on the brand than I did.

She had clearly been brought in- how can I most diplomatically put it?- to backstop my efforts to save the brand.

Not only that. They replaced my all-star Assistant Product Manager, Marian O'Neill, with a much less experienced hire. Was I being set up?

So, it was Bob Klein and me against the world.

That was when we *finally* figured it out.

A part of the market research package Bisquick annually purchased was consumer product usage data. The data came from 1,500 households that used Bisquick and recorded in diaries how they were using the product—specifically, what recipes they were making over a thirty- to sixty-day period.

The diaries were then submitted to the research company, which compiled the data and summarized the results for General Mills. Because product usage trends normally didn't fluctuate very dramatically over time, the data was only purchased once a year. And Bob and I were about eight months into the Bisquick brand erosion before we had any access to updated product usage data.

When the report came in, we attacked it like starving castaways gorging themselves at their first meal after months subsisting on tasteless, dried out tropical fruits on a remote desert island.

What we found was very interesting. And in a way, very ironic.

Bisquick had traditionally built its business—and its multi-million dollars in sales—on the backs of households using it to make biscuits and pancakes. A biscuit recipe uses two and a quarter cups of product. A pancake recipe uses two cups of product.

But recently, the brand's recipe emphasis- in advertising and on the package- had been the "Impossible Pie" recipes. This in an attempt, as mentioned previously, to make Bisquick more relevant to working moms.

The problem was that the "Impossible Pie" recipes only called for **one-half** cup of the stuff.

Eureka!

We had, in a campaign originated by Michelle and continued by me, shifted consumers from using a lot of Bisquick per recipe to using a little.

With the nosedive diagnosed by virtue of Bob's and my sleuthing, recipe service was immediately flipped back to heavier usage recipes. But it takes time to roll out revised recipes, create new advertising, design new packaging, and turn around the aircraft carrier.

Bisquick ultimately rebounded, but for me, the damage was done.

Regarding my career, at least as far as General Mills was concerned, it was both figuratively and literally a case of ***recipes for disaster.***

As I engineered Bisquick's comeback, reversing the business for Michelle, I began looking for a new job. Elsewhere.

"You'll be a VP of Marketing somewhere," she told me. "Just not here."

James Berger, another colleague from the Mills, once said of a company where he subsequently worked, "Your first day of work, they fire a bullet at you, and it's only a matter of time until you get hit."

That's marketing management. Life in the big city. It comes with the territory.

THE FUTURE IS BECOMING APPARENT: EPISODE 2

"Keep looking up...that's the secret of life."

—Charlie Brown

A S I BEGAN MY JOB SEARCH, DENISE AND I DISCOVERED WE WERE GOING TO become parents for the second time. That was a nice counterbalance to the disappointment I couldn't help but feel at the way the Bisquick assignment had turned out.

However, as far as the headhunters and other companies out there were concerned, I had completed my "Second MBA." I had made it to Product Manager at General Mills, and for all they knew, in Bisquick, successfully run a well-known national brand. They didn't have access to the Nielsen data showing Bisquick's struggles, and they just *loved* those Mills credentials.

As a commodity, I was in demand. Marketing wise, I could go wherever, do whatever, with whoever.

Mission, if not Mission "Impossible Pie," accomplished.

I discussed various opportunities at varied points of the compass, but during a summer vacation picnic on Duxbury Beach, Denise and I agreed we wanted to raise our young family on the East Coast.

Conversations began to get pretty earnest with Nestle, headquartered in White Plains, New York, which was looking to create a leaner, meaner, less bureaucratic US marketing organization. That struck me as a pretty refreshing proposition after what I had just experienced at General Mills. A former Betty Crocker colleague, Geoff Winters, was running Nestle's toll house morsels business and doing a bit of internal cheerleading for me.

Sandwiched in between interviews with Bill Talbot, Nestle's headhunter, Martha Gordon, the Nestle HR exec running the search, and a visit to White Plains, I tried one last time to trade off my strength and endurance base at the 1984 Twin Cities Marathon. But my focus wasn't on it, which meant my heart wasn't in it, and I dropped out at mile 12. It would be my seventeenth and final marathon, albeit a DNF.

Thirty-six days later, as Denise went into labor and as we were about to head for the hospital, an offer letter arrived from Nestle via UPS. During the next few hours, I aggressively multitasked, helping Denise with her Lamaze breathing while negotiating with Martha Gordon over the phone.

By the time little Allison Dahle Riehl was born on November 5, weighing six pounds and thirteen ounces. Her dad had a new job, and we had our little girl. Like Pete, she was named after a grandfather, her maternal one, Louis Allison Dahle.

When I tried nicknaming her "Allity," for some reason, it just didn't stick.

As Denise tartly put it, "The 'Re-Pete' idea was kind of cute, Jim, but the 'Re-Allity' idea is incredibly stupid."

The next day, November 6, Ronald Reagan crushed Walter Mondale by an electoral vote of 525 to 13. Reagan was nicknamed "The Great Communicator," but as I basked in my triumphant career rebound, I speculated that, in my negotiations with Nestle, perhaps I might have been an even greater communicator.

I resigned from General Mills the following week and started commuting to White Plains in early December. Back in Minnesota, Denise faced her own challenges, dealing on her own with a newborn and an active two-year-old. When the day finally came for our move in early January, it was clearly time to be a family again.

As the movers loaded our van to head back east after our six and a half years in the Twin Cities, it was twenty degrees below zero. Settling into our seats for the flight to LaGuardia, we were delighted when the pilot declared over the intercom that the temperature was fifty-two degrees warmer in New York.

Things were looking up.

Once we were in the air, while Pete terrorized the flight deck, a number of the passengers begged to hold Allison, our precious, tiny "lap child." By this time, her justifiably exhausted mom was only too happy to oblige. Engaging one of the guest swaddlers in conversation, we learned that Denise's childhood pastor from Illinois, Herb Anderson, was now holding court at the Brick Presbyterian Church on Park Avenue in New York City.

Things *really* were looking up.

Four months later, that's where Allison was baptized.

I guess we were truly coming back home.

FATHER TIME IS UNDEFEATED

"Reach for the stars. You may not catch any, but you won't end up with a handful of mud, either."

—William W. Cease, American Food Service Entrepreneur and Inventor

THE LAST ENTRY IN MY TRAINING LOG WAS AUGUST 7, 1983.

Oh, I kept running, of course. I finished Twin Cities later that fall and DNF-ed Twin Cities the following year.

But August 7, 1983 was the unofficial end for me.

That was when my age, my injuries, and my responsibilities began telling me it had been a good ride, a great ride, but the ride was over.

At first, I didn't listen. I wouldn't listen.

But Father Time is undefeated.

As Bill Rodgers wrote of his Wesleyan classmate and 1968 Boston Marathon champion Amby Burfoot, "For a couple of years after his victory in 1968, Amby entertained optimistic thoughts about repeating his success in the Boston Marathon. But for Amby, our college years—when he was so focused on running and all he did was go to class and do his homework and work in the cafeteria and run—had been conducive to training to be the best. Once he entered the real world and found himself working in an elementary school classroom for seven hours a day, it wasn't as easy to find the time to train and to keep the dream afloat."

Back in 1975, in our Duxbury apartment, the one with the green shag carpet, when I had just met Scott Graham and started training with GBTC, I was exhilarated. *Exhilarated!* I stood in the shower after a run, thinking, "It's totally up to me how far I can take this sport, how good I can get. If I work hard enough, I can run a 2:20 marathon. Maybe faster."

But that's not how it works.

Harking back to *Chariots of Fire*, Harold Abrahams's coach, Sam Mussabini, expressed it best when he declared to Abrahams, "You can't put in what God's left out." Translation: Without the natural talent to be fast, hard work will only take you so far.

I guess "so far" in the marathon for me was 2:43:47.

Sam's statement has its basis in physiology. It seems we are all born with two types of muscle fibers—fast-twitch fibers and slow-twitch fibers. Fast-twitch fibers enable powerful bursts of quick movement like sprinting, while slow-twitch fibers foster endurance-type activities such as distance running. The higher the percentage of fast-twitch fibers an individual has, the faster they can run. Conversely, the higher percentage of slow-twitch fibers, the better the endurance athlete.

Admittedly, I've never had a muscle biopsy. But I have trained at levels approaching those of the world-class GBTC distance runners, and judging from my times on the road and on the track, I'm betting I'm primarily a slow-twitch guy. The differential between my best road race times—around 6 minutes per mile—and my fastest marathon—6:15 per mile—a mere 15 seconds, just wasn't that much.

Consequently, on the assembly line of my life, no additional hard work would put in what God had left out, specifically fast-twitch muscle fibers. And, unlike in Detroit, for me there would be no factory recall.

So, taking stock, what had 18,964 road miles, 115 track workouts, 127 road races, and 17 marathons gotten me?

Self-confidence, a belief in my ability to overcome obstacles, an insatiable work ethic, resilience, and persistence.

I began the journey as a frustrated jock without a sport, repeatedly told I wasn't good enough even to earn a puny high school varsity letter. Through my own diligence, the support of many others, including my wife and my friends, and a number of flat-out lucky breaks, I was able to take my abilities as far as they would carry me, reducing my marathon time by almost an hour and my marathon minute-per-mile pace by over two minutes.

The successes were sweet, the failures chastening, and the comebacks heartening.

Along the way, I learned a lot about myself, trained with and then ate the dust of some of the greatest marathoners of the day, experienced the exhilaration of Boston, New York, and Duluth, and the disappointment of Terre Haute and Brookings. I made lifelong friends, enjoyed incredible experiences I would never have imagined, and created indelible memories of a race well run.

A race I wouldn't trade for anything.

But, as they say, all good things must come to an end.

As for me, in addition to having taken my running about as far as I could, I had a loving wife and two beautiful, blond, and rambunctious little kids to care for, as well as a challenging new job in the suburbs of New York City.

It was finally time to be an adult.

And that was OK.

I had chased down my dream.

EPILOGUE

"In the end, it's not the years in your life that
count. It's the life in your years."

—Abraham Lincoln

An Update on Each of the Individuals Who Influenced this Narrative...

Dick Beardsley

"The Duel in the Sun" with Alberto Salazar at the 1982 Boston Marathon was the peak of Dick's running career. Two months later, he won Grandma's Marathon in 2:14:49 but injured his Achilles tendon in the process and was not competitive at New York that fall. Two failed tendon surgeries and two failed 1984 and 1988 Olympic marathon bids later, he retired from running to build up his Minnesota dairy farm and fishing guide businesses.

In November of 1989, working on his dairy farm, Dick became entangled in a power auger he was using to lift corn into a crib. He suffered severe rib, back, arm, and head injuries and was disabled for five months. In the span of the next three years, in a series of terrible accidents, Dick's car was blindsided by another driver, he was hit by a truck while running in a snowstorm, and he rolled his vehicle over several times.

In the light of all of Dick's accidents, injuries, and remedial surgeries, it was no surprise that he was prescribed pain meds and plenty of them. By 1996, he was hooked, taking eighty to ninety pills a day, a combination of Demerol, Percocet, and Valium. In September of that year, he was arrested for forging a prescription. "It saved my life," Dick recalls on his website. "Getting caught put the brakes on my downward spiral."

After several months in a Fargo, North Dakota psychiatric unit, Dick emerged drug-free in early 1997. He has resumed running and regularly completes sub 2:50 marathons. He also gives motivational speeches and published his autobiography, *Staying The Course*, in 2002.

"Turbo" Tony Benthin

Tony and I met just after I started at General Mills in 1978, and as he recalls, "Jim convinced me I could run even though I had not run in high school or college. My only running experience had been in the US Army Reserve in those wonderful running shoes called Army boots."

"Looking back at my running career," Tony notes, "I guess Jim was right. I could run. My first race was in an 18K in the fall of 1978 where I learned what a side stitch was. I was in my late twenties when I started racing and it became a very important part of my lifestyle for the next twenty years. I ran in races of all distances ranging from 1 mile to 100 K. My racing included twenty-eight marathons and four ultramarathons."

Tony ran the Boston Marathon six times, scoring a 2:33:01 marathon PR there in 1983, and running his last marathon there at the 100th edition in 1996. His ultramarathons included a 50K, two 50-mile trail runs, and a 100 K in 1987 with a time of 8:27:15. Tony met many good friends with whom he still keeps in touch today, and he enjoyed traveling and running in races in ten different states.

He finds it interesting how he and several other friends who were very active runners have had similar health issues later in life. Tony has had prostate cancer and cardiac/coronary issues involving two stents, one in his heart and one in his leg. He has also undergone a ten-hour ablation procedure to treat atrial fibrillation. He knows several other runners who have cardiac issues or joint replacements. "Running was great when it was happening," Tony concludes. "But I really wonder if there is a correlation between it and later health challenges."

Tony and his wife, Kristi, live in Maple Grove, Minnesota.

John Ford

After I left him in Honolulu in 1973, John admittedly was spending way too much time enjoying extracurricular activities, which he insisted were of an academic nature. He received his Bachelor of Science in Zoology about three years later than he should have and jumped straight into a master's program where he focused on tropical insular limnology, whatever that is.

John's senior master's professor suggested he go to Northwestern to pursue a doctorate, but John was simultaneously offered a full-time ecologist position at the Corps of Engineers. It didn't take him long to decide between winters in Chicago or brilliant sunsets on the beach in Bora Bora.

From the Corps of Engineers, he moved to the Department of Interior Fish and Wildlife Service in Honolulu. Over the following decade, he led operations for an environmental/geospatial services firm based in Ojai, California doing business throughout the United States and the Pacific Rim. From there, he was recruited to return to Honolulu, open a storefront for SWCA Environmental Consultants, and build and run their Hawaii and Pacific operations.

Being able to resist anything but temptation, John was married occasionally and fathered two lovely daughters, Marissa and Malina. Then, after being single for twelve years, John unexpectedly met his soulmate, Tayawadee, early one morning at SFO, and the rest is history, including a son, Owen.

"Son Owen is now almost 7 years old, is crazy in love with his older sisters, and has become a little prince at home and in Thailand where his proud grandparents and extended family live. As Marissa and her husband may be expecting their first child shortly, Owen will likely become an uncle by the time he turns 8 or 9 years old. Just the All-American family," John reports.

He, Tayawadee and Owen live in Honolulu.

Dave "Bubba" Gelly

After scoring his 2:58:17 marathon PR at Twin Cities in 1982, Bubba continued his world tour, ultimately running in fifty marathons before morphing into cycling, nowadays averaging 80 miles a week. Before retirement, he served as Head of Corporate Security at General Mills, Fort Howard Paper, Hanes, and Syngenta.

Since dismounting, he has penned the best-selling *Gap* series of novels, *Fancy Gap, Orchard Gap, Piper's Gap,* and *Volunteer Gap*. In his limited spare time, Bubba savors fine wines and dotes on his bride of a half-century, Helen (also known as "Lulu"), while splitting his residential inhabitance between Winston-Salem, North Carolina, and Fancy Gap, Virginia.

Scott Graham

In researching this section of the book, I reached out to Bill and Charlie Rodgers online at the Bill Rodgers Running Center to see if they could put me in touch with Scott, my fellow Plymouth-Carver Intermediate School teacher and the guy who made such a difference in my running career by introducing me to the Greater Boston Track Club. Sure enough, Charlie was back to me within a couple of hours. He said he thought brother Bill would know how to get in contact with Scottie. That's the running community for you.

Two days later, I had Scott's contact information and reconnected with him, learning that, after several more years in the Plymouth-Carver Schools teaching Math, Scott had a brief tenure as a cost accountant for New Balance, Inc. He then returned to his teaching roots, imparting wisdom to young scholars in private schools first in the Dallas area and later in the Bay Area of California, coaching track and cross country in both locales. Along the way, he got his PhD in Educational Research, and he now teaches community college students.

A long-time member of GBTC with a marathon PR of 2:23:37, Scott has remained athletically active, completing duathlons (run-bike-run), and he even now occasionally stops by the local track to put in a few intervals.

Rob "Hark" Harkel

Hark and I met Valparaiso in the summer of 1967. Everyone called him Hark...even my late parents. He was also nicknamed "Eddie Haskell" because of his obsequious politeness to adults—but we'll save that for my next book.

We spent a lot of time at each other's houses. When Hark would visit, he had the rare knack of breaking something or regularly irritating at least one of my four sisters. It was not unusual for him to be the recipient of a stern lecture from my dad...and then be invited for dinner.

Hark attended Indiana University where, as he recalls, somehow he acquired a degree in Economics. To this day his friends and family call it an "Act of God" and "nothing short of a miracle." After spending thirty-plus years selling in the corporate world, in 2007 he accomplished his lifelong dream of entering the music business, founding Brightside Music and producing and promoting national touring acts such as Roger McGuinn, the BoDeans, and the Smithereens.

Rob and his wife Jenny, who is a registered nurse, have been married for forty-four years after actually attending their senior prom together! They have a daughter, Julia, who is a hospice social worker in Indianapolis, and a son Kevin, who works in the energy business in Houston. Julia and her husband recently welcomed Hark's first grandchild, a little girl named Haddie.

Hark and Jenny continue to reside in his hometown of Valparaiso while wintering in Marco Island, Florida.

Phil Hunter

Following HBS graduation, Phil bought a Chevy Chevette with his Visa card and then took a position in Finance with Ore-Ida Foods, the frozen food division of H.J. Heinz in Boise, Idaho. Throughout Phil's eight frenetic years in Boise, he climbed from Assistant to VP of Finance to Product Marketing Manager, while having three kids along the way, learning to fly fish, and teaching skiing at the local ski resort.

Then it was off to the San Francisco Bay area, where he was employed as a consultant at a big six accounting firm, specializing in marketing assignments, before being hired by Apple Computer, Inc. With Apple, Phil's career evolved exponentially as the company itself did. Initially brought aboard to roll out the Macintosh computer into businesses, he progressed through multiple field positions, participating in the introduction of the iMac computer, the iPod, the iPad, and finally the iPhone. After twenty-five years at Apple—as his wife Beth will comment, Phil worked at Apple longer than Steve Jobs—it was time to retire. At his departure, he was responsible for the sales of all Apple products on the West Coast, with the exception of the Apple stores and education products.

As Phil recalls, "It was an up and down and up ride. During one of the descents, I had coronary bypass surgery but bounced back with sufficient vigor that I got another promotion a year later. This left some wag asking if the only way to get ahead at Apple was to work yourself into a heart attack."

Now both retired, Phil and Beth are traveling to all seven continents, supporting some nonprofits, including one in Zimbabwe, and building relationships with their three grandchildren. They live in Walnut Creek, California.

Dave Kispert

Dave was my "brother from another mother" and my brother-in-law who garnered those multiple high school varsity letters. We last saw Dave along with my sister Nicky, Denise, and my parents at the top of Heartbreak Hill at the 1981 Boston Marathon. During that time, he was in the middle of crafting an exemplary teaching and coaching career at Duxbury High School, leading the Dragon football team and, on multiple occasions, the ice hockey team to the Massachusetts state championship tournament.

Dave and Nicky also created *College Choice*, a counseling service that assisted high school students in their college application and selection. It was from there, on the strength of his college consulting, that he briefly pivoted into the publishing business before sadly passing away from cancer in 1995 at the age of 48.

Three days before Christmas that year, Dave was honored at a memorial service by hundreds of attendees, who packed Pilgrim Church in Duxbury, including scores of his former students and student-athletes, who had been inspired by the lessons he taught, the values he stood for, and the example he set.

Bob Klein

As Bob recalls it, thirty-seven years ago, he was rewarded by his advertising agency, Needham, Harper & Steers with the dubious honor of reassignment from the national launch of Bud Light ® beer to Bisquick baking mix from Betty Crocker.

Heading into the assignment with a hangover from the news and too much Bud Light the night before, he was told his new client was a guy by the name of Jim Riehl. Harvard MBA. Marathoner. Married. Two kids. Wicked smart.

Bob and Jim were being tasked by the General to turn around a tired brand in decay. A mammoth profit cash cow being milked into extinction. At the time, Bob was over ten years junior to Jim, bringing the impressive credential of a BA diploma signed by the inimitable University of Wisconsin's Bucky Badger. In retrospect, Bob admits he may have been just a bit intimidated. But soon, much to his surprise and delight, he learned that he and Jim were actually twin sons of different mothers. Different educational pedigrees. For sure. Same logical thinkers.

To quote Bob, it was a simple turnaround: "Want to sell more Bisquick? Get Moms (OK, so that was 1983) to use more Bisquick. How? Make pancakes *every* weekend. Result? The cow started producing like the good ole days. Rocket science? Brain surgery? Nope. Their inspiration lay in their tummies."

Bob's resume thirty-five years later includes 12 EFFIE awards and partnerships with over 100 companies, in which he helped them make a *lot* of money. Bob also reported that he learned first-hand what brain surgery is, whatever that means.

One other thing. To all the runners who are part of Jim's rich pageant of a life, Bob emphatically states that he is not one of them. In seventh grade, he couldn't finish the 600-yard dash. It was the beginning and end of his running career.

Bob and his wife, Jill, reside in Deerfield, Illinois.

Alan Knobel

Following his inaugural marathon at New York in 1977, Alan, my original running muse, returned to Gotham City again in 1978 and also competed in the Revco-Cleveland Marathon in 1978 and 1981. Subsequent athletic pursuits included men's over-thirty soccer, senior swimming and, more recently, tennis.

With twenty years' private entrepreneurial business experience and twenty years in the US Postal Service, Alan and his wife Debbie have two grown children, also distance runners, and five grandchildren and live in Westerville, Ohio.

John Larson

After wrapping up his final year of law school at the University of Pennsylvania, John returned to Ohio to begin work at Squire, Sanders & Dempsey, then the seventh-largest law firm in the nation with 210 lawyers in three offices. He planned to spend a few years as a tax or public finance lawyer until he figured out what might be next. Forty-three years later, he is the senior partner in the public finance practice in what has become a 1,500-lawyer firm with forty-five offices in twenty countries around the world. He has spent his entire career in that practice, at intersection of law, government, finance, public policy, and politics, which serves state and local governments and nonprofit corporations from coast to coast.

Soon after beginning work, he met Jan, and they married on October 20, 1979, a day the Dartmouth football squad celebrated by thrashing Harvard,

10–7. They have enjoyed a rich life together raising two wonderful daughters in Shaker Heights, Ohio.

Dick O'Shaughnessy

After a post-graduate year at The Hill 1949–50, Dick roamed the gridiron from 1951 to 1953 at the University of Michigan, was named All–Big 10 Center in 1952, and served as Wolverine team captain in 1953. Having won the Big 10 heavyweight wrestling championship in 1952 and 1953, off he went into the wild blue yonder, joining the US Air Force for three years, where he served as an electronics warfare officer.

He was married to Winifred "Winnie" Sarr in 1954, who was his wife for sixty-six years. Together they had seven children.

In 1959, O'Shaughnessy returned to The Hill, where he would spend the next thirty-six years teaching Science and Physical Education and coaching football and wrestling. He also served as Dean of Students and Faculty and Assistant Director of The Hill's Summer Camp in Wolfeboro, New Hampshire, and has been inducted into *The Hill School Athletics Founders Hall of Fame*.

Upon retirement in 1996, Dick and his wife, Winnie, restored an eighteenth-century house in Mirror Lake, New Hampshire. When not enjoying visits from his seven children and several grandchildren, Dick embarked upon a second career as a blacksmith and a fly-fisherman until he passed away in December of 2020.

Coach O'Shaughnessy's legacy lives on in the tremendous positive influence he had on so many young people at The Hill. Though he didn't award me a varsity letter sweater, he did foster in me the discipline, perseverance, and resilience that has served me so well in running and in life.

Bill Rodgers

Boston Billy ran sixty marathons in all. He DNF-ed only seven of them and was competitive for a ten-year stretch between 1973 and 1983, during which he won twenty-three of them. He won Boston and New York a mind-boggling four times *each*. His amazing ability to avoid injury was the exception rather than the rule.

The only glory denied him, perhaps, was an Olympic medal because of leg cramps in Montreal in 1976 and because of Mr. Carter's boycott of Moscow in 1980. Other than that, Bill pretty much ran away and hid from every other American marathoner of the era.

He leveraged his celebrity status into a line of running apparel and three retail Bill Rodgers Running Centers, two of them in Boston's Cleveland Circle and Faneuil Hall Marketplace, the last of which closed in 2012. The Center remains an online presence to this day, and as you have already read, helped me reconnect with Scottie Graham. Bill maintains an active personal appearance schedule at road races and running camps and completed his last Boston in 2009 in 4:09:49.

Alberto Salazar

After graduating from Wayland High School and being recruited by Stanford University and the University of Oregon, Alberto headed to Eugene, where he was coached by legendary Ducks coach Bill Dellinger. While at Oregon, Alberto roomed with Rudy Chapa, another gifted runner he had met at a USA-USSR high school track meet in 1975 in Nebraska. Rudy, from Hammond, Indiana, was the son of a Mexican steel mill laborer and the first of his family to attend college.

In 1978, while between years at Oregon, Alberto dueled with Bill Rodgers at the Falmouth Road Race, ultimately suffering a serious case of heatstroke and recording body temperatures as high as 107 degrees before he was stabilized. Alberto was administered the Last Rites and hospitalized. This near-death experience convinced him that he was unbreakable and could "out-tough" any opponent he encountered.

Once he graduated from Oregon, Alberto signed a deal worth $50,000 to run for Athletics West, a club for post-collegiate runners sponsored by Nike. Adidas had been wooing him with the same amount of cash; the only difference was that the Swoosh offered him the possibility of future employment with the company at its Beaverton, Oregon campus, outside of Portland. Alberto liked that idea, so he signed on the dotted line.

As it was for Dick Beardsley, the 1982 "Duel in the Sun" at the Boston Marathon also proved to be the zenith of Alberto's marathoning career. He would win in New York again that fall but then nevermore at the 26.2-mile distance, qualifying for the 1984 US Olympic team but finishing a distant 15th on a hot day in Los Angeles.

Dismayed by his 1984 Olympic performance, Alberto determined to "out tough" his opponents by training harder and longer, increasing his 120-mile weekly regimen to 180 to 200 miles. Soon, this led to a breakdown of his immune system, leaving him ill, injured, and unable to train. After he failed to make the 1988 and 1992 US Olympic marathon teams, he retired from competitive running and took a marketing job at Nike.

Briefly unretired in 1994, Alberto won the 56-mile Comrades Marathon, contested annually in South Africa, then moved from marketing at Nike to coaching. He took the reins of "The Oregon Project," a company-financed program in which Alberto recruited and worked with young, promising runners, hoping to return Americans to prominence in the ranks of international distance running. Some of his charges included Alan Webb, Galen Rupp, Adam and Kara Boucher, and Mo Farah, a British runner who won the gold medal in both the 5,000- and 10,000-meters at both the 2012 London and 2016 Rio Olympics.

In June 2007, Alberto experienced a massive heart attack and was clinically dead, without a pulse, for fourteen minutes, as documented in his autobiography, *14 Minutes: A Running Legend's Life and Death and Life.* Miraculously, he was revived and suffered no ill effects aside from some short-term memory loss.

In June 2015, Salazar was named in a joint BBC Panorama and ProPublica doping allegation investigation, which involved alleged micro-dosing of testosterone and prednisone at the Oregon Project. After appeals, he and Dr. Jeffrey Brown, a colleague, were banned from the sport for four years by the US Anti-Doping Agency effective September 2019. He denied all charges and planned one final appeal to the International Court for Arbitration for Sport.

A month later, *The New York Times* published an op-ed account by high school distance ace and Oregon Project runner Mary Cain, who claimed mental and verbal abuse under Coach Salazar's supervision. In response, Nike closed down their pioneering development program down. A follow up investigation by *Sports Illustrated,* interviewing eight other project athletes, validated Cain's claims, painting "a picture of a toxic culture where female athletes' bodies were fair game to be demeaned publicly." The US Center for SafeSport, with exclusive authority over sexual abuse within the US Olympic community, also suspended Salazar from coaching in January 2020.

In his statement denying those charges, Alberto concluded, "While I disagree with what Mary has said publicly about her treatment by Oregon Project coaches and staff, her underlying message that elite coaching needs more women is a good one."

At last report, Nike was continuing to support Salazar as he appealed his doping suspension.

Jock Semple

Guardian, patron saint, and defender of the Boston Marathon, Jock suffered neither fools nor bandit runners lightly, declaring to *Sports Illustrated* in 1968, "These screwballs! These weirdies! These MIT boys! These Tufts characters! These Harvard guys! They write me askin' should they put on spiked shoes for the marathon!"

We've already seen how Jock tried to prevent Katherine Switzer from running in 1967, how he refused to give me a status update on my entry in 1976, and how he and co-race director Will Cloney lowered the marathon qualifying time in 1977 and again in 1980 to reduce the number of runners.

But it didn't work. By the time Jock passed away from pancreatic cancer at age eighty-four in 1988 in Peabody, Massachusetts, his race boasted 6,758 entries.

After the marathon authorized its first female entries in 1972, Jock reconciled with Katherine Switzer, who visited him in the hospital during his terminal illness.

Frank Shorter

After his graduation from Yale in 1969, Frank entered medical school at the University of New Mexico in Albuquerque, only to withdraw after six weeks because it was interfering with his training regimen. Relocating to Gainesville, Florida in the spring of 1970 to train with the Florida Track Club, he later entered and graduated from the University of Florida of Law School.

As I researched his post-collegiate training techniques, it turned out that Frank—who, in his book *My Marathon: Reflections on a Gold Medal Life,* referred to himself as largely self-coached—was doing exactly the same stuff that Bill Squires had Rodgers, Scottie, Alberto, and me doing three and four years later. Mileage, intervals, and hills.

Frank focused on the 5,000- and 10,000-meters as he exited college and then punted med school. That required him to hammer repeat track interval workouts, both on the European track circuit in the summer of 1969, with Steve Prefontaine, and a year later, with his Florida Track Club teammates Jack Bacheler, Jeff Galloway, and John Parker.

Trading up to the marathon as his primary event, he supplemented his time on the track with mileage, lots of it, at elevation. After triumphing in Japan's prestigious Fukuoka Marathon in 1971, Shorter prepared for the 1972 Olympic trials with a 120-mile weeks of combined long runs at altitude in Vail, Colorado (8,150 feet above sea level) and interval workouts in Boulder (5,328 feet). Frank pithily summarized it this way: "I trained like a 5-K runner while, as a competitor, I placed the bulk of my chips in the marathon."

As we've already seen, this was clearly a formula for success at the Munich Olympics, as Frank touched off the American running boom. He captured Fukuoka again in 1972, 1973, and 1974 before coming up just short at Montreal in 1976 to a chemically assisted Waldemar Cierpinski.

Shorter faced off again against Rodgers at New York in 1976 and Boston in 1977, suffering a foot injury in the latter that would require surgery. At age thirty-three, Frank was past his prime and injured when he rang up a 2:24 at the 1980 US Olympic Trials.

In the meantime, he was leveraging his marathoning cred to develop business interests, including a line of running apparel and a running specialty store in his adopted home of Boulder, Colorado. He also worked as a running commentator for NBC, spoke at race and marathon expos, and gave media interviews.

In January of 1998, Frank had dinner with Dr. Werner Franke, who had spearheaded the investigation into the East German Olympic athletic doping program of the 1960s and 1970s. One week later, Dr. Franke faxed Shorter some documents implicating 1976 and 1980 Olympic marathon gold medalist Waldemar Cierpinski's participation in the project.

Rather than seek to overturn Cierpinski's 1976 Olympic marathon victory and claim for himself a second gold medal, Shorter sought to prevent future athletic drug cheating by recommending to the Clinton administration an independent, government-funded agency that would be responsible for all drug testing and enforcement. This would no longer be the bailiwick of officials within the individual sport federations, who were not always entirely objective.

To Frank's surprise, this led to the creation of the US Anti-Doping Agency, to which in 2000 he was named chairman and board member. He served on the agency until 2003.

Also continuing his active schedule of personal appearances, Frank appeared in November 2010 with Bill Rodgers and Dick Beardsley at a Boys and Girls Town in Springfield, Missouri. Addressing the disadvantaged youth in the audience with entirely unscripted remarks, he suddenly launched into a previously never before detailed account of the abuse he suffered as a child at the hands of his father.

After he had concluded his remarks, a young girl from the audience approached him, saying simply, "That story you told, that's my story. All of those things happened to me. The way you tried to keep one step ahead of your father and worried about your sisters and brothers—that was me you were talking about."

As Frank later wrote in his book, "That day, that girl, snapped my feelings into focus. I had a responsibility to tell my story, which could be of use to people like this young woman."

Word of his revelation slowly spread, and soon Frank was contacted by a journalist from *Runner's World* seeking permission to update his profile incorporating this new and previously untold angle. After a great deal of personal deliberation, Frank agreed to do the article and allowed the scribe to contact his siblings for corroborative purposes.

Frank lives in Boulder, Colorado.

Bill Squires

Coach Squires was another guy who was athletically hungry from an early age. It seems a doctor diagnosed him with a "weak heart" at age seven and consequently sentenced him to complete inactivity, such that his mother wheeled him about in a baby carriage at precisely the time when he longed to run faster and jump higher.

His incarceration lasted four years, until another doc more realistically determined young Billy had a heart murmur that he would outgrow in his teens. As Squires later recounted, "Well that was…I wanted to marry the guy! Geez*! I've got wings now!* I was out of the friggin' room—I wanted to play!"

After winning three Massachusetts state championships in the mile at Arlington High School and being named to the 1952 *Parade Magazine* All-American Team, Bill accepted a scholarship to Notre Dame, where we've already briefly summarized his successes on the trail and the track. Graduating in June of 1956, Bill married Sally Kuhn in July and was drafted into the US Army in August. He spent the next two years in Europe as a part of the CIA, investigating military aircraft crashes to determine their cause and competing in track meets across the continent as a four-minute miler.

In the fall of 1958, Squires accepted a Biology teaching position at Wakefield, Massachusetts High School and that spring became the institute's track and cross-country coach. Shortly thereafter, in 1961, he finished 20th in his first Boston Marathon in 2:47:46, banned from future Bostons due to the fact that he accepted a salary as Wakefield's coach and thus was technically not an amateur, thereby running afoul of the Amateur Athletic Union rules in effect at the time.

In 1963, Billy left Wakefield to become an Associate Professor of Physical Education and, again, coach of track and field at Division III Boston State College. As he perfected his coaching techniques, frequently running right alongside his charges, the Boston State program began to enjoy tremendous success, winning prestigious regional spring outdoor track and field championships.

He also advised running clubs, conducted clinics, and traveled internationally to coach athletes and coaches at all levels. In 1971, Squires was drafted by the government for a second time—on this occasion, by the US State Department—to go to India for three months as coach and consultant to help its coaches and athletes prepare for the 1972 Munich and the 1976 Montreal Olympics.

As his running commitments continued to pile up, including his 1973 agreement to coach the GBTC, Bill continued to run, finishing about 15 minutes ahead of me in 2:48:29 at the 1978 Boston Marathon.

After four GBTC marathoners cracked the top 10 at Boston in 1979—first place Rodgers, third place Bobby Hodge, eighth place Randy Thomas, and tenth place Dickie Mahoney, Squires was approached by the US Olympic Committee about joining the 1980 US team staff as a specialty coach of the 10,000-meter and marathon runners. This offer, of course, became moot when President Carter pulled the plug on American participation in the Moscow Olympics.

Bill retired as full-time coach of GBTC in October of 1980 to assume a similar role with, as he called it, "the new club in town," the New Balance

Track Club, where he tutored Dick Beardsley, among others. He remained active in a consulting role with GBTC until 1985.

Squires retired as professor and coach from Boston State successor institution University of Massachusetts at Boston in 1991. His coaching legacy is overwhelming.

Allow me to quote from his biography, *Born to Coach*, by Paul Clerici: "In 18 cross-country, indoor and outdoor track seasons at Boston State, he accumulated a combined record of 274-84. In addition to that .765 winning percentage, he was named National Association of Intercollegiate Athletes Coach of the Year three times, won 49 team championship titles, and coached four NCAA champions, six New England champions and 16 collegiate All-Americans."

However, Bill is proudest of those he mentored who themselves became teachers and coaches. "I had about 50 kids in total (as coaches/ teachers), and at one time there were about five college coaches. That was something!"

He lives in Reading, Massachusetts.

Chris Wiley

Chris later admitted during junior year at Dartmouth to barely surviving the horror of prepping Jim for his bone graft surgery. As a means of expunging his harrowing mental images of that experience, he busied himself with his pre-med studies.

His future bride, Peg, convinced him to geographically expand his pool of med school applications to California, where, via an unexpected thunderbolt, he was accepted at Stanford Medical School. Soon he found himself wandering, starry-eyed, among majestic eucalyptus trees and beautiful people. He certainly wasn't in New Hampshire anymore!

Peg and Chris were married after his first year of med school, and they remained in the Bay Area for his internship in surgery at the University of California at San Francisco and his residency in anesthesiology at Stanford.

The vision of raising a family in New England drove Chris to drag Peg back to Portland, Maine so he could join the staff at Maine Medical Center. Their firstborn, Michael, appeared shortly thereafter.

After subsequent stints in California and Northern Arizona, the trio returned to New England, and Chris then entered a private practice in western Massachusetts for eight years, at which point second son Ben joined them, and Peg earned her master's degree in English Literature.

His final career move occurred when he joined the faculty at Dartmouth Hitchcock Medical Center, where he remained for twenty-three very fulfilling years. Peg went on to earn her PhD and land a tenured faculty position at Colby Sawyer College.

Retirement for both Chris and Peg came in 2015, along with a move back to Portland, Maine, where both their grown sons, Michael and Ben, and their grandson, Sam, also live.

Allison Riehl Konrad

After her baptism at the Brick Presbyterian Church in New York City, Allison spent her formative years in Green Bay, Wisconsin and New Canaan, Connecticut, where (unlike her father) she lettered as the captain of her high school swimming team. Then it was off to Miami University (Ohio) to major in sociology and business, facilitating her entry into a career in consumer market research. An avid Green Bay Packers fan, Allison currently lives in Manhattan with her husband, Greg, and her son, Chase.

Pete Riehl

Excelling at soccer and ice hockey well into his high school years, Pete also scored the varsity letters his father never did. From there, he attended Rochester Institute of Technology, playing freshman soccer, graduating with a degree in computer science, and demonstrating a technical acumen unseen in previous family generations. Pete now develops software for a New York City investment firm and lives in South Orange, New Jersey with his wife, Annie, and his two sons, Jack and Elliot.

Denise Riehl

While a full-time mom to Pete and Allison, Denise oversaw the construction of the family's two new homes in Monroe, Connecticut and Green Bay, Wisconsin. She continues to facilitate the realization of her clients' residential design dreams through her company, The Riehl Design House, and enjoys frequent trips into the design centers in Manhattan. When not scoping out her next project, Denise can be found sunning by the pool, occasionally hanging out with her three grandsons, or watching a movie with Jim at their place in Fairfield, Connecticut.

Jim Riehl

After five successful years at Nestle, I graduated to a succession of increasingly responsible corporate marketing, sales, and strategic management positions at a series of consumer products and business services companies in the Midwestern and Northeastern United States.

After moving on from General Mills, twice more my career was interrupted, and I spent an extended period, in job search parlance, "on the beach," once due to a merger of unequal firms and once because I landed on an unsalvageable business that subsequently went bankrupt.

More recently, I have done strategy and marketing consulting for small businesses.

Perhaps some of those experiences will be the subject of my next musings. Certainly, as a stand-up comedian might say, there's "plenty of material" there.

At any rate, as I researched *these* musings, I realized may not have possessed the same fleetness of foot as Shorter, Rodgers, Salazar, or Beardsley, but I learned I had more in common with each of them than ever I thought.

With Shorter, I was a preppie who got into running through an impromptu run around campus, then went on to an Ivy League college.

With Rodgers, I shared some of the same reservations about being drafted into the US military and then, for a short time, became a teacher.

With Salazar, I shared the same ineptitude in middle school sports, the "marathon shuffle," and later in life, some heart health issues.

With Beardsley, we both ran because we wouldn't be lettering in high school football, and we were both injured in accidents involving power equipment.

One thing I don't share with any of these guys anymore is the ability to run. Due to orthopedic constraints, these days I'm limited to the stationary bike, the elliptical trainer, and the treadmill. Those things are a poor substitute for the long runs along Duxbury Beach or the thrill of Patriots' Day, but my memories will just have to suffice.

Awaiting our next great adventure, Denise and I are camped out in Fairfield, Connecticut.

PHOTO GALLERY

1967

Jim, jersey number obscured, is third from the right in the front row. At age 15, as offensive guard and linebacker, he's already in trouble, since they always put the shortest, lightest guys in the foreground.

1968

Appearing as Number 60 in the back row, here's Jim as seen in the 1968 Hill-Lawrenceville football program. And that's just about all the visibility he got, as the prep school junior chronically rode the pine.

1973

Captured for posterity in a jigsaw puzzle, bandits Jim (left) and Alan Knobel (right) at the start if the 1973 Boston Marathon. Less than seven miles later, they dropped out, to the extreme disenchantment of the spectators.

1974

All smiles after completing his very first B.A.A. Marathon, Jim poses with Denise in front of their trusty VW Super Beetle. He won't be smiling later, when he takes off his shoe to deal with the huge blister on the bottom of his right foot.

1974

Bill Pollock shows good form.

Inauspiociously misidentified as "Bill Pollock" in *The Duxbury Clipper*, Jim brings it on home to capture 4th place in the 1974 Turkey Trot.

Courtesy of *The Duxbury Clipper*

1976

Garnering their 15 minutes of fame, Jim and Scott Graham are front page news in the *Old Colony Memorial* five days before the 1976 Boston Marathon.

Courtesy of wickedlocal.com

1976

After he survived the 100+ degree "Run for the Hoses" B.A.A. Marathon, Jim and sister Laurie grab the first available photo op outside the Pru.

1976

Seated in the back row out of harm's way, Jim tends to the Section D gong at Harvard Business School

Courtesy of David Vogt

1977

Ailing right hamstring securely wrapped, Jim descends the Queensboro Bridge onto First Avenue in the 1977 NYC Marathon.

Courtesy of Alan H. Knobel

1981

In a new PR of 2 hours, 46 minutes and 38 seconds, Jim crosses the Prudential Center finish line at the 1981 Boston Marathon, albeit right behind a Yalie.

1981

Denise and Jim, happily reunited after Jim's PR at the 1981 Boston Marathon.

1982

A wayward breeze tousles the General Mills banner as the team march-
es in the opening ceremonies of the Corporate Cup Relays in Palo Alto,
CA. Subsequently, the supremely talented competition would similarly
tousle the General Mills team.

Courtesy of C. David Gelly

1982

One of the General Mills Corporate Cup Relays teams, from left: Tony Benthin, Jim, Mike Dahnert, Bill Lombardo and John Eldredge.

Courtesy of C. David Gelly

1982

Jim chasing down his dream at the Corporate Cup Relays.

Courtesy of Lauren R. Martin

1982

Headed downhill in downtown St. Paul, a weary looking Jim shuffles to the finish of the inaugural Twin Cities Marathon.

1983

Primed for their trek to International Falls and whatever adventures might ensue, the Bombardiers pose in front of their RV.

Courtesy of C. David Gelly

1983

Fresh off their victory over Winnipeg's own Meter Eaters, Jim and Bubba Gelly brandish the IF Cup.

Courtesy of C. David Gelly

1983

After triumphing in one of the Richfield, Minnesota Corporate Cup Regional relays, Jim and Tony Benthin share the victory stand with 8-month old "Re-Pete," who is awarded a gold medal just for showing up.

1983

Jim and Bubba Gelly cross swords with other Fortune 500-ers in the 1983 Corporate Cup 10 K Final in Palo Alto, CA.

1983

Jim mans the middle of the pack in one of his 127 road races.

1986

Life after Chasing Down a Dream: Allison, Pete, Denise and Jim in 1986.

Courtesy of C. David Gelly

TABLE 1: MILEAGE*

	Year												Total
	1973	1974	1975	1976	1977	1978	1979	1980	1981	1982	1983	1984	
January	NA	NA	NA	308	298	17	NA	221	390	283	90	NA	
February	NA	NA	NA	371	405	186	NA	230	353	-	NA	NA	
March	NA	NA	NA	452	528	189	NA	378	481	52	8	NA	
April	7	37	27	385	266	364	NA	457	167	109	NA	NA	
May	NA	NA	NA	279	101	281	NA	440	311	131	31	NA	
June	NA	NA	NA	343	310	17	NA	179	134	239	90	NA	
July	NA	NA	NA	341	298	NA	NA	183	144	246	237	NA	
August	NA	NA	32	306	371	NA	NA	258	74	407	68	NA	
September	NA	NA	312	250	426	NA	NA	218	207	325	NA	NA	
October	NA	NA	273	172	307	NA	NA	284	240	127	27	12	
November	NA	4	288	150	255	27	NA	353	331	50	NA	NA	
December	NA	NA	190	270	186	NA	17	282	431	50	NA	NA	
Total	7	41	1,122	3,627	3,751	1,071	17	3,483	3,263	2,019	551	12	18,964

* Only reflects documented mileage run between April 1973 and October 1984. Does not reflect mileage run before or after.

314

TABLE 2: TRACK WORKOUTS

| # | Date | Location | \multicolumn{11}{c}{Interval Distance In Miles} | | | | | | | | | | | Total |
			1	2	3	4	5	6	7	8	9	10	11	
1	1/24/76	Tufts / GBTC	0.375	0.75	1.125	0.75								3
2	1/27/76	Tufts / GBTC	0.25	0.25	0.25	0.25	0.25	0.5						1.75
3	2/3/76	Tufts / GBTC	0.5	0.5	0.5	0.5	0.5	0.5	0.5					3.5
4	2/7/76	Tufts / GBTC	0.5	0.5	0.75	0.5	0.5	1						3.75
5	2/24/76	Tufts / GBTC	0.75	0.75	0.5	0.5	0.375	0.375	0.375	0.375				4
6	3/12/76	Tufts / GBTC	0.5	0.5	0.5	0.375	0.375	0.375	0.375	0.375	0.375			3.75
7	3/16/76	Tufts / GBTC	0.5	1.5										2
8	3/20/76	Duxbury	0.25	0.25	0.25	0.5	0.5	0.5						2.25

315

#	Date	Location	Interval Distance In Miles											Total
			1	2	3	4	5	6	7	8	9	10	11	
9	4/1/76	BC / GBTC	0.25	0.25	0.25	0.25	0.25	0.5						**1.75**
10	4/6/76	BC / GBTC	0.1875	0.1875	0.188	0.1875	0.1875	0.1875	0.375					**1.5**
11	1/19/77	Harvard	0.363	0.363	0.363	0.363	0.363	0.182						**1.997**
12	1/24/77	Harvard	0.363	0.363	0.363	0.363	0.363	0.363	0.363					**2.541**
13	2/2/77	Harvard	0.454	0.454	0.454	0.454	0.363	0.363						**2.542**
14	2/10/77	Harvard	0.454	0.454	0.454	0.454	0.454	0.454						**2.724**
15	2/17/77	Harvard	0.545	0.545	0.545	0.454	0.454	0.454						**2.997**
16	3/3/77	Harvard	0.545	0.545	0.454	0.454	0.363	0.363	0.182	0.182				**3.088**
17	3/9/77	Harvard	0.545	0.545	0.545	0.545	0.545	0.545						**3.27**
18	3/16/77	Harvard	0.363	0.727	1.09	0.727	0.363							**3.27**
19	3/23/77	Harvard	0.545	0.818	1.181	0.818	0.545							**3.907**
20	3/30/77	Harvard	0.5	1	1.5	1	0.5							**4.5**
21	4/7/77	BC / GBTC	0.375	0.375	0.375	0.375	0.375	0.375						**2.25**
22	6/2/77	Harvard	0.25	0.25	0.25	0.25	0.25	0.25	0.25	0.25				**2**
23	6/6/77	Harvard	0.25	0.25	0.25	0.25	0.25	0.25	0.25	0.25				**2**

#	Date	Location	1	2	3	4	5	6	7	8	9	10	11	Total
							Interval Distance In Miles							
24	6/17/77	NY City	0.25	0.25	0.25	0.25	0.25	0.5	0.5					2.25
25	6/20/77	New York City	0.5	0.5	0.5	0.5	0.25							2.25
26	6/24/77	New York City	0.5	0.5	0.5	0.5	0.5							2.5
27	6/28/77	New York City	0.5	0.5	0.5	0.5	0.5	0.5						3
28	7/7/77	New York City	0.5	0.5	0.5	0.5	0.5	0.5						3
29	7/27/77	New York City	0.25	0.25	0.25	0.25	0.25	0.25	0.25	0.25	0.25	0.25		2.5
30	8/2/77	New York City	0.25	0.25	0.25	0.25	0.25	0.25	0.25	0.25	0.25	0.25		2.5
31	8/5/77	New York City	0.25	0.25	0.25	0.25	0.25	0.25	0.25	0.25	0.25	0.25	0.25	2.75
32	8/10/77	New York City	0.25	0.25	0.25	0.25	0.25	0.25	0.5	0.5	0.5			3
33	8/15/77	New York City	0.25	0.5	0.5	0.25	0.5	0.5	0.5					3
34	8/18/77	New York City	0.25	0.5	0.5	0.75	0.5	0.5	0.25					3.25
35	8/24/77	New York City	0.25	0.5	0.5	0.75	0.5	0.5	0.25					3.25
36	8/31/77	New York City	0.25	0.5	0.5	0.75	0.5	0.5	0.25					3.25

#	Date	Location	1	2	3	4	5	6	7	8	9	10	11	Total
37	9/15/77	Harvard	0.25	0.5	0.5	1	0.5	0.5	0.25					3.5
38	9/20/77	Harvard	0.272	0.545	1	0.272	0.545	1	0.545					4.179
39	9/22/77	Harvard	0.25	0.5	1	0.25	0.5	1	0.25					3.75
40	9/27/77	Harvard	0.25	0.5	1	0.25	0.5	1.5	0.25					4.25
41	9/29/77	Harvard	0.25	1	1.5	1	0.25							4
42	10/4/77	Harvard	0.25	0.5	1	0.25	0.5	1.5	0.25					4.25
43	10/6/77	Harvard	0.25	1	1.5	1	0.25							4
44	10/10/77	Harvard	0.25	0.5	1	0.25	0.5	1.5	0.25					4.25
45	10/12/77	BC GBTC	0.375	0.375	0.375	0.375	0.375	0.375						2.25
46	4/25/78	Harvard	0.25	0.5	1	0.25	0.5	1	0.25					3.75
47	4/27/78	Harvard	0.25	0.5	1	0.25	0.5	1	0.25					3.75
48	5/2/78	Harvard	0.5	1	1.5	1	0.5							4.5
49	5/10/78	Harvard	0.5	1	1.5	1	0.5							4.5
50	5/12/78	Harvard	0.5	1	1.5	1	0.5							4.5
51	5/17/78	Harvard	0.5	1										1.5

#	Date	Location	Interval Distance In Miles												Total
			1	2	3	4	5	6	7	8	9	10	11	12	
52	4/16/80	St. Louis Park	0.125	0.125	0.125	0.125	0.125	0.25	0.125						1
53	4/23/80	St. Louis Park	0.125	0.25	0.25	0.25	0.25	0.25	0.25	0.25	0.25	0.125			2.25
54	4/30/80	St. Louis Park	0.125	0.25	0.25	0.25	0.25	0.25	0.25	0.25	0.25	0.25	0.25	0.125	2.75
55	5/3/80	St. Louis Park	0.125	0.25	0.5	0.25	0.5	0.25	0.5	0.25	0.25	0.125			3
56	5/6/80	St. Louis Park	0.125	0.25	0.5	0.25	0.5	0.25	0.5	0.25	0.5	0.125			3.25
57	5/8/80	St. Louis Park	0.125	0.25	0.5	0.25	0.5	0.25	0.5	0.25	0.5	0.25	0.5	0.25	4.125
58	5/13/80	St. Louis Park	0.125	0.25	0.5	0.75	0.25	0.5	0.75	0.25	0.125				3.5
59	5/15/80	St. Louis Park	0.125	0.25	0.5	0.25	0.5	1	0.25	0.125					3
60	5/20/80	St. Louis Park	0.125	0.25	0.5	1	0.5	1	0.5	0.25	0.125				4.25
61	5/22/80	St. Louis Park	0.125	0.25	0.5	1	0.75	1	0.5	0.25	0.125				4.5
62	5/27/80	St. Louis Park	0.125	0.25	0.5	1	1	1	0.5	0.25	0.125				4.75
63	6/3/80	St. Louis Park	0.125	0.25	0.5	1	1.5	1	0.5	0.25	0.125				5.25
64	6/7/80	St. Louis Park	0.125	0.25	0.5	0.5									1.375
65	6/9/80	St. Louis Park	0.125	0.25	0.5	1	1.5	1	1						5.375
66	8/21/80	New Hope	0.125	0.25	0.25	0.25	0.5	0.125							1.5
67	8/28/80	New Hope	0.125	0.25	0.25	0.25	0.25	0.5	0.125						1.75

#	Date	Location	1	2	3	4	5	6	7	8	9	10	11	Total
68	10/8/80	New Hope	0.125	0.25	0.25	0.25	0.25	0.25	0.25	0.25	0.25	0.125		2.25
69	1/22/81	JCC	0.142	0.142	0.142	0.142	0.142	0.142	0.142	0.142	0.142	0.142	0.142	1.562
70	1/24/81	JCC	0.213	0.213	0.213	0.213	0.213	0.213	0.213					1.491
71	1/27/81	JCC	0.213	0.213	0.213	0.213	0.213	0.213	0.213	0.213	0.213	0.213	0.5	2.63
72	1/29/81	JCC	0.284	0.284	0.284	0.284	0.284	0.284	0.284	0.284	0.284	0.284		2.84
73	1/31/81	JCC	0.284	0.284	0.284	0.284	0.284	0.284	0.284	0.284	0.284	0.284	0.284	3.408
74	2/5/81	JCC	0.142	0.284	0.284	0.284	0.5	0.284	0.284					2.062
75	2/10/81	JCC	0.142	0.284	0.284	0.284	0.284	0.5	0.284					2.062
76	2/12/81	JCC	0.142	0.284	0.284	0.284	0.284	0.284	0.284	0.284	0.284	0.284	0.284	3.266
77	2/26/81	JCC	0.142	0.284	0.284	0.284	0.284	0.5	0.284	0.142			0.284	2.204
78	2/28/81	JCC	0.142	0.284	0.5	0.5	1	0.5	0.284	0.142				3.352
79	3/3/81	JCC	0.142	0.284	0.5	0.5	1	0.5	0.284	0.142			0.284	3.352
80	3/5/81	JCC	0.142	0.284	0.284	0.284	0.284	0.284	0.284	0.284	0.284	0.284	0.142	3.124
81	3/7/81	JCC	0.142	0.284	0.5	1	1	1	0.5	0.284	0.142			4.852
82	3/10/81	JCC	0.142	0.284	0.5	1	1.5	1	0.5	0.284	0.142			5.352
83	3/12/81	JCC	0.142	0.284	0.284	0.284								0.994
84	3/17/81	JCC	0.142	0.284	0.5	1	1.5	1	0.5	0.284	0.142			5.352

Interval Distance In Miles

#	Date	Location					Interval Distance In Miles							Total
			1	2	3	4	5	6	7	8	9	10	11	
85	3/19/81	JCC	0.142	0.284	0.284	0.284	0.284	0.284	0.284	0.284	0.284	0.284	0.284	0.142 → **3.124**
86	3/21/81	JCC	0.142	0.284	0.5	1	2	1	0.5	0.284	0.142			**5.852**
87	3/24/81	JCC	0.142	0.284	0.5	1	2	1	0.5	0.284	0.142			**5.852**
88	3/26/81	JCC	0.142	0.284	0.5	1	2	1	0.5	0.284	0.142			**5.852**
89	3/31/81	JCC	0.142	0.284	0.5	1	2	1	0.5	0.284	0.142			**5.852**
90	4/2/81	JCC	0.142	0.284	0.5	1	2	1	0.5	0.284	0.142			**5.852**
91	4/9/81	JCC	0.355	0.355	0.355	0.355	0.355	0.355						**2.13**
92	5/7/81	St. Louis Park	0.25	0.25	0.25	0.25	0.25	0.25	0.25	0.25				**2**
93	5/13/81	St. Louis Park	0.125	0.25	0.5	1	1.5	1	0.5	0.25	0.125			**5.25**
94	5/26/81	JCC	0.142	0.284	0.5	1	2	1	0.5	0.284	0.142			**5.852**
95	5/28/81	JCC	0.284	0.284	0.284	0.284	0.284	0.284	0.284	0.284	0.284	0.284	0.284	0.284 → **3.408**
96	7/6/81	New Hope	0.25	0.5	1	0.5	0.25							**2.5**
97	7/8/81	New Hope	0.25	0.5	1	0.5	0.5	0.25						**3**
98	1/7/82	JCC	0.071	0.071	0.071	0.071	0.071	0.071	0.071	0.071	0.071	0.071	0.071	**0.781**
99	1/9/82	JCC	0.071	0.071	0.071	0.071	0.071	0.142	0.142	0.142	0.142	0.142		**1.065**
100	1/12/82	JCC	0.071	0.142	0.142	0.142	0.142	0.142	0.142	0.142	0.142	0.142	0.142	0.071 → **1.562**
101	1/14/82	New Hope	0.071	0.071	0.142	0.284	0.142	0.071	0.071	0.142	0.142	0.142		**1.136**

#	Date	Location	1	2	3	4	5	6	7	8	9	10	11	Total
102	6/19/82	New Hope	0.125	0.125	0.125	0.25	0.125	0.25	0.125	0.25	0.125	0.25	0.125	1.875
103	6/21/82	New Hope	0.125	0.25	0.125	0.25	0.125	0.25	0.125	0.25	0.125	0.25	0.125	2
104	6/23/82	New Hope	0.125	0.25	0.125	0.25	0.125	0.25	0.125	0.25	0.125	0.25	0.125	2
105	6/30/82	New Hope	0.125	0.25	0.25	0.25	0.25	0.25	0.25	0.25	0.125			2
106	7/2/82	New Hope	0.125	0.25	0.25	0.25	0.25	0.25	0.25	0.25	0.25	0.125		2.25
107	7/8/82	New Hope	0.125	0.25	0.25	0.25	0.25	0.25	0.25	0.25	0.25	0.25	0.125	2.5
108	8/5/82	New Hope	0.125	0.25	0.25	0.25	0.25	0.25	0.25	0.25	0.25	0.25	0.125	2.5
109	8/26/82	New Hope	0.125	0.25	0.5	1	0.5	0.25	0.125	0.25				3
110	9/2/82	New Hope	0.125	0.25	0.5	1	0.5	0.25	0.125	0.25				3
111	9/16/82	St. Louis Park	1	1	1	0.25								3.25
112	6/23/83	New Hope	0.25	0.25	0.5	0.25	0.25							1.5
113	7/7/83	New Hope	0.125	0.25	0.5	1	0.5	0.25	0.125					2.75
114	7/14/83	New Hope	0.125	0.25	0.5	1	0.5	0.25	0.125	0.125				2.875
115	8/2/83	New Hope	0.125	0.25	0.5	1	0.5	0.25	0.125					2.75

TOTAL MILES 354.861

322

TABLE 3: ROAD RACES

#	Date	Event	Location	Miles	Time	Per Mile	Place	Out Of
1	4/16/73	Boston Marathon	Boston, MA	6.7	DNF	NA	NA	NA
2	4/15/74	Boston Marathon	Boston, MA	26.2	3.40.00	8.24	NA	NA
3	11/17/74	Turkey Run	Duxbury, MA	4.0	22.50	5.42	4th	NA
4	4/5/75	Jaycees 10.4 Mile Race	Duxbury, MA	10.4	59.48	5.75	12th	NA
5	4/15/75	Boston Marathon	Boston, MA	26.2	3.08.30	7.12	NA	NA
6	8/3/75	Gurnet Beach Run	Duxbury, MA	6.2	40.52	6.36	38th	NA
7	8/9/75	Scituate Road Race	Scituate, MA	6.0	37.19	6.13	20th	NA
8	10/12/75	New England 15 KM Race	Manchester, NH	9.3	56.00	6.01	NA	NA
9	10/13/75	4.7 Mile Run	Bridgewater, MA	4.7	25.55	5.31	NA	NA
10	11/22/75	Turkey Run	Duxbury, MA	4.0	22.15 *	5.34	3rd	NA
11	11/30/75	Philadelphia Marathon	Philadelphia, PA	26.2	2.54.46	6.40	NA	141
12	2/1/76	9.75 Mile Race	Lynn, MA	9.75	59.47	6.08	39th	NA
13	2/15/76	Newark Distance Run	Newark, NJ	12.0	1.14.24	6.12	NA	NA
14	2/29/76	9.32 Mile Run	Providence, RI	9.32	56.03	6.01	35th	NA
15	3/7/76	NEAAU 25 KM Championship	Holliston, MA	15.6	1.33.57 *	6.01	44th	NA
16	3/28/76	NEAAU 30 KM Championship	Schenectady, NY	18.6	1.53.04 *	6.05	96th	359
17	4/19/76	Boston Marathon	Boston, MA	26.2	3.08.39	7.12	634th	1,942

#	Date	Event	Location	Miles	Time	Per Mile	Place	Out Of
18	4/24/76	Jaycees 10.4 Mile Race	Duxbury, MA	10.4	1.00.57	5.52	18th	94
19	5/9/76	Western Reserve Marathon	Hudson, OH	26.2	2.55.38	6.42	23rd	209
20	6/18/76	Kingston Road Race	Kingston, MA	5.8	32.50	5.40	29th	120
21	7/18/76	Marshfield 20 KM Race	Marshfield, MA	12.4	1.15.02	6.03	33rd	116
22	8/22/76	Gurnet Beach Run	Duxbury, MA	6.2	36.45	5.56	28th	NA
23	10/10/76	New England 15 KM Race	Manchester, NH	9.3	57.10	6.09	NA	NA
24	10/17/76	12.15 Mile Road Race	Hanover, NH	12.15	1.15.04	6.11	12th	92
25	2/6/77	9.75 Mile Race	Lynn, MA	9.75	59.38	6.07	NA	NA
26	3/6/77	NEAAU 25 KM Championship	Holliston, MA	15.6	1.34.06	6.02	68th	241
27	3/12/77	Fresh Pond	Cambridge, MA	2.5	13.58	5.35	33rd	120
28	3/20/77	9.3 Mile Race	Brighton, MA	9.3	51.54 *	5.36	51st	215
29	3/27/77	9.3 Mile Race	Lexington, MA	9.3	NA	NA	NA	NA
30	4/3/77	9.69 Mile Race	Wellesley, MA	9.69	57.47	5.58	61st	561
31	4/18/77	Boston Marathon	Boston, MA	26.2	2.51.53	6.34	521st	2,766
32	4/23/77	Norwell Clip Along	Norwell, MA	10.0	1.00.30 *	6.03	6th	NA
33	7/3/77	Chicago Distance Classic	Chicago, IL	12.4	NA	NA	NA	NA
34	7/17/77	Marshfield 20 KM Race	Marshfield, MA	12.4	1.21.52	6.36	21st	113
35	7/30/77	Gurnet Beach Run	Duxbury, MA	6.2	39.41	6.24	NA	NA
36	8/21/77	Falmouth Road Race	Woods Hole, MA	7.0	41.39	5.57	205th	2,820
37	8/28/77	Around Cape Ann 25 KM	Gloucester, MA	15.6	1.42.43	6.35	24th	371

#	Date	Event	Location	Miles	Time	Per Mile	Place	Out Of
38	9/25/77	Schlitz Lite Classic	Waltham, MA	13.1	1.21.40	6.14	135th	NA
39	10/2/77	Freedom Trail Road Race	Boston, MA	8.0	47.30	5.56	121st	3,000
40	10/23/77	New York City Marathon	New York, NY	26.2	2.46.59	6.22	279th	3,664
41	4/17/78	Boston Marathon	Boston, MA	26.2	3.02.49	6.59	2,172nd	4,391
42	4/30/78	Marsh Post 12-Miler	Boston, MA	12.0	1.13.59	6.10	30th	NA
43	5/7/78	Charles River Run	Boston, MA	7.0	44.00	6.17	NA	NA
44	7/17/78	Marathon Marathon	Terre Haute, IN	17.0	DNF	NA	NA	NA
45	11/5/78	Longest Day Marathon	Brookings, SD	26.2	3.20.00	7.38	NA	NA
46	3/16/80	St. Pat's 5-Mile	Minneapolis, MN	5.0	31.58	6.24	NA	NA
47	3/22/80	Hopkins 25 KM Run	Hopkins, MN	15.6	NA	NA	NA	NA
48	4/12/80	Fred Kurz Memorial 10 Mile	Minneapolis, MN	10.0	1.01.28	6.09	NA	NA
49	4/19/80	Unboston Marathon 10 KM	Minneapolis, MN	6.2	37.07	5.59	NA	NA
50	4/26/80	Get In Gear 10 KM	Minneapolis, MN	6.2	37.20	6.02	NA	NA
51	5/17/80	Syttendai Mai 16.3 Mile Run	Grantsburg, WI	16.3	1.51.20	6.50	NA	NA
52	5/24/80	Lowry Hill Climb	Minneapolis, MN	5.0	30.10	6.02	NA	NA
53	5/31/80	St. Louis Park Mini-Marathon	St. Louis Park, MN	4.0	23.07	5.47	NA	NA
54	6/14/80	Do It Downtown 10 KM	Minneapolis, MN	6.2	40.10	6.29	NA	NA
55	6/21/80	Grandma's Marathon	Duluth, MN	26.2	2.47.11	6.23	153rd	2,375
56	7/3/80	Tartan Terrible	St. Paul, MN	4.75	28.34	6.01	NA	NA
57	7/20/80	Raspberry 5-Mile Run	Hopkins, MN	5.0	30.50	6.10	NA	NA

#	Date	Event	Location	Miles	Time	Per Mile	Place	Out Of
58	7/23/80	Aquatennial 8-Mile Run	Minneapolis, MN	8.0	49.27	6.11	NA	NA
59	8/23/80	Steve Smith Track 10-Mile	New Hope, MN	10.0	1.03.07	6.19	NA	NA
60	8/30/80	Minnesota AAU 20 KM	Brooklyn Center, MN	12.4	1.19.18	6:24	NA	NA
61	9/20/80	Dannon 15 KM	Minneapolis, MN	9.3	56.14	6.03	NA	NA
62	10/5/80	Freedom Trail Road Race	Boston, MA	9.3	50.08	6.16	NA	NA
63	10/11/80	Run For Your Life 15 KM	Minneapolis, MN	9.3	58.04	6.14	NA	NA
64	10/25/80	Fall Finale 10 KM	St. Paul, MN	6.2	37.15	6.00	NA	NA
65	11/8/80	Plymouth Jaycees 10 KM	Plymouth, MN	6.2	38.14	6.10	5th	68
66	2/7/81	Snowflake 10 KM	Coon Rapids, MN	6.2	41.03	6.37	NA	NA
67	2/14/81	Park Board 3 Mile	Minneapolis, MN	3.0	18.17	6.06	NA	NA
68	3/15/81	St. Pat's 5-Mile	Minneapolis, MN	5.0	30.04 *	6.01	NA	NA
69	3/28/81	Hopkins MDRA 7 Mile	Hopkins, MN	7.0	42.56	6.08	NA	NA
70	4/4/81	Hopkins 25 KM Run	Hopkins, MN	15.6	PPD/DNF	NA	NA	NA
71	4/20/81	Boston Marathon	Boston, MA	26.2	2:46.38	6.22	1,401st	6,881
72	5/2/81	Boulder Dash	Plymouth, MN	4.0	23.59	6.00	20th	284
73	5/9/81	Run For New Life	Minneapolis, MN	5.6	32.34	5.49	NA	NA
74	5/17/81	The Main Course	Chicago, IL	6.2	36.30 *	5.53	NA	NA
75	5/30/81	Lake St. to Water St. Easy Race	Excelsior, MN	13.1	1.21.00	6.11	NA	NA
76	6/6/81	Corporate Cup Regionals / Open Relay / 3 Mile Leg	Richfield, MN	3.0	17.31	5.50	4th	NA

#	Date	Event	Location	Miles	Time	Per Mile	Place	Out Of
77	6/6/81	Corporate Cup Regionals / Men's 3,000 Meter	Richfield, MN	1.875	10.41	5.42	1st	NA
78	6/7/81	Do It Downtown 10 KM	Minneapolis, MN	6.2	37.17	6.01	NA	NA
79	6/20/81	Grandma's Marathon	Duluth, MN	26.2	2.43.47 *	6:15	216th	3,202
80	6/25/81	Pepsi 10 KM Run	Syracuse, NY	6.2	37.02	5.58	NA	NA
81	7/11/81	Tonka 10 KM Run	Minnetonka, MN	6.2	39.56	6.26	NA	NA
82	7/18/81	Corporate Cup Finals / Open Relay / 3 Mile Leg	Palo Alto, CA	3.0	17.20 *	5.47	NA	NA
83	7/18/81	Corporate Cup Finals / Men's 3,000 Meter	Palo Alto, CA	1.875	10.24 *	5.33	NA	NA
84	7/19/81	Corporate Cup Finals / 10 KM Open	Palo Alto, CA	6.2	37.30	6.03	NA	NA
85	7/22/81	Aquatennial 8-Mile Run	Minneapolis, MN	8.0	49.00	6.07	NA	NA
86	8/8/81	Race Day 10 KM Run	Minneapolis, MN	6.2	38.08	6.21	NA	NA
87	8/16/81	Corn Days 4 Mile Run	Long Lake, MN	4.0	23.52	5.58	NA	NA
88	8/30/81	CDC Team Challenge 10 KM	Minneapolis, MN	6.2	39.20	6.21	NA	NA
89	10/24/81	Fall Finale 10 KM	St. Paul, MN	6.2	42.00	6.46	NA	NA
90	NA	Y To Y 20 KM Run	Minneapolis, MN	12.4	1.17.00	6.13	NA	NA
91	5/23/82	Do It Downtown 10 KM	Minneapolis, MN	6.2	40.32	6.32	NA	NA
92	6/6/82	Grand Old Days 5 Mile Run	Wayzata, MN	5.0	32.31	6.30	NA	NA
93	6/6/82	Race To The Place	St. Louis Park, MN	5.2	36.47	7.04	NA	NA
94	6/13/82	A. G. Classic 10 KM Run	Syracuse, NY	6.2	39.47	6.42	NA	NA

#	Date	Event	Location	Miles	Time	Per Mile	Place	Out Of
95	6/26/82	Corporate Cup Regionals /Men's 3,000 Meter	Richfield, MN	1.875	11.05	5.55	NA	NA
96	6/26/82	Corporate Cup Regionals / Men's Team Mile	Richfield, MN	1.0	5.38	5.38	NA	NA
97	6/27/82	Corporate Cup Regionals /10 KM Open	Richfield, MN	6.2	39.50	6.25	NA	NA
98	7/4/82	Firecracker 10 KM Run	Plymouth, MN	6.2	41.02	6.37	NA	NA
99	7/10/82	Tonka 10 KM Run	Minnetonka, MN	6.2	37.52	6.06	NA	NA
100	7/24/82	Chariot Cup Finals / Open Relay /2 Mile Leg	Palo Alto, CA	2.0	11.40	5.50	NA	NA
101	7/25/82	Chariot Cup Finals / 10 KM Open	Palo Alto, CA	6.2	37.33	6.03	NA	NA
102	8/15/82	Corn Days 4 Mile Run	Long Lake, MN	4.0	24.21	6.05	NA	NA
103	8/21/82	Steve Smith Memorial Track 10-Mile	New Hope, MN	10.0	1.02.59	6.18	NA	NA
104	8/28/82	Airport Half Marathon	Bloomington, MN	13.1	1.19.31 *	6.04	NA	NA
105	9/4/82	Minnesota TAC 20 KM Run	Minneapolis, MN	12.4	1.17.22	6.14	NA	NA
106	9/12/82	City of Lakes 25 KM Run	Minneapolis, MN	15.6	1.37.22	6.23	NA	NA
107	9/18/82	Dannon 15 KM	Minneapolis, MN	9.3	55.42	5.59	89th	NA
108	9/25/82	Fall Finale 10 KM	St. Paul, MN	6.2	44.00	7.06	NA	NA
109	10/3/82	Twin Cities Marathon	Minneapolis, MN	26.2	2.48.18	6.25	NA	NA

#	Date	Event	Location	Miles	Time	Per Mile	Place	Out Of
110	1/15/83	Freeze Your Gizzard Blizzard 10 KM	International Falls, MN	6.2	NA	NA	NA	NA
111	NA	Frigid Five	St. Paul, MN	5.0	NA	NA	NA	NA
112	3/19/83	St. Pat's 5-Mile	Minneapolis, MN	5.0	NA	NA	NA	NA
113	NA	Healthy, Wealthy & Wise 5 KM Run	Minneapolis, MN	3.1	NA	NA	NA	NA
114	5/14/83	Syttendai Mai 16.3 Mile Run	Grantsburg, WI	16.3	1.42.41	6.18	NA	NA
115	5/28/83	Lake St. to Water St. Easy Race	Excelsior, MN	13.1	NA	NA	NA	NA
116	6/4/83	Do It Downtown 10 KM	Minneapolis, MN	6.2	NA	NA	NA	NA
117	6/18/83	Corporate Cup Regionals / Open Relay / 2 Mile Leg	Richfield, MN	2.0	11.40	5.50	NA	NA
118	6/18/83	Corporate Cup Regionals / Executive Relay / 1 Mile Leg	Richfield, MN	1.0	5.30	5.30	NA	NA
119	6/19/83	Corporate Cup Regionals /10 KM Open	Richfield, MN	6.2	37.14	6.00	NA	NA
120	6/25/83	Easy Does It 5 Mile Run	Plymouth, MN	5.0	30.36	6.07	NA	NA
121	7/9/83	Saucony 10 KM Run	Minneapolis, MN	6.2	38.38	6.14	NA	NA
122	7/16/83	Kaiser Roll 10 KM Run	Bloomington, MN	6.2	38.43	6.15	NA	NA

#	Date	Event	Location	Miles	Time	Per Mile	Place	Out Of
123	7/23/83	Corporate Cup Finals /Open Relay / 2 Mile Leg	Palo Alto, CA	2.0	11.24 *	5.42	NA	NA
124	7/23/83	Corporate Cup Finals /Men's Team Mile	Palo Alto, CA	1.0	5.22 *	5.22	NA	NA
125	7/24/83	Corporate Cup Finals / 10 KM Open	Palo Alto, CA	6.2	39.32	6.23	NA	NA
126	10/2/83	Twin Cities Marathon	Minneapolis, MN	26.2	2.58.43	6.49	487	4,795
127	9/30/84	Twin Cities Marathon	Minneapolis, MN	12.0	DNF	NA	NA	NA
		Total Miles		1,258.4				

*Personal Record

TABLE 4: MARATHONS

#	Date	Event	Location	Miles	Time	Per Mile	Place	Out Of
1	4/16/73	Boston Marathon	Boston, MA	6.7	DNF	NA	NA	NA
2	4/15/74	Boston Marathon	Boston, MA	26.2	3.40.00	8.24	NA	NA
3	4/15/75	Boston Marathon	Boston, MA	26.2	3.08.30	7.12	NA	NA
4	11/30/75	Philadelphia Marathon	Philadelphia, PA	26.2	2.54.46	6.40	NA	141
5	4/19/76	Boston Marathon	Boston, MA	26.2	3.08.39	7.12	634th	1,942
6	5/9/76	Western Reserve Marathon	Hudson, OH	26.2	2.55.38	6.42	23rd	209
7	4/18/77	Boston Marathon	Boston, MA	26.2	2.51.53	6.34	521st	2,766
8	10/23/77	New York City Marathon	New York, NY	26.2	2.46.59	6.22	279th	3,664
9	4/17/78	Boston Marathon	Boston, MA	26.2	3.02.49	6.59	2,172nd	4,391
10	7/17/78	Marathon Marathon	Terre Haute, IN	17.0	DNF	NA	NA	NA
11	11/5/78	Longest Day Marathon	Brookings, SD	26.2	3.20.00	7.38	NA	NA
12	6/21/80	Grandma's Marathon	Duluth, MN	26.2	2.47.11	6.23	153rd	2,375
13	4/20/81	Boston Marathon	Boston, MA	26.2	2.46.38	6.22	1,401st	6,881
14	6/20/81	Grandma's Marathon	Duluth, MN	26.2	**2.43.47** *	6:15	216th	3,202
15	10/3/82	Twin Cities Marathon	Minneapolis, MN	26.2	2.48.18	6.25	235th	3,511`

331

#	Date	Event	Location	Miles	Time	Per Mile	Place	Out Of
16	10/2/83	Twin Cities Marathon	Minneapolis, MN	26.2	2.58.43	6.49	487th	4,795
17	9/30/84	Twin Cities Marathon	Minneapolis, MN	12.0	DNF	NA	NA	NA

Total miles **402.5**

*Personal Record

ACKNOWLEDGMENTS

SUCCESS IN LIFE, AND PERHAPS WHATEVER EMINENCE *CHASING DOWN A Dream* achieves, is a function not of my savvy storytelling but rather of the collaboration of a bunch of bright and talented individuals who benevolently invested the time to get involved either in my personal evolution or in the project itself.

Accordingly, I offer the following acknowledgments...

First of all, the sincerest thank you with love to my late parents, **Julia van der Voort Riehl** and **James H. Riehl, Sr.** for making this adventure possible, for their love, their sacrifices and for all the opportunities they made available to me.

Second, a shout out to my four sisters—**Nicky Kispert Kurz, Susie Stewart, Laurie Martin, and Liz Ritz**—who each contributed in a personal and unique way to this memoir:

- Nicky, who along with boyfriend and then husband Dave Kispert, introduced me to the notion of varsity letters, lots of them, and to the State of Massachusetts, and who influenced my decision to go into teaching.
- Susie, whose Christmas, 1975 gift to me was a tome filled with blank pages entitled *The Nothing Book*, which became my training log and documentation motherlode as I penned this account.
- Laurie and Liz, the only true athletes in the family:

- Laurie, who excelled in field hockey, volleyball, softball, and as tennis captain and best All-Around Athlete at Ferry Hall/Lake Forest Academy in Illinois.
- Liz, who distinguished herself in basketball, tennis, and as volleyball MVP at the Culver Academies in Indiana.

And then my gratitude to my intrepid first round editors, who brought to their reading of the manuscript a different perspective, resulting in many material and meaningful changes:

- **Scott Graham**—One of the true highlights of writing *Chasing Down a Dream* was reconnecting with Scottie. He provided invaluable insights into those GBTC workouts and was a true safety net when my recollections of Bill Rodgers, Alberto Salazar, and Coach Squires became a bit hazy.
- **Rob Harkel**—Despite insisting his attainment of a college degree was "nothing short of a miracle," Rob read the manuscript faster than anyone else and offered up a plethora of worthwhile suggestions that made for a better storyline and a tighter read.
- **Phil Hunter**—Kudos to Phil, who encouraged me to share more of the personal feelings and motivations behind both my running and some of the other adventures related in these pages, hopefully making this memoir a bit more of an intimate journey.
- **John Larson**—John provided priceless legal insights into the publishing of this, my first book, as well as enthusiastic encouragement for the story I was attempting to relate. He also sourced incisive intellectual property counsel who provided invaluable guidance.
- **Anne Marcus**—With her background in media and publishing, Anne not only offered many worthwhile perspectives on the manuscript but provided beneficial guidance on going to market as well.

Also, my appreciation to others who contributed or verified historical factoids and updated profiles for the Epilogue, including **Tony Benthin, John Ford, Dave Gelly, Scott Graham, Rob Harkel, Phil Hunter, Nicky**

Kispert Kurz, Bob Klein, Alan Knobel, John Larson, Laurie Martin, Winifred O'Shaughnessy, Liz Ritz, Susie Stewart, and **Chris Wiley.**

A word of gratitude to **Dave Gelly, Alan Knobel, Laurie Martin, Denise Riehl, Dave Vogt,** *The Duxbury Clipper* and wicked.local.com for their help pulling together the book's photo section to prove that, yes, Virginia, this stuff really did happen.

I also want to thank **Charlie Rodgers** for reconnecting me with Scott Graham, and shout outs to **Libby Alexander, Amby Burfoot, C. David Gelly, Scott Graham, Bill Rodgers** and **Bill Squires** for their book testimonials.

Kudos to my Palmetto Publishing team, **Jack Joseph** and **Stephanie Stupalski**, who provided peerless support in navigating me through my initial publishing experience with zero angst and agitation.

Hats off to my ex-neighbors and marketing and digital media mavens at BCM Media, **Brenda** and **Shaun McKenna**, who have proved to be of tremendous assistance in my efforts to bring *Chasing Down a Dream* to the attention of readers everywhere.

And finally, my acknowledgment of:

- **Tim Berners-Lee**, a computer scientist who actually did invent the internet, contrary to the popular myth that its father was Al Gore,
- **Wikipedia**, which enabled my rapid research of a myriad of obscure subjects, and
- **YouTube**, which gave me access to many vintage archived Boston Marathon, Olympic Marathon, and New York City Marathon videos.

Until my next publication, adios.

BIBLIOGRAPHY

Amdur, Neil, *New York Times, "Cusack Captures Marathon,"* April 16, 1974.

Amdur, Neil, *New York Times, "Seko of Japan Captures Boston Marathon,"* April 21, 1981.

Amdur, Neil, *New York Times*, "Two World Records Set as 13,360 Finish Marathon," October 26, 1981.

Berkow, Ira, *New York Times, "Corporate Races Get Competitive,"* July 20, 1981.

Boston Athletic Association, *Racer's Recordbook*, 1976 Boston Marathon Official Computer Results.

Boston Athletic Association, *Racer's Recordbook*, 1977 Boston Marathon Official Computer Results.

Boston Athletic Association, *Racer's Recordbook*, 1978 Boston Marathon Official Computer Results.

Boston Athletic Association, *Racer's Recordbook*, 1981 Boston Marathon Official Computer Results.

Clerici, Paul, *Born To Coach: The Story of Bill Squires, The Legendary Coach of The Greatest Generation of American Distance Runners,* Meyer & Meyer Sport (UK) Limited, 2020.

Cohen, Peter, *The Gospel According To Harvard Business School*, Garden City, NY, Doubleday & Company, Inc., 1973.

Conrad, John, *Eugene Register-Guard*, *"A Nice Run in the Park for Shorter,"* May 23, 1976.

Eaton, Perry, Boston.Com, *"Boston's Late, Great Eliot Lounge was the Marathon's Unofficial Finish Line,"* April 15, 2016.

Elger, Dave, *Dave Elger on Running, Racing and Training*, *"The Marathon Collapse Point Theory,"* September 14, 2009.

Falls, Joe, *The Boston Marathon*, New York, NY, Collier Books, 1977.

Fixx, James E., *The Complete Book of Running*, New York, NY, Random House, 1977.

Harris, Bruce, *The Nothing Book: Wanna Make Something of It?*, New York, NY, The Crown Publishing Group, 1974.

Henderson, Harold, *ChicagoReader.Com*, *"A Spinach Plant Grows in DeKalb,"* September 3,1987.

Higdon, Hal, *Boston: A Century of Running*, Emmaus, PA, Rodale Press, 1995.

Knight, Phil, *Shoe Dog: A Memoir By The Creator of Nike*, New York, NY, Scribner, 2016.

Newlin, Bill, *Old Colony Memorial*, *"PCIS Teachers to Run in Boston Marathon Monday,"* April 15, 1976.

Reilly, Lucas, Big Questions/MentalFloss.Com, "Why are Marathons 26.2 Miles Long," November 14, 2018.

Rodgers, Bill and Shepatin, Matthew, *Marathon Man: My 26.2-Mile Journey from Unknown Grad Student to the Top of the Running World*, New York, NY, Thomas Dunne Books, St. Martin's Press, 2013.

Salazar, Alberto and Brant, John, *14 Minutes: A Running Legend's Life and Death and Life*, New York, NY, Rodale Press, 2012.

Shapiro, Jim, *On The Road, The Marathon: The Joys and Techniques of Marathon Running*, New York, New York, Crown Publishers, Inc., 1978.

Shorter, Frank and Brant, John, *My Marathon: Reflections on a Gold Medal Life*, New York, NY, Rodale Press, 2016.

Stracher, Cameron, *Kings of The Road: How Frank Shorter, Bill Rodgers and Alberto Salazar Made Running Go Boom*, Boston, MA and New York, NY, Houghton Mifflin Harcourt, 2013.

ThisBigWildWorld.Com, "The Most Minnesotan Things Ever," November 2, 2019.

1975 Marathon Handbook, Mountain View, CA, World Publications Group, Incorporated, 1975.